BRIGHTON
in Diaries

BRIGHTON
in Diaries

PAUL K LYONS

The
History
Press

First published 2011

The History Press
The Mill, Brimscombe Port
Stroud, Gloucestershire, GL5 2QG
www.thehistorypress.co.uk

British Library Cataloguing in Publication Data.
A catalogue record for this book is available from the British Library.

ISBN 978 0 7524 6222 6

Typesetting and origination by The History Press
Printed in EU for The History Press.

Contents

Introduction

When Brighton and Hove was granted city status by Queen Elizabeth II as part of the millennium celebrations in 2000, it marked three centuries of extraordinary growth – from small fishing village to one of Britain's largest and most dynamic places to live and visit. Today it boasts old-world and alternative shopping quarters, two universities and a large foreign student population, one of the finest piers in the country, as well as an atmospheric pier ruin, miles of wide beaches with clean water and busy promenades, magnificent Regency architecture, stunning picturesque curves of terraced houses on the many hills, an arts festival second only to Edinburgh, a large and colourful gay community which puts on a magnificent parade for all in the summer, and an open, innovative and busy music scene.

Go back more than 300 years, and Brighthelmstone, as it was then known (among various other spellings), was little more than a small harbour-less fishing town or village, without much protection from the weather or from French and Dutch raiders. The village's first claim to any fame at all came in the mid-seventeenth century when the young and future King Charles II, escaping from Oliver Cromwell's Roundheads, took refuge there for one night before secretly making his way the following morning to Shoreham where he boarded a coal-carrying coaster which carried him to safety in France. Ten years later, on returning to England, he recounted his adventures to another young man, Samuel Pepys, who recorded the details in his now-famous diary.

Terrific storms in 1703 and 1705 did great damage to the place. A description was written down by John Warburton who visited the coast in the early-eighteenth century. Having dismissed Hove as 'a ruinous village' which the sea is daily eating up, he writes:

A good mile further going along the beach I arrived at Bright-hem stead, a large ill-built irregular market town, mostly inhabited by seafaring men who choose their residence here as being situated on the main and convenient for their going on shore on their passing and repassing in the coasting trade. This town is likely to share the same fate with the last, the sea having washed away the half of it; whole streets being now deserted, and the beach almost covered with walls of houses being almost entire, the lime or cement being strong enough, when thrown down, to resist the violence of the waves.

Other travellers' accounts – letters and retrospective narratives – of visiting Brighton start to emerge in the early part of the eighteenth century. John H. Farrant, an expert on Sussex's history, has analysed these for the magazine *Sussex Genealogist and Local Historian*. The author of *Robinson Crusoe*, Daniel Defoe, for example, may have visited as early as 1712, when he found it 'a poor fishing town, old built, and on the very edge of the sea'. A little later, during a visit around 1730, Revd John Burton (writing in Greek) described the men of the town as 'hardy and industrious, and very skilful in naval matters and reported to be very dextrous in defrauding the revenue', but also noted that the appearance of the town was 'miserable'.

Soon afterwards, though, the town underwent rapid growth. This was largely thanks to Dr Richard Russell whose medical theories about the benefits of seawater transformed Brighton into a health resort. Writing in the late eighteenth century, Thomas Walker Horsfield put it this way in *The History, Antiquities, and Topography of the County of Sussex*: 'Science invited fashion and fashion [. . .] has in the short space of half a century transformed the poor fishing village of bright Helmston into one of the gayest and grandest of our favourite abodes.'

One man drawn to Brighton by its growing reputation was Peregrine Phillips. Not much is known about him, except that he was a lawyer by profession, and the father of a famous West End actress, Mrs Crouch. Coming from Little Hampton, he did not much like Brighton at first, but it grew on him and he stayed for a couple of weeks in August 1778, and then came back the following August.

And it is thanks to Phillips that we have the first *bona fide* and substantial record of Brighton written in diary form. A brilliant diary it is too. Phillips took his pen and paper with him wherever he went, and wrote 'On the Clift' or 'Upon the Sands' or 'On the Steyne'. He records anything and everything – from the sublime to the ridiculous – amusing anecdotes of people and colourful description of places. Moreover, one gets the sense that he loved his own diary voice, and took great pleasure in giving opinions on subjects large and small.

While Phillips was probably more typical of the professional and middle classes, high society had also begun to flourish in Brighton, thanks in part to King George III's brother, the Duke of Cumberland, being a regular visitor. Thus, literary types, such as Henry and Hester Thrale and Dr Samuel Johnson, were drawn south to the coast. And with them came one Fanny Burney, a young writer of talent. Her first book published anonymously – *Evelina* – was a sensation, and she herself, when uncovered as the author, became a society star. More than a century later, Virginia Woolf called her 'the mother of English fiction', but today, she is also celebrated for her diaries, which she wrote assiduously for most of her life. They are justly famed for their literary quality as much as for their descriptions of society. Although she later married and became known as Madame D'Arblay, at the time of her visits to Brighton she was still very much a young woman interested in young men!

Fanny Burney's diaries, in their most extensive edition, run to twelve volumes. Joseph Farington, a painter known in his day for topographical drawings but celebrated now for his diaries, betters that. Yale University published them in sixteen volumes, with a separate 1,000 page index. Farington, too, was drawn to Brighton, though he did not have much to say about the place. By 1802, the Prince of Wales had already become well-established. A first stage of the Pavilion had been built some years earlier, and the building of a second stage was underway. That year, Farington told his diary, the Prince was 'much about, riding and walking' and 'takes much interest in building'.

Chronologically, the next diarist to have left behind interesting remarks about Brighton is anonymous. His or her diary is quoted in a history of Brighton by John Ackerson Erredge, the first substantial (and very entertaining) history of the town in fact. It was originally published in 1862, and was recently republished with a learned introduction by John Farrant. The anonymous diary entries are all from 1805 or 1807, apart from one in 1810, and have been included here along with samples of Erredge's commentary – on the history of The Steine, for example, and the spread of 'virulent pastimes'.

In late 1810, parliament deemed King George III's mental health to be so unstable that it transferred his regal powers to his son, George, who formally became Prince Regent; until 1820 when his father died, and then he became king. This so-called Regency period (1811–1820) saw three very different politicians – who are remembered for their diaries – visiting Brighton.

Sylvester Douglas, later Lord Glenbervie, was hobnobbing, gadding about, and filling his diary with amusing anecdotes. More serious, even though they sound like a double act, were Creevey and Croker. Creevey was a Whig, and Croker a Tory, but both wrote diaries published respectively as *The Creevey Papers* and *The Croker Papers*.

Creevey was in Brighton in the autumn of 1811, dining at the Pavilion most nights, but at the same time was hardening his political stance against the Prince Regent's political appointments. During that visit, indeed, he fell out with the Prince, and subsequently lived in Brussels for several years. Charles Greville, a more famous diarist, said 'old Creevey is a living proof that a man may be perfectly happy and exceedingly poor. I think he is the only man I know in society who possesses nothing.' Creevey, though, fixed his own very minor place in history by being the first civilian to interview the Duke of Wellington after the Battle of Waterloo.

Croker's diary entries are taken from a few years later, in 1818, and show him as a more cynical observer than Creevey. One entry finds him complaining about the money the prince is spending on the Pavilion: 'It is, I think, an absurd waste of money, and will be a ruin in half a century or sooner.' In another, he comments on the Prince's long-term female companion: 'One reason why Mrs Fitzherbert may like this place is that she is treated as queen, at least of Brighton.' The Prince had married the widow Maria Fitzherbert in 1785, but as the marriage had not been approved by his father or the Privy Council it was null and void.

Gideon Mantell was a very different sort of man, a surgeon by profession, but energetic and restless, often dissatisfied with his lot. He was born and brought up in Lewes, where he took over a successful practice. Ambition drove him to move his family home to the centre of Brighton where he hoped to attract rich patients from within the King's entourage or the high society surrounding it. However, the nobility in Brighton became more intrigued by the collection of fossils, including dinosaurs before they were so named, in his home. His diaries are a delight, partly because he was such an active man, and partly because he was a keen observer of life. Typical of how his diary benefited from this restless energy was the time he raced to Brighton (he was not yet living there) to watch the sea during a tremendous gale and to brave walking on the Chain Pier: 'The awful grandeur of the scene more than compensated for the inconvenience of our situation.'

One of the most important nineteenth-century British diarists, Charles Greville, visited Brighton often in the 1820s, usually on the King's business but also to visit the racecourse. As a clerk to the Privy Council, he was, essentially, a high level civil servant. As such, one might expect his diaries to be more discrete than those of a leading politician, for example. But they are not. They are wonderfully indiscrete, so much so that when they were published after his death, both the Prime Minister at the time, Benjamin Disraeli, and Queen Victoria were outraged. Here is Greville on an early visit to Brighton: 'I was curious to see the Pavilion and the life they lead there, and I now only hope I may never go there again, for the novelty is past, and I should be exposed to the whole weight of the bore of it without the stimulus of curiosity.'

Henry Edward Fox was another diarist who visited Brighton in the 1820s, during the reign of King George IV. He certainly spoke, rather wrote, his mind too, describing the English countryside as being full of 'Lilliput ostentation', and the Pavilion as a fairies' palace. He also described, with some relish, a contentious report of him embracing 'Lady L' on the steps of the Chain Pier.

Walter Scott was a literary giant, the first real writer of historical novels, and the world's first author of bestsellers. Some consider his diaries to be as brilliant as his novels, and it is a great shame that he did not start the diary habit until 1825, shortly before a financial crisis that would leave him in serious debt until his death in 1832. Scott did not like Brighton very much – he called it 'a city of loiterers and invalids' – and his visits during this latter period of his life were all connected with his daughter, Sophia, who had married a close friend, the writer and editor John Gibson Lockhart. Their first born child was sickly, and was taken to Brighton for his health, and it was there that a second son, Walter, named after his grandfather, was born.

Whereas Walter Scott famously faced up to his financial difficulties, Thomas Raikes – labelled as 'dandy and diarist' by the *Oxford Dictionary of National Biography* – ran away to Paris for a decade to escape his financial troubles. While there, he kept a regular diary, though sometimes the entries are less about his present life, and more about the past, his life in England, including time at court with the King in Brighton. And he has colourful stories to tell, about race days and the betting scene on The Steine, and about a quarrel at the Castle Inn which led to a duel in which one of the participants fought naked.

After so many upper-class types, it comes as a refreshing change to see Brighton through the eyes of a more ordinary person. William Tayler was brought up in rural Oxfordshire but, for want of work, became a servant. On New Year's Day in 1837 he decided to improve his writing and spelling by keeping a diary; and, though he had tried to keep a diary before, this was the first time he kept the resolution. Thus, when his employer decided to spend the summer in Brighton, the enterprising Mr Tayler, who used all his spare time to explore the new place, had plenty to write about. Despite his atrocious spelling, he wrote with a lively clear voice that conjures up pictures more interesting, or not even seen, by many of his better educated fellow diarists. Gideon Mantell may have braved ferocious waves on the Chain Pier, and Henry Fox may or may not have embraced Lady L. on its steps, but it falls to William Tayler to say what it looks like: 'Went on the pier. This is a kind of bridge projecting into the sea a quarter of a mile. It's a great curiosity as it's hung on chains.' And his description of election day in Brighton could hardly be bettered.

The somewhat stiff and serious Henry Crabb Robinson was a literary type, one who knew good art and theatre when he saw it. He was also a faithful diarist and kept historically useful notes on the London cultural scene. By the time he began visiting Brighton, George IV had died and his younger brother William had taken the throne. Although King William IV did continue to use the Pavilion (Mantell, in his diary, describes this King's first entry into Brighton along London Road), he only lasted until 1837. His successor, Queen Victoria, disliked Brighton, and the Pavilion was sold by the government to the town in 1850. By this time, though, nearly half a century of royal patronage had seen Brighton grow into a large, rich, thriving town.

Although Robinson's visits span some thirty-five years, it was his interest in a brilliant young preacher that took him regularly to Brighton in the early 1850s. This is how he described Frederick William Robertson in his diary: 'The best preacher I ever saw in a pulpit; that is, uniting the greatest number of excellences, originality, piety, freedom of thought, and warmth of love. His style colloquial and very scriptural. He combined light of the intellect with warmth of the affections in a pre-eminent degree.' After his death, Robinson and Lady Byron, who was another of the preacher's fans, worked together to publicise his teachings and publish his sermons.

Xue Fucheng has the distinction of being the only foreign diarist in this book, and very foreign he was too. China, which had followed an isolationist policy for so long, was under great pressure from world powers to open up its markets to trade and its culture to new ways. Somewhat belatedly, the ruling Qing Dynasty decided to send ambassadors abroad to liaise with, and learn more about, these powers. Xue Fucheng, a distinguished academic, was dispatched to Europe, where he stayed a few years in London. While there, he tried hard to understand, and sometimes copy, the traditions of the local inhabitants. One of these was to take a summer holiday by the seaside. Which is how Xue Fucheng and his family and his interpreter spent several weeks in Brighton, and how one day on the 'new pier' he watched 'a performance of a flea circus and marvelled at a flea pulling a cart around.'

Around the same time that Xue Fucheng was learning about the British way of life, and taking a summer holiday in Brighton, Henry Peerless, a Brighton businessman, was beginning to discover the joys of using his summer holidays to travel around Britain and discover different seaside resorts. Because he only kept a diary during his holidays, the references to his home town are largely confined to leavings and returnings. He does, however, also take great delight in comparing, usually favourably, Brighton's attractions to those of the places he's visiting. Thus, although Bournemouth may appear more modern and have more natural beauties, 'our greatest asset still is that only 52 miles separates us from the great metropolis'.

Four authors are next, all of them well-known, and all extraordinary, but very different, diarists. Arnold Bennett is famous for his novels set in the English Midlands, and for his naturalist style. He spent a few months one winter in Brighton, during which time he was writing *Clayhanger*, the first of his famous Clayhanger series. Moreover, his experience in and of Brighton then contributed significantly to the second novel in the series, *Hilda Lessways*. His voluminous diaries have been compared to Pepys, and to the great Parisian diarists of the realist/naturalist movement, Edmond and Jules Goncourt.

'I have always thought it would be unwholesome of me to attempt to write a diary. I'm sure it will make me think my life drab and strain after sensation to make copy for my autobiography.' This is how Lady Cynthia Asquith begins her first diary, but there is very little evidence in it of her needing to 'strain after sensation'. Her life during the First World War – the only period of her diaries to be published – appears to have been full of movement, people and challenges of one sort or another. Her husband, the Prime Minister's son, enlisted in the army and was stationed for a while in Brighton. Their children were also lodged there at times, while she herself moved around – 'cuckooing' as she called it – without a proper home. She has been described as one of the most fascinatingly beautiful women of her time, but also as the greatest flirt that ever lived. Her diaries provide a startlingly open and self-absorbed account of a life so privileged on the surface but affected deeply and painfully by the pressures of marriage, children, war, and her own intense social needs.

Virginia Woolf, one of the most famous of twentieth-century British novelists, was also a diarist of some distinction. She lived for much of her short life near Brighton at Rodmell and often visited to go shopping. She loved browsing the second-hand books shops or taking afternoon tea, though could be impatient with the ordinary people she found there, and once wrote about Brighton as 'a love-corner for slugs'. For much of her life she was on intimate terms with Vita Sackville-West, who was married to Harold Nicolson. They lived further east in Kent at Sissinghurst. Nicolson, too, was a diarist of the first rank, though he mentioned Brighton only a couple of times in his diary – notably when he came to dispose of the ashes of his mother-in-law, who had lived in Brighton.

During the Second World War many people across the country were encouraged to keep diaries by a social research organisation called Mass Observation. The organisation has been through a number of changes since then, but holds a large volume of papers from during and after the war which are stored in the Special Collections department of the University of Sussex. Within the archive are two A4-sized volumes titled 'Boots Scribbling Diary', one for 1940 and the other for 1941, kept by Olive Stammer. At the time she was in her early thirties and unmarried. Her brother, George, was away serving in the army. The two diaries are packed full of Olive's daily notes, mostly announcements by the British government or major news items from abroad. However, she also recorded local events, such as 'Mine washed up at Hove. Traffic diverted', and her own experiences such as, 'Saw soldier motor cyclist laying London Road this morning with broken leg, lorry cut out of Baker St on wrong side.'

A vivid contrast to Olive Stammer's sober record of the early years of the war is provided by Tony Simmonds and his exuberant teenage language about the latter years, including VE day: 'People just went mad – dancing, singing, chanting, shouting – the crowd just surged this way and that [. . .] fire crackers, flares and even pre-war "jumpers" were thrown about the streets – even into busses – all policemen "had their eyes shut". ' Extracts from Tony's diaries can be found in a book of war memories published by a Brighton community publisher, QueenSpark, and online thanks to the most excellent community website, My Brighton & Hove.

Much more recently, in 2007, a number of organisations – including QueenSpark, My Brighton & Hove and Mass Observation – collaborated in a project called 'Letter in the Attic'. Following an appeal to the public, some 800 unpublished personal items, such as letters, diaries and photos, were collected, archived and digitalised. The earliest of them go back to the first half of the nineteenth century. The collection, which can now be searched and viewed online, is also the basis of an online exhibition and a set of educational resources. Surprisingly, perhaps, it contains relatively few diaries. Short extracts from three diarists are included here: Hinda Harris who was keen on the cinema during the war; Jane Lucas who was a student in the 1970s; and Sharon Fosdyke who passed through Brighton in the early 1990s on a tour of the south coast.

In his mid-fifties, Des Marshall moved from his familiar haunts in Camden, London, to live in Brighton, and stayed a little over two years. His life hitherto had not been easy, chronically ill as a child and chronically vulnerable to mental illness as an adult, he was always at odds with society, and constantly searching for answers. In 1994, he says, he met a man calling himself Urban Robinson Crusoe: 'Small, nervous, thin faced, he didn't look very well.' And, he explains, it was Crusoe – not Marshall – who kept a diary. Less than five years later, it was published by Saxon Books with the title *Journal of an Urban Robinson Crusoe*. Marshall, *aka* Crusoe, chronicles the life he finds at street level, and in trying to explain this life to himself, he paints a surprisingly accurate portrait of modern Brighton as a 'tinsel town' where 'anything goes' and people 'seem very excited and distracted'.

Ten years later, and almost to the present day, Ross Reeves is very much a typical Brighton resident: young, good-looking, gay, alternatively but very well-dressed, into music, and likely to move on after a while. Having started to write a diary while travelling all over the world, he found he couldn't stop. He came to Brighton in 2004, and felt like he'd arrived at his home. His unpublished diaries are beautifully written. Although, like many diarists, he writes about friends and relationships often, and analyses his own behaviour, he also gives lovely insights into modern-day life in the city, such as when he and his friends celebrated Guy Fawkes night – on an allotment: 'We managed to light up the allotment valley in fantastic colours. Had a great night, buzzing and dancing until the early hrs of course.'

Like Ross, my own commitment to keeping a diary evolved when I was travelling, though that was a quarter of a century earlier, in the 1970s. On my return from distant parts, I made friends with Rosy and Andrew who soon moved with their young children to live in Brighton. I was a regular visitor, drawn by their warm personalities and open house. Later, when I was still living in London for work, my partner and young son moved to North Laine for a few years, and I became a half-time resident, loving the beach, and the sea, and the parks, and the festivals, and the music, and the pubs, and the nearby Downs.

This book, thus, is essentially a collection of cameos of people, famous and ordinary, young and old, serious and cynical, but with Brighton always setting the scene: like a play, perhaps, in which, despite a medley of brilliant actors and a plot full of intriguing story-lines, it is the set, the backdrop that really steals the show.

Notes about the texts

Diary extracts quoted throughout the book, and only diary extracts, are indented, and do not have quotation marks. Other quotations, of which there are many (editor's comments, biographical material, other material by the diarists) are in the same font as the narrative but within quotation marks.

Although the original diary texts have been kept as close to the original as found in the published version used, I have made minor editorial alterations here and there.

Mostly I have left the spelling and punctuation as I found it, mistakes and inconsistencies included. But, as I have not consulted original handwritten documents, all spellings and punctuation, whether old-fashioned or mistakes, originate from the published versions, and may or may not have been modified in some way from the originals.

I have not always kept faithful to the paragraph spacing within diary texts as found in the published versions they are taken from – opting sometimes to include/exclude paragraph breaks.

More significantly, perhaps, I have cherry-picked extracts without indicating precisely what's been left out. While generally speaking I have used [. . .] to indicate text missing in the middle of an extract, I have not done so for text left out from the beginning or end of a chosen extract. (NB: Original texts themselves sometimes include trailing dots so where these are part of the quote they are not enclosed in square brackets.) Similarly, in a sequence of dated extracts, I have not indicated where whole entries might have been omitted.

Also, I have tried to impose some consistency on the use of quotation marks within diary texts, using double quotation marks where diarists have quoted speech or other texts. For the names of books, plays etc. I have opted for a standard use of single quotation marks within diary texts (although within my own commentary, as is modern practice, I have used italics).

Otherwise, where not confusing or useful, I have tried to replicate the use of capitals and italics within the diary texts as I found them.

Round brackets within a diary text are part of the quotation. Square brackets, however, are not. They are always about providing relevant information. Sometimes this information is provided in the original publication itself in a square bracket (a missing word perhaps), or else as a footnote (and occasionally I quote the footnote verbatim, in single quotation marks). Here and there, though, I have also used square brackets to clarify the meaning of a word, or to give more information on a person.

I have also chosen to impose consistency on the dates, so these are never part of the quotation itself; where a location is included, however, on the next line, this does form part of the quote.

All side headlines are my own.

Paul K Lyons,
2011

Acknowledgements

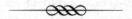

I am indebted for their help to the library staff at Brighton's Jubilee Library and History Centre, and at the University of Sussex Special Collections, and to John Farrant.

Thanks to: Oxford University Press for permission to quote from *The Journal of Gideon Mantell, Surgeon and Geologist* as edited by E. Cecil Curwen; to the Marylebone Society for kindly allowing me permission to use extracts from *Diary of William Tayler, Footman, 1837* as edited by Dorothy Wise; to Palgrave Macmillan for permission to quote from *The European Diary of Hsieh Fucheng: Envoy Extraodinary of Imperial China* as edited by Douglas Howland, translated by Helen Hsieh Chien and published by 119St Martin's Press; to Edward Fenton for generously allowing me to use extracts from *A Brief Jolly Change* published by Day Books; to Orion Books for permission to quote from *The Journals of Arnold Bennett 1896-1928* as edited by Newman Flower and published by Cassell; to Random House for permission to use extracts from the diaries of Cynthia Asquith (Hutchinson) and the diaries of Virginia Woolf (Hogarth Press); and to Juliet Nicolson for kindly allowing me to quote from her grandfather's diaries.

The Olive Stammer diaries are held by the University of Sussex Special Collections which granted permission for their use. Despite best efforts, however, no copyright holder has been traced.

I am very grateful to Tony Simmonds for allowing me to include extracts from his wartime diary, and for patiently answering my questions; as well as to Jane Lucas and Sharon Fosdyke who let me make use of their contributions to the 'Letter in the Attic' project, and to Sophie Harris who allowed me to use some diary entries she had chosen for the same project but which were written by her aunt, Hinda Harris. Many thanks also to QueenSpark, the Brighton and Hove community publisher which organised the 'Letter in the Attic' project, for help in contacting the diarists. Des Marshall and his publisher were kind enough to allow me use of extracts from *Journal of an Urban Robinson Crusoe* published by Saxon Books. A special thank you to Ross Reeves who generously (and patiently) allowed me to look through his private diaries and choose some extracts for publication.

Last but not least a multitude of thanks to Hat and JG for their advice, time and many other helpful contributions.

Pictures and picture acknowledgements

Chapter 1: Samuel Pepys, engraving by Geoffrey Kneller; Chapter 2: 'A Modern Hell' from Egan's *Real Life in London,* illustrated by Rowlandson and Alken; Chapter 3: Frances d'Arblay by Henry Colburn, London, 1842; Chapter 4: Joseph Farington from a drawing by George Dance; Chapter 5: 'Packing up after a Country Ball', by Richard Dighton, Library of Congress, LC-USZ62-85550; Chapter 6: 'Merrymaking on the Regent's Birthday', 1812, by George Cruikshank, Library of Congress, CLC-DIG-ppmsca-04317; Chapter 7: The Pavilion, Brighton, by Henry Wallis, in Dugdale's early Victorian collection *Curiosities of England*; Chapter 8: 'The Rival Queens' (Mrs Fitzherbert on the left being held by the Prince of Wales) by S. W. Fores, Library of Congress, LC-USZC4-6452; Chapter 9: Gideon Mantell by J. J. Masquerier (used by permission ©19thcenturyscience.org); Chapter 10: George IV (1828 statue in Brighton – photograph © Paul K Lyons); Chapter 11: Brighton Chain Pier in the 1820s, courtesy of Royal Pavilion and Museums, Brighton & Hove; Chapter 12: Walter Scott (artist unknown), Library of Congress, LC-DIG-ppmsc-07693; Chapter 13: Tattersalls, as seen in Egan's *Real Life in London*, illustrated by Rowlandson and Alken; Chapter 14: Brighton beach (old postcard); Chapter 15: Henry Crabb Robinson, engraving by William Holl; Chapter 16: Brighton beach (and bathing machines), Library of Congress, LC-DIG-ppmsc-08043; Chapter 17: Brighton beach and pier, Library of Congress, LC-DIG-ppmsc-08044; Chapter 18: Arnold Bennett by Oliver Herford, Library of Congress, LC-USZ62-100959; Chapter 19: 'Rally around the Flag', published by the War Office in 1914, Library of Congress, LC-USZC4-11310; Chapter 20: Virginia Woolf by Roger Fry (photograph © Paul K Lyons); Chapter 21: Olive Stammer's diary by permission from Special Collections, University of Sussex (photograph © Paul K Lyons); Chapter 22: Tony Simmonds (photograph used by permission from Tony Simmonds); Chapter 23: Brighton Pavilion (photograph © Paul K Lyons); Chapter 24: Brighton street (photograph © Paul K Lyons); Chapter 25: Ross Reeves by Keith Elliot (photograph © Keith Elliot); Chapter 26: Barbara and Fred (Paul's parents) on Brighton Pier in 1951 (photograph used by permission).

1

Samuel Pepys and Charles II walking on the quarterdeck

The first reference to Brighton – or Brighthelmstone as it was then – in any diary occurs as early as 1660, thanks to a precocious young man called Sam, who would in time become the most famous diarist in history, and Charles who was in the process of returning to England to be King. At the time, Samuel Pepys was with a fleet of ships, led by his relative Sir Edward Montagu, that had sailed to the Netherlands to bring the future Charles II back from exile. There was 'a fresh gale and most happy weather', and Charles was walking on the quarterdeck recounting the details of his escape, nearly a decade earlier, after the Battle of Worcester. Sam was listening, avidly, almost in tears.

In the 1640s, King Charles I was engaged in a fierce struggle for power with the English and Scottish Parliaments. Having been defeated in the First Civil War (1642-1645), he remained defiant by trying to make an alliance with Scotland. This provoked the Second Civil War (1648-1649) which Charles also lost. Then, having been captured and convicted for high treason, he lost his head too. While the monarchy was being abolished and Oliver Cromwell was establishing a republic called the Commonwealth of England, Charles I's son, Charles, was on the run. He made his way north to Scotland, where he was proclaimed Charles II King of Scots.

There he formed an army of Scots Royalists, 12,000 strong, and, in 1651, marched south, hoping to raise military support in England against the Parliament. He met with little opposition, but was unable to enlist many new recruits either. He occupied Worcester on 22 August, and the next day was proclaimed King. Less than a week later, Cromwell arrived with 30,000 men, and a few days after that, they attacked the city. On 3 September, Cromwell's Roundheads finally and brutally crushed the Royalist army thus bringing the Civil War to its end. Charles managed to escape, first to Boscobel nearby where he famously hid in a tree, and then he was on the run again, this time for six weeks, often hiding in barns and disguised as a countryman. He arrived in Sussex on 14 October, passing through Arundel and Beeding, before reaching Brighton. He stayed one night and then sailed from Shoreham to safety in

France. It would be nine years before his return to England and his restoration to the English throne.

The story of Charles II's adventurous and romantic escape through and from England was initially written by Thomas Blount, a lawyer and lexicographer, and published as early as 1660, the year of Charles II restoration to the monarchy, but has been republished many times. Later volumes include a narrative of his escape told by Charles to Samuel Pepys in 1680, of which Pepys made a written record, long after he'd stopped keeping a diary. Here is part of that narrative in which Charles II tells the story of his stay in Brighton, and of several people who recognised him there!

King Charles's version of his escape

'We went to a place, four miles off Shoreham, called Brighthelmstone, where we were to meet with the master of the ship, as thinking it more convenient to meet there than just at Shoreham, where the ship was. So when we came to the inn at Brighthelmstone we met with one, the merchant who had hired the vessel, in company with her master [Nicholas Tettersell, or Tattersell], the merchant only knowing me, as having hired her only to carry over a person of quality that was escaped from the battle of Worcester without naming anybody.

And as we were all sitting together (viz, Robin Philips, my Lord Wilmot, Colonel Gunter, the merchant, the master, and I), I observed that the master of the vessel looked very much upon me. And as soon as we had supped, calling the merchant aside, the master told him that he had not dealt fairly with him; for though he had given him a very good price for the carrying over that gentleman, yet he had not been clear with him; for,' says he, 'he is the king, and I very well know him to be so.' Upon which, the merchant denying it, saying that he was mistaken, the master answered, 'I know him very well, for he took my ship, together with other fishing vessels at Brighthelmstone, in the year 1648' (which was when I commanded the king my father's fleet, and I very kindly let them go again). 'But,' says he to the merchant, 'be not troubled at it, for I think I do God and my country good service in preserving the king, and, by the grace of God, I will venture my life and all for him, and set him safely on shore, if I can, in France.' Upon which the merchant came and told me what had passed between them, and thereby found myself under a necessity of trusting him. But I took no kind of notice of it presently to him; but thinking it convenient not to let him go home, lest he should be asking advice of his wife, or anybody else, we kept him with us in the inn, and sat up all night drinking beer, and taking tobacco with him.

And here I also run another very great danger, as being confident I was known by the master of the inn; for as I was standing, after supper, by the fireside, leaning my hand upon a chair, and all the rest of the company being gone into another room, the master of the inn came in, and fell a-talking with me, and just as he was looking about, and saw there was nobody in the room, he, upon a sudden, kissed my hand that was upon the back of the chair, and said to me, 'God bless you wheresover you go! I do not doubt, before I die, but to be a lord, and my wife a lady.' So I laughed, and went away into the next room, not desiring then any further discourse with him, there being no remedy against my being known by him, and more discourse might have but raised suspicion. On which consideration, I thought it best for to trust him in that manner, and he proved very honest.

About four o'clock in the morning, myself and the company before named went towards Shoreham, taking the master of the ship with us, on horseback, behind one of our company, and came to the vessel's side, which was not above sixty ton. But it being low water, and the vessel lying dry, I and my Lord Wilmot got up with a ladder into her, and went and lay down in the little cabin, till the tide came to fetch us off.'

Of Tettersell and The George

There are two other sources of information about Charles's escape as far as Sussex and Brighton are concerned: Colonel Gunter's narrative printed in Parry's *An Historical and Descriptive Account of the Coast of Sussex*, and Sir Richard Baker's *Chronicles of the Kings of England* which is thought to rely on a version of events provided by Tettersell, captain of the escape ship, a coal carrying coaster. Through these sources we know that Charles and his group left on horseback for Shoreham at 4 in the morning; that Tettersell managed to bargain a high price of £200 for the use of his ship; and that the inn was called The George.

There is a little more to know about both Tettersell and The George. Apart from his £200, Captain Tettersell did very well out of the escapade. Once Charles II was restored to the throne, he was granted a pension of £100 per year, and his ship, *Surprise*, was transferred into the Royal Navy's fleet and renamed *The Royal Escape*. His memorial is the oldest in the churchyard of Brighton's St Nicholas.

As for The George, there has been much debate down the centuries as to the actual building where Charles slept. In the 1880s, Frederick E. Sawyer, a well-known and prolific writer on Brighton's history, argued with painstaking evidence that it was not, as was generally assumed at the time, The King's Head in West Street (having been renamed in honour of the King's stay). He found evidence that The King's Head was not even an inn in the mid-seventeenth century, but part of a tenement, and that there had been a pub called The George in Middle Street – on the site of number 44 – and that this, therefore, must have been where Charles stayed. Despite Sawyer's research, the idea that Charles stayed at The King's Head in West Street is widely reiterated in tourist literature.

Today, more than 350 years later, there are two significant cultural celebrations of Charles II's great escape story. One is the Monarch's Way, a 615 mile footpath which traces Charles's route from Worcester to Shoreham. The other is the annual Royal Escape Race from Shoreham to Fécamp in France which, according to the Sussex Yacht Club, draws large mixed fleets of hard-core racers, family cruisers and gaff rigged classics.

Pepys and his diary

All of which is to stray from Pepys – the most famous diarist in the English language. Indeed, it's no exaggeration to suggest that he is to diaries what Shakespeare is to plays. Although born in humble circumstances, the son of a tailor, Pepys was also related to nobility. By dint of his family connections, hard work, intelligence, and considerable social skills, Pepys rose quickly through the civil service ranks eventually to become Chief Secretary to the Admiralty under both Charles II and James II. In 1662, he was briefly imprisoned in the Tower of London on suspicion of spying for

France and of being a Papist, but later on became an MP, and president of the Royal Society (serving as such when Isaac Newton published his *Principia Mathematica*).

Pepys started keeping a diary on New Year's Day in 1660, and stopped in May 1669 – because he felt that writing was bad for his ailing sight. But in those ten years, he not only provided a gloriously detailed picture of the Restoration period, but a first-hand account of several important historical events, not least the Second Anglo-Dutch War, the Great Plague, and the Great Fire of London. With meticulous detail and literary skill he recorded everything, from tragic to the comic, from his own weaknesses and frailties to grand affairs of state. Indeed, the diaries reveal a man as comfortable presenting Navy affairs to Parliament as philandering with servant girls.

Written in a shorthand code, the diaries were not deciphered or published until the 1820s. Other editions followed in the nineteenth century, but it was not until the 1970s and 1980s that Robert Latham and William Matthews transcribed and edited the complete diary for publication in nine volumes published by Bell & Hyman, London, and the University of California Press, Berkeley. Most of this edition is now available on the internet thanks to *The Diary of Samuel Pepys* website run by Phil Gyford, which also has a Pepys encyclopaedia, in-depth essays, and a lively forum for debate.

So, finally then, thanks to Sam, here is that first reference to Brighton in a diary.

The master of the house did know him

23 May 1660

The Doctor and I waked very merry, only my eye was very red and ill in the morning from yesterday's hurt. In the morning came infinity of people on board from the King to go along with him. My Lord, Mr Crew, and others, go on shore to meet the King as he comes off from shore, where Sir R Stayner bringing His Majesty into the boat, I hear that His Majesty did with a great deal of affection kiss my Lord upon his first meeting. The King, with the two Dukes and Queen of Bohemia, Princess Royal, and Prince of Orange, came on board, where I in their coming in kissed the King's, Queen's, and Princess's hands, having done the other before. Infinite shooting off of the guns, and that in a disorder on purpose, which was better than if it had been otherwise. All day nothing but Lords and persons of honour on board, that we were exceeding full. [...]

After dinner the King and Duke altered the name of some of the ships, viz the *Nazeby* into *Charles*; [...] That done, the Queen, Princess Royal, and Prince of Orange, took leave of the King, and the Duke of York went on board the *London*, and the Duke of Gloucester, the *Swiftsure*. Which done, we weighed anchor, and with a fresh gale and most happy weather we set sail for England. All the afternoon the King walked here and there, up and down (quite contrary to what I thought him to have been), very active and stirring. Upon the quarterdeck he fell into discourse of his escape from Worcester, where it made me ready to weep to hear the stories that he told of his difficulties that he had passed through, as his travelling four days and three nights on foot, every step up to his knees in dirt, with nothing but a green coat and a pair of country breeches on, and a pair of country shoes that made him so sore all over his feet, that he could scarce stir.

Yet he was forced to run away from a miller and other company, that took them for rogues. His sitting at table at one place, where the master of the house [in Brighton], that had not seen him in eight years, did know him, but kept it private; when at the same table there was one that had been of his own regiment at Worcester, could not know him, but made him drink the King's health, and said that the King was at least four fingers higher than he. At another place he was by some servants of the house made to drink, that they might know him not to be a Roundhead, which they swore he was. In another place at his inn, the master of the house, as the King was standing with his hands upon the back of a chair by the fire-side, kneeled down and kissed his hand, privately, saying, that he would not ask him who he was, but bid God bless him whither he was going. Then the difficulty of getting a boat to get into France, where he was fain to plot with the master thereof to keep his design from the four men and a boy (which was all his ship's company), and so got to Fecamp in France. At Rouen he looked so poorly, that the people went into the rooms before he went away to see whether he had not stole something or other.

2

Peregrine Phillips takes an excursion or two

The oldest published diary of any significance relating to Brighton was written by an intelligent and amusing, if slightly pompous, lawyer called Peregrine Phillips. Having gone on holiday to Little Hampton in the summer of 1778, he decided, almost on a whim, to travel to Brighton. A few days after arriving, his diary reveals little joy in the decision: 'The principal business going on among the great vulgar, is gaming: after all, as many sharpers, undoubtedly resort to these places, reservedness in general may be somewhat excusable; but yet, must remark, this makes Brighthelmston a very disagreeable place to me: to select parties it may be pleasurable, but not belonging to any such, am sincerely sorry I left Little Hampton.'

Much had changed since Charles II's escapade over a century earlier. England had united with Scotland to become a single country (1707), Britain had begun transporting convicts to Australia (1718), Sir Robert Walpole had become Britain's first Prime Minister (1721), Dr Samuel Johnson had published his *Dictionary of the English Language*, and America had declared its independence (1776). Brighton too had changed, and was no longer a simple fishing village, as Phillips's observations show. Historians point very specifically to a turning point in Brighton's fortunes – the arrival, from nearby Lewes, of Dr Richard Russell.

Dr Russell and glandular diseases

Born in 1687, Russell studied abroad in Leiden and Rotterdam before becoming – by the mid-1720s – a well-established physician. He was particularly interested in glandular diseases, and slowly developed ideas on how they could be treated by drinking, and bathing in, seawater. His thesis, first published in Latin and then in English, was widely acclaimed, and his practices attracted many followers. He is credited, thus, with playing an important supporting role in encouraging the fast-growing mania for visiting the seaside.

By the early 1750s, Russell was so successful that he could afford to build a large house on the Steine (on the site of what is now the Royal Albion Hotel) for the reception of patients. After his death in 1759, this house was rented to seasonal visitors, one of whom, twenty years later, was the Duke of Cumberland, brother of King George III. In September 1783, the Prince Regent and future George IV visited his uncle there, thus triggering what would become forty years of royal patronage for the once humble fishing village.

Peregrine Phillips was one of the many tourists attracted to Brighton by its growing reputation and improving social status, though he arrived there a few years before the Prince Regent's first visit, and stayed about two weeks. Phillips decided to have his travel diary privately printed, not long after the journey was complete, and he called it *A Sentimental Diary, Kept in an Excursion to Little Hampton, Near Arundel, and to Brighthelmstone, in Sussex*. It was sold by two booksellers in London, J. Bew of Pater-Noster-Row; and M. Davenhill, Cornhill. His own name, however, did not appear anywhere in the book.

The following year, 1779, and despite his opinion of Brighton as a 'disagreeable place', Phillips was back, diary in hand. And before that year was out, he was at the printers again, publishing his diaries from both years in a two-volume set with an amended title (and different spelling): *A Diary Kept in an Excursion to Little Hampton Near Arundel And Brighthelmston in Sussex in 1778; And also to the latter Place in 1779*. Subsequently, they were also published together in one book. Although there is still no sign of a named author or editor in these later editions, Phillips does reflect, in brief, on his purpose in printing/publishing the diaries.

The pulse of the public

'To the Editor of the Diary published in 1778', he writes, 'Thanks to you, Sir, for your publication of my DIARY last year! Your intent was good and your reasons for so doing amply sufficient; altho' several imperfections in the copy you found were afterwards materially done away, and several additions were made during a short residence abroad. By your means, Sir, I felt the pulse of the public: the reception I met with, and am now to meet with, must govern my own opinion. If encouragement follows, it may occasion some future attempts to amuse the reading part of the world; a body of people who will always let an author into the secret, if he has mistaken his talents.'

And he concludes: 'Having this season again visited BRIGHTHELMSTON, and continued the DIARY, those who shall be inclined to become my readers, may now peruse a compleat copy of the whole. I am, Sir, Your much obliged, And very humble Servant. The Author. London Nov 1779'.

Not much is known about this Peregrine Phillips. Intriguingly, a 1780 copy of the diary held by the Brighton History Centre has a handwritten note written in one of the front pages stating 'These volumes were written by Peregrine Phillips father of Mrs Crouch of Drury Lane Theatre.'

Mrs Crouch of Drury Lane

Mrs Crouch, or Anna Maria Phillips as she was born, became a very well-known singer and actress. She married a naval officer called Crouch, but the relationship did not survive long, and for much of her life she lived and worked with an Irish singer called Michael Kelly. She is also thought to have had an affair with the Prince of Wales. She died young, in her early 40s, in Brighton. There, she was buried in St Nicholas's churchyard, and an inscription, written by Kelly, on her tomb reads:

'The remains of ANNA MARIA CROUCH during many years a performer at DRURY LANE Theatre. She combined with the purest taste [as] a Singer the most elegant Simplicity as an Actress. Beautiful almost beyond parallel in her person. She was distinguished by the powers of her mind, they enabled her when She had quitted the Stage to gladden life by the charm of her conversation and refinement of her manners. She was born April 20th 1763 and died on 2nd October 1805. This stone is inscribed to her beloved memory by him whom she esteemed the most faithful of her friends.'

What we do know about Phillips is because of the fame of his daughter, not because of his own reputation in any field, or as a diarist. Details of Anna's life, in the *Oxford Dictionary of National Biography* (DNB), reveal that she was born in Gray's Inn Lane, the third of six children of Peregrine Phillips, a lawyer and official of the Wine Licence Office (of Welsh paternal and French maternal descent), and his wife, a Miss Gascoyne, the daughter of a Worcestershire farmer.

Joseph Farington, a landscape painter and another diarist with Brighton connections (see Chapter 4), mentions Phillips briefly in a diary entry from 1800. He says he was an attorney, but 'a man in a low way in that profession', but that he had been in the mercantile sea service before he became a solicitor. Towards the end of her short life, the DNB adds, Anna installed her father in a cottage off the King's Road, in Chelsea.

And that's about all. He was a keen, wry observer of human behaviour, a most forward-thinking commentator on social issues, and not a bad storyteller either. His language may seem occasionally flowery or over-wrought by modern day standards, but it is rarely boring or without purpose. Here then are substantial extracts from *A Diary Kept in an Excursion to Little Hampton Near Arundel And Brighthelmston In Sussex in 1778; And also to the latter Place in 1779.*

Volume I – Phillips decides to go to Brighton

22 August 1778
On the Sands

Mr Napier is come on the beach, to take his leave; by accident, says, he has my address; 'twas given him by a gentleman with whom he spent the preceding evening, at the Dolphin; that he had told the stranger he had just before drunk tea with us at our apartments, and of course where I was. The stranger was to go off early this morning – have lost my tide in going after him – he is gone. Who is this stranger? The elderly gentleman first mentioned, as part of the stage-coach company going to Brighthelmston. This person proposed taking a postchaise to Little Hampton, to see me, yet he has just been in the same village, and could not so much as send a messenger, or leave an address for me to find the ladies by, at Brighthelmston: but there I will go, if it is only to upbraid this man with receding from a serious promise. How the old fool has mortify'd me! What! could not I make a more forcible and lasting impression? Do the ladies – will they approve of this neglect? Well, I shall know all in a few days. And so, according to Congreve, this is THE WAY OF THE WORLD, is it? This also is a just emblem of human life.

27 August 1778
Crown and Anchor
Took leave of Mr and Mrs Lewis – left Little Hampton with more than one sigh – arrived in the evening at the Crown and Anchor, in Brighthelmston, for the first time in my life.
All is confusion and consequence here –
The building of Babel and Vanity Fair.
Enquired at the post-office, but found my stage-coach acquaintance had not left his address, according to repeated voluntary promises: emblem of human life further verified. Lay at the above tavern.

Libraries on the Steine

28 August 1778
The same
Walked on the Steine. Mr Thomas and Miss Widget both have libraries, and are very obliging people; cannot say a great deal in favour of either of their libraries, but believe they would be much better, was there not a want of spirit somewhere else. Saw the assembly-rooms; the new one, near the Steine, is extremely grand, tho' the ceiling and ornaments are by no means so elegant and high-finished as those in the buildings called Portland Place, in London. Found out the four persons who came down with me to Steyning; reproached them with insincerity, and then left them. Spent the evening with Wilson who had been to Lewes. Lay at the Crown and Anchor again. MEM. *The charge two shillings a night for lodging; too much, at least when one lives at the same house. Will remove to a private lodging tomorrow.*

Of the army and Englishmen in America

29 August 1778
The same
Friend Wilson has left me – additional reason for removing. A major in the army, one who calls himself a jolly companion, dined with us – would help every one, and officiously push the bottle about, calling constantly for a fresh one before the former was finished. The assurance with which this conduct was supported for once succeeded, and I was fully resolved to give no occasion to sneer at the Londoner as a milksop, and also to avoid such company in future. In the course of our being together, the major gave Success to his Majesty's arms in all quarters of the world! Refused to join in the toast: declared, that had it been to any person's health, I would have conformed, but in the present case, as I had all along believed the Englishmen settled in America had been unjustly treated, would not. Being determined, it was waived by the officer, who urged, that he eat his Majesty's bread, and thought it his duty; that a soldier's principal virtue was obedience. Observed, that I apprehended this to be a mistake, being assured that he and his master both eat the bread of the public; and that, if he thought it his duty to do whatever he was bid, it furnished me with further reasons why the army establishment should not be encreased, among the rest, least some of them should be bid to cut my throat.

Came here with a view of restoring health, and not to impair it, so bargained with a woman for a lodging in Middle-street Lane; conveyed my effects there, when found her husband had let the apartment, in the interim, to another person, who was a policeman: it being after dark, wished the man and his wife had a closer correspondence, at least in this respect. The good woman went with me to a poor man's house, in Ship-street, who has a large family; took a small bed-room the sooner on that account, tho' the music is rather too powerful, for the cherubims and serafims continually do cry: this, added to the spiritual songs and hymns which some females in the next house are continually chanting, make up something like a concert – wish I could say it consisted of concords.

A *disagreeable place*

30 August 1778
The same
Had a design to acknowledge I had lain tolerably well; but my landlord having just informed me the bed has been lain upon not only by lords and knights, but also esquires, upon further recollection, I say – very well; only hope, in such cases, it was placed for such personages, at least, in a better bed-chamber.

Have surveyed this town thoroughly; like the place well enough, but abominate both townsmen and visitors. The townsmen look upon all strangers as lawful prize, a sort of God-sends, as the Cornish-men call wrecks, those whom he has suffered to be afflicted, or to afflict themselves – such as needs must when the devil drives. The townsmen seem to have forgot that the ocean encircles an island; another such season as the present, however, may clear up this mystery, tho' not, perhaps, to their entire satisfaction. The people who come to bathe appear reserved and sullen, of course unsociable, as if the principle complaint they laboured under was pride; and as to the efficacy of sea water in such cases, have given my opinion before. The principal business going on among the great vulgar, is gaming: after all, as many sharpers, undoubtedly resort to these places, reservedness in general may be somewhat excusable; but yet, must remark, this makes Brighthelmston a very disagreeable place to me: to select parties it may be pleasurable, but not belonging to any such, am sincerely sorry I left Little Hampton.

The town is built on spots, in patches, and for want of regularity does not appear to advantage; every man, as to building, seems to have done what appeared right in his own eyes. Here is no magistracy; if there is an affray, the parties must go as far as Lewes, which is much the prettier town, to have it settled. Upon recollection, this town may be the quieter for having no trading justices resident on the spot. Am since informed, a gentleman in the commission of the peace attends here occasionally from Lewes. There can be no antiquities, for Brighthelmston was only a small obscure village, occupied by fishermen, till silken Folly and bloated Disease, under the auspices of a Dr Russel, deemed it necessary to crowd one shore, and fill the inhabitants with contempt for their visitors.

Competition is good for the public; against cruelty to animals

31 August 1778
The Clift

Breakfasted at the New Ship: the Old Ship has too much custom. Incline to encourage an opposition, for wherever that is the case, the public are best suited.

A young mouse has fallen down a step into my room – so young, it cannot get up again: am resolved not to kill it. What right have I wantonly to prejudice the smallest link in the great chain of animated nature? It has done me no injury – it hath purloined none of my provender; for I am unprovided – am only a lodger. Have told my landlady, however, 'tis here, by way of quieting my conscience, and she seems to care little about that, or anything else – so what is it to me? It is certainly no affair of mine.

Mr and Mrs Lloyd are this instant arrived, and have found me out: have communicated my grievances; and "griefs, when divided," as the old song says, "are hush'd into peace." But a plague attends it; they set off, after dinner, for the hamlet of Hammersmith, in the vicinity of the metropolis.

The dead alderman

A gentleman riding slowly past, have just said to Mrs Lloyd, he is very like Alderman Crosby; but it cannot be him, for, by the news-paper accounts of last week, he is dead. He calls me by my name: I shake hands with the alderman, so am sure it is not a departed spirit, and with much satisfaction ask the quondam state-prisoner, how he does. "Tolerably well for a dead man," is the answer: he has not looked better for some years. If, by the bye, the news-papers take such liberty with any man, as to kill him, the proprietors are certainly bound to restore him to life again, thro' the same vehicle.

The Lloyd's have left me.

1 September 1778
The Settle

Mr Griffiths, of Drury-lane play-house, with much civility, at my request, conducts me to the Theatre in North-street in which company he is concerned; am fearful the manager is most concerned at – the badness of the season, for here seems a plentiful lack of company. But, not to play too much upon words, it is a pretty building, something larger than that at Richmond, and seems well adapted to its intended uses.

Do not dine to-day, the reason for which forbearance may be disclosed to-morrow. Mean soon to visit the lineal descendants of Thespis.

Outwitted by a Brighthelmston dog

2 September 1778
The New Ship
The Lloyd's had left me a cold roast duck, and being determined to write at home all day, I fetch it from the George in West-street, where they quartered. Thoughtful to select fresh matter for the Diary, or, passing along thro' Middle-street-lane, thinking, if the reader pleases, like Dr Last's parson, of – nothing at all, with my newly acquired property, I felt a smart tug, and turning round, observed a huge dog making off with all practicable speed, and, to my entire confusion, with my duck in his mouth. Must confess I was agitated by a variety of passions, among which none of the smallest was rage, to be outwitted, or rather over-reached, by even a Brighthelmston dog. Well, there was but short time for deliberation, and it is plain, from the circumstance, I was badly gifted, as to presence of mind. What was to be done? by the aid of four feet he ran fastest, in a moment more would turn the corner, and be out of sight; perhaps too, poor devil! the thief might be steeped, tho' not in poverty, according to Shakespeare, yet in hunger, up to the very lips: I knew where to procure another duck – he might not, at that particular juncture; I knew also, almost by experience, that hunger would extinguish all principle, and that hospitality was below water-mark at Brighthelmston. In short, I refrained from raising the hue and cry, or even attempting to promote a pursuit.

I went home, determined to mortify myself, for my carelessness, by recording this, and former adventures, until dark. Did so: sallied forth, and ordering a small dish of fish, at the New Ship, made one good meal pass for dinner and supper. MEM *Waiter and master (the former seems the latter) hardly care if they serve a wayfaring passenger or not, unless he wears a horse, or carries a carriage about with him.*

A beached tuna

3 September 1778
On the Beach
A monstrous fish, called a *Tunie*, but not much unlike a shark, lays on the shore, wearing two double rows of large masticators: it has broke the net, and, towards mending same, the fishermen collect money of the curious. But is not this impolite, especially as such exhibitions happen very frequent? for might not such a voracious monster come, or be toss'd nearer in, and fish in its turn for human white-bait? Ask a fisherman about this, who, with an arch leer, assures me they are forbid coming nearer in shore than six or seven miles, which, without doubt, I swallow implicitly, "Mark, how the toe of the peasant doth kibe the heel – (I was going to say) of the courtier."

4 September 1778
At the Theatre
In the evening went to Mr Griffiths's benefit, the West-Indian, by desire of Lady Mills; much, but pleasingly disappointed, because the company performed a great deal better than, from information, I had been taught to expect; the ladies also were, what all stage-ladies not always are, extremely decent.

A gentleman soldier

5 September 1778
At the Sign of the King and Queen, in North-Row
Saw the militia exercise – very well indeed – for new-raised levies: I look upon them with pleasure; they are the natural defence of the nation. The word of command is "Quarters!" They disperse. A private man near me mutters "I have exchanged the Pen, master, for Brown Bess." Turning towards him, he addresses me by my name, saying he had been an attorney's clerk about ten years, but having an extravagant, ailing wife – (Query, Might not she have had an idle, drunken husband?) – and so, it being long vacation, he had accepted ten guineas to serve under his Grace, the Duke of Richmond, rather than under the keeper of a jail for debt; that he and his Grace had differed at first, the law-soldier contending, that, by having belonged to the law, he was a gentleman, and the Duke acknowledging he was a gentleman, but then insisting it was in virtue of his now being a gentleman soldier, and therefore he must conform to duty accordingly; that he had done so, much to the approbation of his officers, and was in hopes soon of obtaining a halbert [a two-handed pole weapon]. In truth, the man exercised well, so gave him credit for one half of his narrative; for my new acquaintance acknowledged he had twice been in the black hole, and once tried by court-martial, within two months for doing of – nothing, to be sure. The gentleman, at any rate, got an extra cup of ale, in consequence of the conference.

Lewd plays

6 September 1778
The Castle-Inn
Went to Lady Huntingdon's chapel in the evening; the minister, a gentleman, and scholar, but apt to wax warm, and like some other extempore preachers, at such times, capable of uttering – almost nonsense. He told us, that divine grace was bestowed, unmerited, nay, unsolicited; that in a book, before the beginning of the world, it was recorded who should be saved, and who should not. Strange doctrine, in my apprehension. Oh! the incomprehensibility of incomprehension! He attacked the neighbouring buildings, where lewd plays were acted, and, with a loud voice, pointed at, and seemingly charged me with having been there. I answer'd, "It was certainly true."

He then said, "he doubted not but I should go there again." My reply was, "Probably I may." He then spoke louder, and said "Perhaps you will turn into ridicule what you have heard here."

"Nothing more likely," rejoined I; "part of it is too much deserving."

MEM. *My part of this dialogue was internal, and therefore not heard by the rest of the congregation.*

Hutton, one of the successors to Mr Foote, who was perdue in a corner, went away muttering, that he would take off the minister at his benefit. I advised him to the contrary. (MEM. *He took my advice.*) There seems to me, faults on both sides. Why should the sons of the Sock perform such an obnoxious piece as the *Epilogue to the Minor*?

How to persuade a father against his son going to sea

7 September 1778
My own Apartment
My landlord is persuading his eldest son, and of course heir-apparent, a young prince Crispin, to go to sea. Desire the father to visit the churchyard, and upon various monuments of youth he may observe the following inscription:
Parents and Friends, weep not for me,
Tho' I was drowned in the Sea!
and then, after due deliberation, if chose to renew his persuasions, he must use his pleasure. The poor man seemed overwhelmed in thought, and much struck. Perhaps the lad may suffer no further solicitation on this account, unless his father should turn out to be a staunch predestinarian.

Mr Alderman Bull, of London, is building a house on the Clift, a window semi-circular, like that at Baltimore of Bolton house, is in each story. Am told he meets with many obstacles in the execution of his design. Surely it is for the interest of these people to have such men become resident among them; but he is denied a convenient entrance to his building. (A cellar-window to the adjoining house projects before his street-door.)

Devil's Dyke

8 September 1778
On the Downs
Breakfast with a brother [attorney] by occupation, and his family; a very worthy, sociable set. Have been with them to view the Devils Dyke, but am more pleased with the prospect of an extensive valley on the opposite side of the hill, among the wealds of Sussex; the plots of scattered villages, immersed among trees, and truly picturesque: contrasted with Old Ocean, and the barren downs round Brighthelmston – altogether, it has a fine effect.

A fisherman's wife upon the cliff

9 September 1778
My own Apartment
Dined with the same company at Shoreham, where we could get nothing to eat. No fish. Such a fishing-town! Well, patience! Bread and cheese, with bad beer; wine, so-so. MEM. *The young women looked sour, upon our asking if it was a corporate town, and whether the CHRISTIAN CLUB used to dine at this house; tho' there is no other, fit to accommodate CHRISTIANS or heathens in: no, nor this either, as Sir Phelim McGrath might be tempted to add.*

"If money comes in, as believe it won't – I'll buy me a comfortable under-petti-coat against next winter," said a fisherman's wife this morning upon the clift, who to appearance seemed miserably poor. Whether any, or what assistance I lent her towards such an acquisition, is nothing to the reader; but, if nothing was given, am fully convinced it ought to have been otherwise; as certainly snatched a smack of her manner, in the following remark, which was made immediately after:

"If I should come to Brighthelmston again (said I to myself) as I firmly believe I never shall – I'll manage my matters more comfortably next time; besides, I shall not only know better, but perhaps be better known."

"O yes!" methinks the eager housekeepers say, "if we know him, we'll throw him over the cliff."

"If you should," say the proud visitors "we'll not inquire after the low fellow: the fishermen swear they'll shew him on the beach for a monster" – not of ingratitude, at least, I hope.

But to proceed: the world, among numberless other vile comparisons, may be compared to a large tinderbox, containing plenty of tinder, with flints and matches; if you carry a proper steel about with you, you may strike a light wher-ever, and when, you please.

A young maiden dressed plain but neat

Tis towards the close of day; the sky lours, the wind blows, the roaring billows, exchanging their natural green for white heads, in curling sheets, dash upon the pebbled beach, and retire with a whistling, hollow noise – they foam in rapid succession. Awful, yet just imagery of the true Sublime! In deep contemplation on so tremendous a subject, am leaning over the rail on the edge of the clift, near the bottom of Middle-street.

A brigantine, that, by frequent trips to Newcastle, supplies this place with coals, for fear of privateers, is close in shore, riding hard, and lengthening out her cable for relief. Not far off, on my right-hand, stands Mr Davis, chief owner: is apprehensive she may not ride it out – but confides, under God, in his partner, the captain, who is on board. On my left, and very near me, reclining anxiously towards the labouring vessel, is a young maiden dressed plain but neat. Her earnest countenance, clasped hands, and whole frame agitated, as if in contact with the troubled wave, denote a troubled mind: she heaves forth many a sigh, and in a tremulous tone of voice, expressive of her fears, informs me – her true-hearted William is on board.

"See, sir," says she, "there he stands! Now, now he waves his silk handkerchief towards us!" Then, with a smile, which ought to deprecate the wrath of the most savage power, she said, exultingly, "I gave him that handkerchief! Poor creature! Am sure I never throw a coal on the fire without thinking of him!" She then put her handkerchief, another of the same pattern, to her eyes. Having been at work below, methought he looked black, like Othello, while she seemed innocently enamoured, like Desdemona. May their fate be unlike!

The brig had ridden safe

10 September 1778
The same
Was early on the clift; found the brig had ridden safe, and, after my morning's bathing, went on board, to shake hands with honest William, who is quite the character – as hearty a fellow as ever broke biscuit with his elbow, or lent hand to empty a can of slip. Am pleased with my new acquaintance: it is pure nature; and "thou, Nature, art my goddess".

Of bathing machines

13 September 1778
On the Clift
Took the liberty of surveying all the bathing-machines. Fine ladies going – fine ladies coming away. Observe them at the instant of bathing. How humiliating! They appear more deplorable than so many corpses in shrouds, and put me in mind of the old dialogue between Death and the Lady. Methinks the guide is saying, in the character of Death,

> Fair lady, lay your costly robes aside,
> Nor longer think to glory in your pride!

Surely, such considerations might assist to abate the pride of an helpless, infirm animal, tho' a fine lady. But away with such gloomy sentiments! The ladies certainly appear to be on a level with the meanest of their sex, agreeable to the old proverb, quoted by Mrs Winifred in Humphrey Clinker, on another occasion, viz. That "all cats in the dark are grey." And now, hey for London.

Volume II – Phillips once more at Brighthelmston

21 August 1779
Written at Steyning
Travelled in a stage-coach towards the sea-coast of Sussex; the company very agreeable. [...] and towards evening found myself once more at Brighthelmston.

22 August 1779
My own Apartments
Most of the morning reposed myself after my journey, and in the evening walked about town, to observe what alterations had been made in the course of twelve months. The Crown and Anchor tavern in East-street is shut up. In the evening walked on the Steyne, and drank tea at Shergold's assembly-rooms.

More on the Steine librarians

23 August 1779
In Bowen's Library
There is a sort of rivalry between the two Librarians on the Steyne, as to their subscription books; which shall most justly deserve the title of the book of Numbers. There is a constant struggle between them, which shall be most courteous; and the effects are those usually consequent upon an opposition. Sir Christopher Caustic, this morning was turning over the leaves, at Bowen's [Bowen's Library, which used to be Widget's, at the south end of the Steyne], which contains the names of the subscribers. Mr Bowen, [...] with offered pen and ink, craved the honour of an additional name: this being his first season, and having been purposely misinformed by some would be witty wag; "Sir," said Mr. Bowen, displaying, all the time, two irregular rows of remarkably white teeth, 'yours will stand immediately after that of the Honourable Charles James Fox, Esq., and before that of Mrs Franco★, the rich Jew's lady★★. Esquire W___d's was to have been on the medium line, but, poor gentleman! he is unfortunately detained near London, on emergent business.' (★ A lady of easy virtue, who spent last season here with Mr France; the present with whom she can; ★★ A fungus, well known by the name of Billy the Beau, who without any foundation has lavished several thousand pounds at this place, and is now in the King's-Bench prison, to the great grief of sundry usurers.)

In Thomas's Library
Mr Thomas, the other librarian, must be noticed in turn. He hath been years enough practising small talk with the ladies and gentlemen upon the Steyne, and hath arrived to a surprising degree of precision in pronouncing French-English. He is now reading the news-papers to some of his subscribers with an audible voice, and repeatedly calls a detached body of troops a corpse; a tour he improves into a tower, and delivers his words with a most promiscas manner.

Mr Diarist is coming this way

26 August 1779
The Alcove
Sometimes a droll incident occurs. This morning I edged away – we are on the edge of the ocean you know – towards the alcove at the east end of the bottom of the Steyne, wherein were seated two Elders, and perhaps, a chaste Susanna; at any rate, she was not naked. On my approach they departed hastily, and I joined the deserted lady – in discourse, by observing that the town was thin, and that I heard trade in general was very bad.

"Very bad, indeed, Sir," said she; "I suppose you are a fellow sufferer. You belong to the players, Sir, don't you?"

"My dear," replied I, "why should you think so?"

"Because you are seldom without a book in your hand."

"Do few read besides players, then?"

"Yes, Sir, I beg pardon; I had another reason; but you'll excuse me."

"Indeed I will not my dear."

"Why then, Sir, as you advanced towards us, one of those elderly gentlemen – by their discourse I believe they are parsons – said to the other, 'Come, Sir, let us be gone, or we shall be taken off; Mr Diarist is coming this way.' Now, Sir, if that is your name, tho' I have never seen it yet in the play bills, was it wonderful that I should imagine you to be one of the gentlemen players." I assured her, nevertheless, that I was not entitled to that honour; and here you may imagine our conference ended.

Genteel company, and small talk

27 August 1779
Under the Front of Bowen's Library
The company encreases fast, and is very genteel; nevertheless, you may measure the wealth and rank of some by the degree of insolence they assume: tho' this rule, like most others, is not universal; for Lady ___ of ___ ___, a star of the first magnitude in the polite hemisphere, surrounded by her macaroni satellites, with each two watches, (one on each thigh,) and two tassels dangling from the two hind triangular corners of each of their hats, is poor to an extreme, as most gamblers generally are – yet she is insolent to an equal extreme. To be sure, no person of rank, or rank person, at Brighthelmston, can pretend to dispute the palm with ___ ___'s lady. The matter of the ceremonies, however assiduously and obsequiously he may bow, and small talk with her Ladyship, would find himself baffled in the search, in the pursuit, and in the ending of the chance, after such another competition of pride and insolence, after such another automaton of vanity.

28 August 1779
"Small talk! Mr Diarist," methinks you say; "what do you mean by small talk? You have mentioned it twice." Oh, 'tis of various sorts, and so common as scarcely to require an explanation; but take a specimen. My Lady Totterdown is addressing the Honourable Sir Harry Harebrains:

"Have you been in this morning, Sir Harry?"

"Yes, my Lady."

"Was it rough?"

"Very."

"Did you stay long in?"

"A short time; a few moments only."

"How far did you go in?"

"As far as I could with safety; your Ladyship knows I am no swimmer. You was not at the rooms last assembly-night, my Lady."

"No, Sir, I was engaged with a private party at Mrs Limberham's; we played rather deep to be sure, but I love to play deep: I play deeper sometimes."

"Do you so, my Lady?" Cetera defunt.

29 August 1779
On a Tomb-stone, in the Church-yard

Have been this morning to the sailor's land mark – to the only church in the town – and collected a number of novelties. The Doctor was pleased to inform us, in a religiously political, or politically religious discourse, that when men tremble they are generally afraid; when they are in danger they should strive to extricate themselves; and that hope is the expectant of many great and singular good events.

Like a Venetian carnival

30 August 1779
My own Apartments

Among others of the musical profession down here are [...] also persons of consequence, tho' not professors, who frequently amuse themselves with drawing a bow, &c. and the delicious concerts, which are almost every evening performed at one private house or another, are enough to remind the street passenger of a principal ingredient in, or more properly at, a Venetian carnival.

Weeding the mental garden

4 September 1779
In the Old Settle

I have several times mentioned raffles, horses, houses, phaetons, child's rattles, books, baubles, caps and bells; of which latter articles, have one on my head, and another on my hand. You'll observe them instantly, Sir, or Madam, Master, or Miss, if you should please to turn your eye this way. Every article of convenience, every trinket of luxury, is transferred by this uncertain, quick mode of conveyance. Not a shop without its rattle-trap – rattle, rattle, rattle, morning and evening. Here may be seen – walk in and see – an abridgement of the wisdom of the world. The pomps and vanities are at large, varying like yon evanescent clouds.

Observe the fond parent, initiating her forward offspring in the use of the dice-box, and setting herself the example; yet may she wonder, at some future day, and think her throw in life's raffle extremely severe, that a propensity to that and similar habits should continue and encrease. Mind, reader! if the next generation should be worse than the present (which a cynic would say can hardly be), and this little book should live so long; take notice, the Diarist avers, is owing to a false love, to a foolish fondness, which prevents weeding the mental garden early, when the first shoots of vice and folly, being young and tender, are easily plucked up by the roots; for want whereof, age gives precedence to youth, and ignorance takes the lead of knowledge.

There are no boys or girls now: from infancy they are all young ladies and gentleman. There is scarce a family without a spoilt child or children in it. When in leading-strings, maid-servants have been charged not to let see the moon, for fear they should long for it, which, tho' it might be raffled for, could not be delivered over to the winner, and when grown up, too many of them, desirous of plunging into an ocean of pleasure, are almost ready to push the parent from her proper seat. After all, this evil may be the natural contrast to the too rigid treatment of youth in the last age. Extremes are ever bad, and ever to be avoided as much as possible; but, according to the scholastic maxim, in avoiding Scylla with difficulty we steer clear of Charybdis. "So you have flung away the book, Miss, have you? Well, Miss, perhaps Mamma may be able to prevail on you to take it up again; and yet as the situation grows critical, I'll not wait to be a witness, peradventure, of my own disgrace; so farewell, Madam."

A missing boy

5 September 1779
At the Bottom of the East-end Windmill
How careful ought youth to be! Had the supreme satisfaction of being instrumental towards saving the life of a fellow-creature. The son of an Irish gentleman of fortune, an Eton scholar, about ten years of age, had been sent to the Castle Tavern, to fetch his father to dinner, but had been missing ever since, and evening was approaching fast. Another gentleman and lady, coming along the sands, from Rottingden, said, that they saw such a youth above two miles from Brighthelmston, underneath the Clift. I searched after some of his distressed, inquiring friends; related what I had heard; and advised the sending instantly a stout man and horse from Shergold's: as the tide was flowing in fast, not a moment was to be lost. They did so, and the child was brought in safe, just at dusk. Some one else took the merit of conveying the information, and of giving the advice; a common case: but no matter for that; the fond parent's anxiety was removed; the principal object of his apparent happiness was saved; and the extent of my view was amply circumscribed by the glorious line of humanity. Well! never mind it, thought I; my friend Sancho's [Ignatius Sancho, a native of Africa, who kept a shop in Westminster] heart will beat in unison, however, when he reads this.

6 September 1779
On the Steyne
This morning, his Grace of Manchester, who wears a benevolent heart, was pleased to commend my assiduity and presence of mind.

Escalating property prices

7 September 1779
On the Clift

Am viewing my worthy friend Mr Bull's house, or rather box, upon the Clift, between Ship-street and Black-Lion-street. He beckons me in, and shews it throughout. It is one pretty room to the height of three stories with a semi-circular window comprising most of the front, and on each floor overlooking the sea all ways, which makes the situation most delightful. The ground whereon it stands is copyhold – indeed the ground in and about Brighthelmston is mostly so – measuring nearly eighteen feet square. The fine is both certain and small. About fifty years ago, this piece of land was sold for four pounds; thirty years since, a purchaser gave eleven; and, about this time two years, the Alderman bought it for one hundred pounds, to build upon. What an influence of improvement! MEM. *The nuisance of a sloping cellar-door, just before the door of his house, is continued, to the disgrace of the Committee appointed by a late act of Parliament, which gives sufficient authority.*

Mr Bull is, with much justice, partial to this retreat, and has furnished it neatly, comfortable to its size; nor do I believe he would exchange it for that of his Grace of Marlborough on the Steyne – indeed he told me so – much less do I believe he would lett his house out for hire, as greater men have done – but some great men (The Duke of Marlborough, tho' his income is immense, letts his house out, even to different families at the same time) can afford to do very little things.

An old well

8 September 1779
Among the Boats on the East Side of the Steyne

An old well is half open among the boats; a little child has just now waddled off the Steyne towards it. I ran to prevent mischief, and succeeded. Have remonstrated against this dangerous neglect in vain. There are one dry and two wet wells open thereabouts. When a child of fortune or two shall have been lost therein, the wells may be boarded over. The Commissioners by the Act have sufficient powers, and collect money enough to answer its purposes; yet the Clift side is all along covered with rubbish, offensive to the sight and smell. Indeed, there is no occasion to search much for nuisances, obstructions, and inconveniences, in this place. MEM: *Since the above complaint, some loose boards have been laid across one of the wet wells.*

The selfishness of bathees

9 September 1779
Upon the Sands

Selfishness, like pride, is natural, and may be meritorious: to a precise point it is a virtue, beyond which it become vicious, the additional criminality whereof encreases rapidly and proportionately. The preference given to self, operates so wisely as to be necessarily beneficial to others; which proves, that "self-love and social are the same." Like a stone thrown upon the surface of a placid pond, the head of a family is incircled singly; another more distant circle, tho' fainter, comprises his nearest relatives, upon an equal line; these are succeeded by others, progressively more faint, being his more distant relations – acquaintance – the inhabitants of the parish, county, and kingdom, wherein he dwells; and the last circular line, tho' naturally most faint, comprehends and embraces the whole human race. What could occasion such a train of thought? The selfishness of the Bathees at Brighthelmston. Each man runs to a machine-ladder, as it is dragging out of the sea, and scuffles who shall first set foot thereon: some send their footmen and contend by proxy; others go in boots, or on horse-back, to meet the machines: so that a tolerably modest man, on a busy morning, has generally an hour and an half, perhaps two hours time, for contemplation on the sands, to the detriment of his shoes as well as the diminution of his patience – nay, he must have the time, whether he will or not; tho' he possesses still the power of using it as he pleases: and this at present is my way, the second morning, successively, that I have been treated thus. To proceed – for I am not likely to be accommodated soon I see – have been long induced to rank selfishness among the temporary national grievances, and that an inordinate lust thereof is the source of the most capital evils sustained by society.

11 September 1779
My own Apartments
Have matched the bathers and bathees this trip however, have corrected them all handsomely, without quarrelling – have given them the slip; but take the particulars: About 6 am, I drew along the sands, the machine of which I had become seized by prescriptive right, by legal possession, having deposited part of my wearing apparel therein, tho' I had requested the assistance of the marine centaur, the man on horseback, in vain. As the tide was flowing, I soon plunged into the sea, stretched a long way out into the offing, and continued rolling and laughing among my brother porpoises, to think what a loss the company on shore would sustain for want of one machine out of seven, it being a very fine busy morning. The bathers halloo'd and bawled in vain; for I could not, indeed would not hear them. After swimming backwards and forwards along the shore, about four miles in the whole, the tide setting strong to the eastward all the time, I returned about nine; and Smoaker, growling like a bear with a sore head, swore bitterly, he believed I had been to France or Holland, and, cooling by degrees, desired to know the news. I told him the Dieppe Monsieurs had laughed heartily at the mode of retaliation I had instituted at Brighthelmston; that they grinned at the account stated, and allowed that the bathers ought to behave like bathers, and the bathees like gentlemen: moreover, that they had whispered, if the above did not succeed, they would come over, and settle the point between us; upon which I had instantly returned, without another word, lest I should incur the charge of treasonable correspondence.

12 September 1779

The same

Yesterday's exploit has produced an amendment. Shame sometimes follows close at the heels of reflection. A man may now be accommodated nearly in turn, which was all that was wished. Have since found no considerable cause of complaint. It proves that an individual may be useful to a community.

Wedding customs

13 September 1779

In the Churchyard

A new man and wife have just passed me. The town's-people preserve some customs here that smack of great antiquity, and seem peculiar to the county of Sussex. At a marriage there are strewers, who strew the way from church, not only with flowers, but with sugar-plums and wheat. Why sugar-plums and wheat, I wonder? Many ceremonies have been retained longer than the history of their origin or foundation.

[According to John Ackerson Erredge, a nineteenth-century Brighton historian – see Chapter 5 – this system of strewing the bride and bridegroom was still being pursued in the 1860s, 'not merely by the friends of the happy pair – all couples just married are pronounced to be happy – but by a constant group of women with children in their arms, who scatter their corn, &c., with blessings, in proportion to the harvest of coin they reap.']

A floating prison ship

14 September 1779

Near the Windmill, at the West-End

The Shoreham floating-jail [the name given by locals to a vessel used to house civilians pressed into joining the army] is in the offing, and the fishermen flee to their hiding places, where some of them have pined, with their almost starving families, for months – and no wonder. When impressed, they are ironed and stowed aboard the tender for several weeks, 'till a full compliment of slaves, I mean free-born Englishmen, are crowded together, who afterwards disembogued on board a man of war, having probably an epidemical distemper on board, which last article frightens the wretches from all bounties. The survivors are sent to fight for their remaining liberties and properties, and their families become parish–burthens. Hark ye! you rich and powerful, are not the connections of these casual children of CALAMITY tender as your own? Consider, is this doing as you would think it right to be done by. Know any of you, what the next age may produce? What your own immediate posterity may be reduced to? How soon "the WHEEL" may "come full circle?"

A long story follows, over the next few days' diary entries, in which Phillips tells of meeting the woman on the Clift, from a year ago, now married to William, but who has been pressed on board the ship, *The Tender*, and how he resolves to save him from that fate.

Defending Brighton against French privateers

23 September 1779
In the Battery of Twelve Guns
Some French privateers are said to be hovering about in the offing, and we hear now and then a report of firing. Provoking! They will not come within reach of the only four guns that may be fired with safety. I mean, when properly loaded with powder and ball – a salute is nothing. The rest are well known to be honey-combed. The small craft, then, may be cut off with impunity. What a pity that a couple of light fix-pounders cannot be spared by the Board of Ordnance to protect the coast! Those, with men or horses, might be dragged along the Clift, and prevent every sort of mischief to be dreaded from such despicable picaroons; instead whereof, two horse-soldiers, in long scarlet cloaks, ride along the coast, [...] The utility of this parade I leave to be enlarged upon by some future Diarist.

Mushrooms on the Steyne

24 September 1779
In the old Settle, farthest from the Steyne
Have frequently asked, in vain, the cause of the large and small ringlets worn in the grass upon the Steyne, and on the sides of the Downs, for the legend of Fairy-dancing was too childish to be satisfactory, and could not find a naturalist in the place; even Mr Thomas could not tell. Doctor Mitchell is coming up Craig's Lane, I meet him about the middle, and propose the question. He begins to explain the cause.

"It is determined at last, Sir," says he, "to be a mushroom business: the seeds" – at this moment, unfortunately for my inquiry, subscribers perhaps, coming along, drew off his attention, and I was left in haste, while he formed the sign of the Salutation in conjunction with a Gentleman, to the back of whose head was fixed a bag, and his side a sword. The Ladies also - I walked off, saying to myself, "Had I been a subscriber now, and leaning out of my own chariot, this business might have ended otherwise."

SLANDER, good heavens! – nothing by slander! An infantine rumour, having been begot by the Prince of Darkness, conceived by Falsehood, nursed by Malice, and conveyed by Whisper up North-street, shall crawl down West-street, creep along the Clift, and fly through East-street upon the Steyne, gathering additional strength every foot of the way. Venomous Reptile! never at rest, till satiated with the defamation of Innocence.

Surviving a storm on the Steyne

26 September 1779
In the Alcove
To prove, once more, how little attention is shewn to the convenience of the genteelest company, in regard even to their most favourite spot, the Steyne, take the following account: In the afternoon, which was remarkably fine, sat under

the Piazzas in the front of Mr Bowen's Library; but soon after it began to rain, thunder, and lighten to an extreme. A gentleman seeming alarmed at its sudden approach and violence, I remarked, "that the storm was nothing to what it would be." Having been silent till then, and speaking with rather a sententious sort of gravity, was sorry to observe, what I had said had taken effect to alarm several ladies who were present. The storm, however, increased to a much greater excess, the Library was locked up, and the key in Mr Bowen's pocket at Lewes.

Thus we continued, the lightning flashes as if the air was on fire, and the rain pouring hard for several hours, so as to overflow the ground. The ladies were obliged to be mounted upon common chairs; and, in endeavouring to accommodate the tenderest and most lovely part of the creation, I discovered they were persons of the first condition; three of them in particular, displayed such fortitude, true politeness, and extreme affability, as sufficiently indicated by their high station in life. The D___ D___ of A___ said to her daughter, "Lady Ch___, you are fond of an adventure, what think you of this?" Their situation was certainly uncommon, and I studied to make it as tolerable as possible.

At last their coach was procured, and I had the honour of handling some of the finest ladies in the universe, to their carriage. To stoop under a very low rail, was mortifying, but necessary, to avoid a flood of water. "Things that love night, love not such nights as these," thought I; and yet, again, "Sweet are the uses of ADVERSITY!" Though I was wet through, I thought myself next morning amply recompensed by complimentary thanks from both mother and daughter near the sea-side.

Parrots talking politics

During the storm, and while we were confined as before related, two silly, chattering fellows, taking advantage of our situation, talked nonsense to the ladies, which must give those who were not used to such company, an ill impression of the middling order of the people. I felt hurt on this account, and wished much for an enlivening conversation; but, to add to my chagrin, the creatures wanted to engage me in politics, which I waved on pretence of the weather, and was never more offended at the prostitution of terms or science. Instead of reading and discriminating, if political disputants, in general, as they are called, can remember, that there are three constitutional estates in this realm, that there is such a part of the world as North America, that the words Liberty and Licentiousness have a different meaning, and if they can acquire, like parrots, a few set phrases, it is now-a-days called talking politics. Quote the opinions of a Locke, or a Sidney, and the sneering whisper circulates instantaneously of – What a Boor! The debating societies, which spring up like mushrooms in the hot-bed of the Metropolis, may or may not rectify this evil. Time will shew all – but it is a talking age; aye and a writing one too, as my Reader might say. My reply, however, in such case, should only be, Courteous Reader, once more farewell.

27 September 1779
Took a farewell review of the Assembly-Rooms, the Steyne, the Sea, and the Town; and, entering a post-chaise, quitted Brighthelmston for London.

3

That's she, that's the famous Miss Fanny Burney

A week or two after Peregrine Phillips 'quitted Brighthelmston', Fanny Burney, not yet famous, but becoming so, arrived for the first time.

Frances Burney was born in 1752 at King's Lynn, Norfolk, the daughter of Charles Burney, a musician and man of letters. The family moved to London in 1760, where Charles was part of a busy literary circle, but her mother died when Frances was just 10. Fanny, as she was known, was a precocious child, educated at home with the help of her father's extensive library and of his friends. One of these was Samuel Crisp who encouraged her to write journal-letters, in which she carefully reported on the social world around her family, which came to include the painter Joshua Reynolds, Samuel Johnson, and Henry and Hester Thrale.

Apart from her diary, Fanny also wrote fiction, but in secret, as this was not considered a suitable activity for respectable females. In early 1778, when only 26, and with the help of family intermediaries, Fanny's first novel, *Evelina, or, A Young Lady's Entrance into the World* was published anonymously. It was an instant success and led London society to speculate on the identity of the writer – widely assumed to be a man.

The author of Evelina *discovered*

When discovered as the author of *Evelina*, Fanny was taken up in her own right by literary and high society, in particular she became more friendly with the Thrales and Johnson. But the success of her second novel, *Cecilia*, was overshadowed by the deaths of friends and her mentor Crisp in the first half of the 1780s. During the second half of the same decade, she entered the royal household as a Keeper of the Robes for Queen Charlotte; but they were unhappy years and she was allowed to resign in 1791. Two years later, she married Alexandre d'Arblay, and they had one son.

Hoping to recover property lost during the French Revolution, d'Arblay moved his family to France in 1802, but the resumption of the Napoleonic War left them stranded there for a decade. While in France, Fanny made medical history by writing about her mastectomy without anaesthesia. Later, she also remained with her husband on the Continent while he was still fighting with French Royalists.

He died in 1818, and thereafter Fanny focused on editing the memoirs of her father and her own writings, especially her diary and letters. She died in 1840.

Evelina is now considered a classic and is still in print, and Fanny's reputation has grown over the years to the point where she is considered by some to be the first woman to make writing novels respectable (Virginia Woolf called her 'the mother of English fiction') and to have paved the way for the nineteenth century writers such as Jane Austen. She is also celebrated today, though, for her extraordinary diaries, famed not only for their literary quality but for their social content.

The diaries were first edited by her niece, Charlotte Frances Barrett, and published by Henry Colburn in seven volumes in the 1840s as *Diary and Letters of Madame d'Arblay*. A fuller and less bowdlerised version was edited by Joyce Hemlow and published in 12 volumes in the 1970s and 1980s by Clarendon Press – *The Journals and Letters of Fanny Burney (Madame d'Arblay), 1791-1840*.

To nobody will I write my journal

Fanny's own introduction to her diary, written when just 15, is worth reproducing:

> To have some account of my thoughts, manners, acquaintance and actions, when the hour arrives at which time is more nimble than memory, is the reason which induces me to keep a Journal – a Journal in which I must confess my every thought, must open my whole heart.
>
> But a thing of the kind ought to be addressed to somebody – I must imagine myself to be talking – talking to the most intimate of friends – to one in whom I should take delight in confiding, and feel remorse in concealment: but who must this friend be? To make choice of one in whom I can but half rely, would be to frustrate entirely the intention of my plan. The only one I could wholly, totally confide in, lives in the same house with me, and not only never has, but never will leave me one secret to tell her. To whom then must I dedicate my wonderful, surprising, and interesting adventures? – to whom dare I reveal my private opinion of my nearest relations? my secret thoughts of my dearest friends? my own hopes, fears, reflections, and dislikes? – Nobody.
>
> To NOBODY, then, will I write my Journal! since to Nobody can I be wholly unreserved, to Nobody can I reveal every thought, every wish of my heart, with the most unlimited confidence, the most unremitting sincerity, to the end of my life! For what chance, what accident, can end my connections with Nobody? No secret can I conceal from Nobody, and to Nobody can I be ever unreserved. Disagreement cannot stop our affection – time itself has no power to end our friendship. The love, the esteem I entertain for Nobody, Nobody's self has not power to destroy. From Nobody I have nothing to fear. The secrets sacred to friendship Nobody will not reveal; when the affair is doubtful, Nobody will not look towards the side least favourable.

The bulk of Fanny's diaries is taken up with observations of and gossip about the people she knows and meets, especially young men, but here are some entries from two visits she made to Brighton, one not long after she had been exposed as the author of *Evelina*, and another three years later, 1782, the year she published her second novel,

Cecilia. These extracts are taken from the first two volumes of a six-volume edition of *Diary & Letters of Madame D'Arblay* (1778-1840) published by Macmillan in 1904.

Of Thomas and Bowen on the Steyn (again)

12 October 1779

Our next stage brought us to Brighthelmstone, where I fancy we shall stay till the Parliament calls away Mr Thrale [Member for Southwark].

The morning after our arrival, our first visit was from Mr Kipping, the apothecary, a character so curious that Foote [Samuel Foote, a dramatist and actor who died in Brighton in 1777] designed him for his next piece, before he knew he had already written his last. He is a prating, good-humoured, old gossip, who runs on in as incoherent and unconnected a style of discourse as Rose Fuller, though not so tonish.

The rest of the morning we spent, as usual at this place, upon the Steyn, and in booksellers' shops. Mrs Thrale entered all our names at Thomas's, the fashionable bookseller; but we find he has now a rival, situated also upon the Steyn, who seems to carry away all the custom and all the company. This is a Mr Bowen, who is just come from London, and who seems just the man to carry the world before him as a shopkeeper. Extremely civil, attentive to watch opportunities of obliging, and assiduous to make use of them – skilful in discovering the taste or turn of mind of his customers, and adroit in putting in their way just such temptations as they are least able to withstand. Mrs Thrale, at the same time that she sees his management and contrivance, so much admires his sagacity and dexterity, that, though open-eyed, she is as easily wrought upon to part with her money, as any of the many dupes in this place, whom he persuades to require indispensably whatever he shows them.

He did not, however, then at all suspect who I was, for he showed me nothing but schemes for raffles, and books, pocket-cases, etc., which were put up for those purposes. It is plain I can have no authoress air, since so discerning a bookseller thought me a fine lady spendthrift, who only wanted occasions to get rid of money.

In the evening we went to the rooms, which, at this time, are open every other night at Shergold's, or the New Assembly Rooms, and the alternate nights at Hick's, or the Ship Tavern. This night they were at the latter.

There was very little company, and nobody that any of us knew, except two or three gentlemen of Mr Thrale's acquaintance, among whom was that celebrated wit and libertine, the Hon. Mr Beauclerk, and a Mr Newnham, a rich counsellor, learned in the law, but, to me, a displeasing man.

Almost everybody but ourselves went to cards; we found it, therefore, pretty stupid, and I was very glad when we came home.

([Editor's notes:] Shergold's was the Castle Inn, in Castle Square, pulled down in 1823; Hick's, the Old Ship Tavern in Ship Street. Both had Public Rooms, where Dress Balls and Card Assemblies were held throughout the Season. The Hon. Topham Beauclerk, 1730-1780, Johnson's friend, and, grandson of the first Duke of St Albans was an original member of the Literary Club.)

Mrs Thrale's daughter and the author of Evelina

While Mrs Thrale, Mrs Dickens, and I were walking about after tea, we were joined by a Mr Cure, a gentleman of the former's acquaintance. After a little while he said,

"Miss Thrale is very much grown since she was here last year; and besides, I think she's vastly altered."

"Do you, sir," cried she, "I can't say I think so."

"Oh, vastly! – but young ladies at that age are always altering. To tell you the truth, I did not know her at all."

This, for a little while, passed quietly; but soon after, he exclaimed,

"Ma'am, do you know I have not yet read 'Evelina'?"

"Have not you so, sir?" cried she, laughing.

"No, and I think I never shall, for there's no getting it; the booksellers say they never can keep it a moment, and the folks that hire it keep lending it from one to another in such a manner that it is never returned to the library. It's very provoking."

"But," said Mrs Thrale, "what makes you exclaim about it so to me?"

"Why, because, if you recollect, the last thing you said to me when we parted last year, was 'Be sure you read 'Evelina'.' So as soon as I saw you I recollected it all again. But I wish Miss Thrale would turn more this way."

"Why, what do you mean, Mr Cure? do you know Miss Thrale now?"

"Yes, to be sure," answered he, looking full at me, "though I protest I should not have guessed at her had I seen her with anybody but you."

"Oh, ho!" cried Mrs Thrale, laughing, "so you mean Miss Burney all this time."

"What? – how? – eh? – why is that – is not that Miss Thrale? is not that your daughter?"

"No to be sure it is not – I wish she was!"

Mr Cure looked aghast, Mrs Dickens laughed aloud, and I, the whole time, had been obliged to turn my head another way, that my sniggering might not sooner make him see his mistake. As soon, I suppose, as he was able, Mr Cure in a low voice repeated, "Miss Burney! so then that lady is the authoress of 'Evelina' all this time." And, rather abruptly, he left us and joined another party.

I suppose he told his story to as many as he talked to, for, in a short time, I found myself so violently stared at that I could hardly look any way without being put quite out of countenance, particularly by young Mr Cumberland, a handsome, soft-looking youth, who fixed his eyes upon me incessantly, though but the evening before, when I saw him at Hick's, he looked as if it would have been a diminution of his dignity to have regarded me twice.

This ridiculous circumstance will, however, prevent any more mistakes of the same kind, I believe, as my 'authorshipness' seems now pretty well known and spread about Brighthelmstone.

(The very next morning as Miss Thrale and I entered Bowen's shop, where we were appointed to meet Mrs Thrale, I heard her saying to him, as they were both in serious and deep confabulation: "So you have picked up all this, Mr Bowen, have you?" then, seeing me, "Oh, ho!" she cried, "so one never is to speak of anybody at Brighthelmstone, but they are to be at one's elbow."

"I presume," quoth I, "you were scarcely speaking of me?"

"No, but I was hearing of you from Mr Bowen."

And when we left the shop she told me that he had said to her, "Oh, ma'am, what a book thrown away was that! All the trade cry shame on Lowndes. Not, ma'am, that I expected he could have known its worth, because that's out of the question; but when its profits told him what it was, it's quite scandalous that he should have done nothing! quite ungentlemanlike indeed!"

There's a bookseller for you, Susy!)

A *childish chaos of absurdity and obscenity*

20 October 1779

Last Tuesday, at the request of Lady S, who patronised a poor actor, we all went to the play, which was Dryden's 'Tempest' [the theatre was in North Street], and a worse performance have I seldom seen. Shakspeare's 'Tempest', which for fancy, invention, and originality, is at the head of beautiful improbabilities, is rendered by the additions of Dryden a childish chaos of absurdity and obscenity; and the grossness and awkwardness of these poor unskilful actors rendered all that ought to have been obscure so shockingly glaring, that there was no attending to them without disgust. All that afforded me any entertainment was looking at Mr Thrale, who turned up his nose with an expression of contempt at the beginning of the performance, and never suffered it to return to its usual place till it was ended!

The play was ordered by Mrs Cumberland. These poor actors never have any company in the boxes unless they can prevail upon some lady to bespeak a play, and desire her acquaintance to go to it. But we all agreed we should not have been very proud to have had our names at the head of a play-bill of Dryden's *Tempest*.

Two young beaus laughing

26 October 1782

My journey was incidentless; but the moment I came into Brighthelmstone I was met by Mrs Thrale, who had most eagerly been waiting for me a long while, and therefore I dismounted, and walked home with her. It would be very superfluous to tell you how she received me, for you cannot but know, from her impatient letters, what I had reason to expect of kindness and welcome.

I was too much tired to choose appearing at dinner, and therefore eat my eat upstairs, and was then decorated a little, and came forth to tea.

Mr Harry Cotton [a relative of Mr Thrale] and Mr Swinerton were both here. Mrs Thrale said they almost lived with her, and therefore were not to be avoided, but declared she had refused a flaming party of blues, for fear I should think, if I met them just after my journey, she was playing Mrs Harrel [a character from 'Cecilia'].

Dr Johnson received me too with his usual goodness, and with a salute so loud, that the two young beaus, Cotton and Swinerton, have never done laughing about it.

Mrs Thrale spent two or three hours in my room, talking over all her affairs, and then we wished each other *bon repos*, and retired. *Grandissima* conclusion.

Oh, but let me not forget that a fine note came from Mr Pepys, who is here with his family, saying he was *pressé de vivre*, and entreating to see Mrs and Miss T, Dr Johnson, and Cecilia, at his house the next day. I hate mightily this method of naming me from my heroines, of whose honour I think I am more jealous than of my own.

That's she, that's the famous Miss Burney

27 October 1782

The Pepyses came to visit me in form, but I was dressing; in the evening, however, Mrs and Miss T took me to them. Dr Johnson would not go; he told me it was my day, and I should be crowned, for Mr Pepys was wild about 'Cecilia'.

"However," he added, "do not hear too much of it; but when he has talked about it for an hour or so, tell him to have done. There is no other way."

A mighty easy way, this! however, 'tis what he literally practises for himself.

We found at Mr Pepys' nobody but his wife, his brother, Dr Pepys, and Dr Pepys' lady, Countess of Rothes. Mr Pepys received me with such distinction, that it was very evident how much the book, with the most flattering opinion of it, was in his head; however, he behaved very prettily, and only mentioned it by allusions; most particularly upon the character of Meadows, which he took various opportunities of pronouncing to be the "best hit possible" upon the present race of fine gentlemen. He asked me whether I had met with Mrs Chapone lately; and when I said no, told me he had two letters from her, all about me, which he must communicate to me.

We did not stay with them long, but called upon Miss Benson, and proceeded to the Rooms. Mr Pepys was very unwilling to part with us, and wanted to frighten me from going, by saying,

"And has Miss Burney courage to venture to the Rooms? I wonder she dares!"

I did not seem to understand him, though to mistake him was impossible. However, I thought of him again when I was at the Rooms, for most violent was the staring and whispering as I passed and repassed; insomuch that I shall by no means be in any haste to go again to them. Susan and Sophy Thrale, who were with their aunt, Mrs Scot, told Queeny, upon our return, that they heard nothing said, whichever way they turned, but "That's she!" "That's the famous Miss Burney!" I shall certainly escape going any more, if it is in my power.

Lady Shelley and Lady Poole were there, and were very civil, and looked very pretty. There was also a Mr Coxe, brother to the writer, a very cultivated man, a great scholar, a poet, a critic, and very soft-mannered and obliging. He is, however, somewhat stiff and affected, and rather too plaintive in his voice.

Ladies distracted by Cecilia

28 October 1782

Mr Pepys had but just left me, when Mrs Thrale sent Susan with a particular request to see me in her dressing-room, where I found her with a milliner.

"Oh, Miss Burney," she cried, "I could not help promising Mrs Cockran that she should have a sight of you – she has begged it so hard."

You may believe I stared; and the woman, whose eyes almost looked ready to eat me, eagerly came up to me, exclaiming,

"Oh, ma'am, you don't know what a favour this is, to see you! I have longed for it so long! It is quite a comfort to me, indeed. Oh, ma'am, how clever you must be! All the ladies I deal with are quite distracted about 'Cecilia', and I got it myself. Oh, ma'am, how sensible you must be. It does my heart good to see you."

Did you ever hear the like? 'Twas impossible not to laugh, and Mrs Thrale has done nothing else ever since.

At dinner we had Dr Delap and Mr Selwyn, who accompanied us in the evening to a ball; as did also Dr Johnson, to the universal amazement of all who saw him there; but he said he had found it so dull being quite alone the preceding evening, that he determined upon going with us; "for," he said, "it cannot be worse than being alone." Strange that he should think so! I am sure I am not of his mind.

Mr H Cotton and Mr Swinerton of course joined us immediately. We had hardly been seated five minutes before Mr Selwyn came to me, from some other company he had joined, and said, "I think you don't choose dancing, ma'am?"

"No," I answered.

"There is a gentleman," he added, "who is very ambitious of the honour of dancing with you; but I told him I believed you would not dance."

I assured him he was right.

[More than twenty pages of similar society gossip follow, with no reference particularly to Brighton.]

Into the ocean we plunged

20 November 1782

Mrs and the three Miss Thrales and myself all arose at six o'clock in the morning, and 'by the pale blink of the moon' we went to the sea-side, where we had bespoke the bathing-women to be ready for us, and into the ocean we plunged. It was cold, but pleasant. I have bathed so often as to lose my dread of the operation, which now gives me nothing but animation and vigour. We then returned home, and dressed by candle-light, and, as soon as we could get Dr Johnson ready, we set out upon our journey, in a coach and a chaise, and arrived in Argyll Street at dinner time. Mrs Thrale has there fixed her tent for this short winter, which will end with the beginning of April, when her foreign journey takes place.

4

Joseph Farington,
Englishman and painter

Joseph Farington, like Fanny Burney, is remembered today as much for having written an entertaining and interesting diary as for any other achievement. But, whereas, Burney's diary focus was almost largely social and literary, Farington's interests were focused on the art world, and also embraced current events and politics.

Born in Leigh, Lancashire, Joseph was the second of seven sons of William Farington, the local vicar, and Esther Gildbody. After studying in Manchester, he went to train with Richard Wilson in London and won several prizes, awarded by the Society of Artists, for landscape drawings. He joined the Royal Academy when it was founded in 1769, and remained an active member for most of his life.

In 1776, he married Susan Mary Hamond, a relative of the Walpole family, but they had no children. When she died, in 1800, Farington suffered a breakdown, and was unable to draw or paint for some months.

The greatest calamity

24 February 1800

This day the greatest calamity that could fall upon me I suffered in the death of the best, the most affectionate, the most amiable of women, my beloved wife. Unexpected indeed was the blow, long had I reason to consider her delicate frame with apprehension, but as she had encountered the severity of many winters so I fondly hoped she might do this and that a more favorable season would restore Her strength. The time was now come when this hope was to be fruitless. Yesterday evening she was declared to be better, but in the night a change took place & at 3 o'clock this day I witnessed the departure of what I held most dear on earth. Without a sigh, with the appearance of only gentle sleep, did my beloved expire, to be received by that God to whom Her duty had been exemplary. May He in his mercies dispose my heart to follow the example of Her who discharged every duty so as to excite the love & respect of all, so that those remaining years which it may please God to allow to me may be devoted to His service and I may be rendered fit to hope for the mercies of my Creator through the mediation of Jesus Christ our blessed Lord Saviour.

3 April 1800
This day I added this continuation of my journal, which I could not do before since that period when I was deprived of the great blessing of my life.

11 April 1800
Mr Crozier called on me this morning and strengthened my mind with conversation and advice suited to my situation. He told me the consequence of continuing in the desponding way I have been in wd. be mental derangement or a nervous consumption. Both in a moral & religious view He shewed it to be my duty to get the better of my grief and that must be by having recourse to Society & to exercise & amusements – that medicine wd. do little for me.

His painting and his diaries

It is difficult to make a real appraisal of Farington's paintings, Evelyn Newby says in the *Oxford Dictionary of National Biography*, as they are scattered in many private and public collections, and rarely appear in art sales. But Farington's forte lay in the careful and accurate topographical drawings he prepared of British views for engravings which proved popular among tourists. Having lived in the north of England in the latter part of the 1770s, a first folio of such works, published in 1785, was titled *Views of the Lakes of Cumberland and Westmorland*. A decade later came *History of the River Thames* in two volumes. He also contributed to other series of artworks, notably *Britannia Depicta* and *Magna Britannia*, neither of which, though, were ever completed due to excessive costs. He died on a visit to his brother Richard in Lancashire, in December 1821, as the result of a fall downstairs from the gallery of Didsbury church.

Farington is particularly remembered today for his diary, which he started writing in 1793 and continued until the day of his death. It provides a vivid picture of the London art world in the late eighteenth and early nineteenth centuries, and much else besides – society, politics, literary events, and his journeys in England and abroad.

According to Newby, Farington wrote a diary for his own amusement and as an *aide-mémoire*. The manuscripts were passed down through the artist's family until sold at auction in 1921 to the *Morning Post* (a conservative newspaper published in London from the 1770s to 1937 when it was acquired by the *Daily Telegraph*). They were then edited by the newspaper's art critic, John Greig, for serialisation, before being published by Hutchinson & Co in four volumes between 1922 and 1928. In 1934, the originals were gifted to George V, and are now housed in the Royal Library at Windsor Castle. Between 1978 and 1984, Yale University published the diaries in sixteen volumes; and much more recently, in 1998, it issued a 1,000 page index of those volumes compiled by Newby.

The following extracts are taken from the second of the Hutchinson volumes.

No customs tax on paintbrushes

10 October 1802

At ¼past four o'Clock we dined & at Ten at night went on board the Packet which soon got under way. There were 15 people Passengers. In the Great Cabin there were 12 Bed places in two rows; the lowest very near the ground. I got an Upper Bed place & abt ½past 10 laid down, as did most of the Passengers. The night passed comfortably enough as I did not suffer the least inconvenience from the motion of the vessel. At eight oClock in the morning we were well on our way. A Calm of three Hours had delayed us in the night, but we now proceeded at the rate of 5 or 6 miles an hour. The Weather was Cloudy, but pleasant.

I had some conversation with one of the Passengers a Scotch Gentleman who was returning after having made a tour in France and Italy. He said when He arrived at Calais from England He purchased a Horse and rode the whole way from that town to Genoa where He disposed of his Horse & went on by other conveyances. He noticed how very generally the land in France was in a state of Agriculture, but He thought the people appeared to be but indifferent farmers. He mentioned how detested the French are by the Italians, and the English respected. He had coasted along part of the Shores of Italy in one of their Coasting vessels which He described as having subjected him to greater endurance than He had ever before suffered. It was the most disagreeable situation that can be imagined. He travelled from Genoa to Pisa, 150 miles, on Mules & had very bad accommodation on the way. The weather in Italy in the Summer was extremely hot.

We arrived off Brighton abt. a quarter past 2 oClock in the afternoon, when a Custom House boat came along side & took out all our Baggage, and the Passengers, and landed us at Brighton at three oClock. The fare from Dieppe to Brighton was a guinea and a half for each person, and two shillings 6d. to the Crew. We were conducted to the Custom House Office and our Trunks were more strictly examined than they had before been at any place. Some painting Brushes which I had brought over were detained. We each paid 3s. 6d. for this examination and our Trunks were then carried to the Old Ship Inn which we made our Head-quarters. On going to the Custom House Office again after their hurry of business was over, we found them disposed to let our Brushes pass with paying duty as being articles of little value, nor did we pay any additional fee.

When I landed on the Beach John Offley was standing before me. Seeing a Vessel coming in from France He walked down to meet it thinking it possible that I might be a Passenger. We also met Mr Sharpe, who had been with us at Paris, and had lately brought his family to Brighton. Fuseli, Halls and myself dined together at the Inn & Sharpe came to tea. Fuseli's anxiety & impatience to be in London had now so encreased that not being able to procure places in the Coach for tomorrow morning He & Halls at Eleven oClock set off in a Post Chaise. He said "His mind was in London" and He must go. He was there at breakfast the following morning.

Englishmen and Frenchmen compared

Our excursion was thus completed. Our absence from England had been but short and I could not have expected that on returning any very sensible impression would have been made upon my mind. I had not prepared myself for any other than what France would make upon me. It proved otherways. I felt on my return a difference the most striking; it was expressed in everything; and may be explained by saying that it was coming from disorder to order. From Confusion, to convenience: from subjection to freedom. I no longer saw the people covered with the patches of necessity, or the ridiculous mixtures of frippery imitations of finery with the coarse clothing of poverty. All appeared appropriate and substantial, and every man seemed respectable because his distinct & proper Character was consistently maintained. What must be the nature of that mind that would not feel grateful that it was his Lot to be an Englishman; a man entitled from his Birth to participate in such advantages as in no other country can be found

Such a state for man must naturally have an influence upon the manners of a people. It certainly was manifest to me that the difference in the deportment of the English when compared with the French, is as great as the causes which produce it. I could not be insensible to that Air of independence bordering upon haughtiness, which is manifested in the English Character, but is little seen among the people I had left. Wealth, and Security, and the pride of equal freedom, together habituate the mind to a conscious feeling of self importance that distinguishes the people of England from those of other Countries. But if this effect is produced, if there is less of what is called the Amiable, it is amply made up by a quality of a much higher kind, which is integrity. That is a word which the English may apply to their character by the consent of the whole world more universally than any other nation that exists in it.

The American who was at Dieppe rendered the panegyric of an Englishman unnecessary. He had been an inhabitant of France; Had traversed Germany; and was acquainted with Italy. He had experienced the varieties of each Country, and formed his judgment upon it. His decision was, "that each of the Countries had something to be admired, and something to be approved; But that there was but One England in the World."

The Prince is much about

14 October 1802
Went to breakfast at Mr Kirby's, the Marine House where I engaged to board at 2 guineas a week. After breakfast walked upon the East Terrace. Saw the Prince, also Lord Thurlow & his daugr. Mrs Brown, and Lord Elenborough to-day. The Prince is much abt. riding & walking. His established companions are Admiral Payne, who has an apartment in the Pavilion, in which, being much a valetu-denarian, he has a fire even in July; Trevies, the Jew; Day, who was formerly in India; and Cole Coningham. When the Prince is invited to dine out at Brighton it is usual to ask those persons also.

20 October 1802
While we were walking, the Prince with Mrs Fitzherbert were also on the Steine together, and called on Lord Thurlow. Lord & Lady Elenborough were also there. She of rather a tall size, and her aspect is mild & agreeable. Lord Elenborough is abt. 52 years of age. He was at Cambridge and took his degree when Mr Keddington did. Lord Thurlow has now all the appearance of an old man, being very gouty & infirm.

Things that can happen in Brighton

13 September 1803
In conversation this evening Mr Evans mentioned the singular circumstance of a countryman of his, who gained a fortune by being mistaken for another man. Bob Wilson, as He was called by His friends, had a property of about £400 a year, which being gay and a man of Show, He was supposed rather to have diminished. He came to England, and went to Brighton, with a view to try what confidence & dressing well would do. A short time before He went to Brighton there had been a Mr Wilson, an Irishman, there whose person was remarkably handsome, and who had been proclaimed by the Ladies to be the

most captivating of his Sex. The reports of him reached other places and Miss Townshend, a daughter of the Countess of Dalkeith by the late Right Honble. Charles Townshend, had heard his praises, at a time when she was preparing to go to Brighton. On her arrival there she went to the rooms, at the very time that Bob Wilson first made his appearance there, and after the much talked of Mr Wilson had left the place.

Bob was the best dressed man in the room, and his air & manner easy & confident, but his face remarkably plain. It happened however that Miss Townshend heard his *name*, and Her imagination doing the rest, she fancied she saw in Bob all that she had heard in praise of Mr Wilson. Bob saw the attention with which she regarded him, was introduced to Her danced with her, and in Ten days or a fortnight ran away with & married Her & got £10,000; and Her Brother dying, an estate said to be £3,000 per annum.

The Prince's stables

20 July 1804
[William Porden, the architect, said] He was building stables at Brighton for the Prince of Wales, of a Circular form in imitation of the famous Corn Market at Paris which was burnt in 1803. The Prince at present takes much interest in building. [The stables are now a hall known as the Dome which adjoins Brighton Museum.]

5

Erredge's history of Brighton and an anonymous diarist

History of Brighthelmston or Brighton as I View It and Others Knew It (With a Chronological Table of Local Events) written by John Ackerson Erredge and published in 1862 is considered the first substantial book devoted wholly to Brighton, past or present. Here is the startling preface to that book:

'The publication of the *History of Brighton* had proceeded, with the most gratifying success, through ten monthly numbers, when it was suddenly interrupted by the lamented decease of the Author – Mr J A Erredge. Death came upon him, not stealthily, but in its most awful form. It surprised him literally at the desk. Whilst talking cheerfully to the publisher, the hand of Death was laid upon him, and he fell dead to the ground; the ink of these pages was still wet whilst the Author was extended on the floor a corpse. So terrible an occurrence for a brief space delayed the publication of the work, but fortunately for the family of the author, the MS was nearly completed, and his sons were enabled, from the materials left by their lamented father, to compile the few last pages and send the two concluding numbers through the press. The *History of Brighton* is now completed, and whatever shortcomings may be detected in the two concluding numbers, which had not the advantage of being corrected by the Author, will no doubt be pardoned by a generous public.'

So, Erredge had died before his history was complete, but the finished work, which is very detailed and idiosyncratic, but also extremely informative and interesting to read, has become something of a classic. Indeed, in 2005, the original edition was republished by Brambletye Books with a new introduction by John Farrant, an expert on the history of Sussex. Farrant not only provides a biography of Erredge, who spent many years working for the *Brighton Observer*, but also carefully analyses Erredge's sources, i.e. all the earlier sources of information about Brighton's past.

To give a flavour of Erredge's book here are a few of his chapter titles: 'The Romans at Brighton', 'The Workhouse', 'The Attack on Brighthelmston by the French, in 1545', 'The Incursions of the Sea on the Town', 'The Old Churchyards', 'Brighton Camp and the Tragedies of Goldstone Bottom', 'The Theatres', and 'On and about the Race-course'.

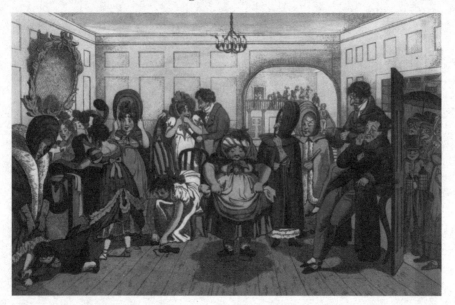

The mysterious Mr Bew

In compiling his history, Erredge occasionally draws on extracts from two 'private diary' manuscripts in his possession. One of the authors he describes as 'Mr Bew, who afterwards lived in East Street, was dentist to George IV, and, in conjunction with Mr Frederick Vining, lessee of the Theatre Royal Brighton.' However, all the entries ascribed to Mr Bew can be found exactly to the word (although not to the date, since some of these have been mixed up) in Peregrine Phillips' diary (see Chapter 2). Farrant states that all the extracts used by Erredge from a diary kept in 1778 and 1779 'are, in fact taken, not from a manuscript, but from Peregrine Phillips.'

One possible explanation for Erredge's mistake or sloppy journalism could have resulted because no author is named on the printed editions of Peregrine Phillips' diary. However, there is a Bew mentioned on the title page, as one of two booksellers stocking the diary. It is not inconceivable that Erredge knew of (or discovered) a Bew in Brighton and wrongly assumed he was the author. (Whether this is the explanation or not, Erredge doesn't seem to have questioned why anyone living in East Street, Brighton, would be undertaking 'an excursion' to the place.)

Erredge gives no clue as to the identity of the second diarist, but the extracts are almost all from 1805 and 1807, and are all to be found in only two of the thirty-one chapters: 'Fortifications of the Town' and 'The Steine and its Tributaries'.

Fortifications of the Town

'In consequence of the frequent incursions of the French, and the inhabitants being harassed by frequent alarm, the town resolved, in 1558, to erect fortifications, to afford them some protection for the future.' So begins Erredge's chapter on the town's fortifications. After several pages, he continues:

'Towards the latter end of the year 1793, two new batteries were commenced for the defence of the town; one on the West Cliff, which mounted eight 36-pounders, and the other on the East Cliff, which mounted four of the same weight. The guns of these batteries were of French casting, ship guns, taken from the French fleet captured by Lord Howe, in his memorable victory of the 1st of June, 1794.

The latter of these batteries was at the bottom of the Marine Parade, opposite the south-end of German Place; but after being in position about ten years – as the explosions of the guns and the encroachments of the sea had made the walls dangerous – it was removed. The west battery was opposite Artillery Place.

The Sea Fencibles, volunteers, during the war with France used to practice at this battery. They were accustomed, also, to exercise with boarding-pikes, in Belle-vue field, now Regency Square. Colonel Moore's volunteers went through their initiation drill, with faggot-sticks, on the ground behind the battery house, Artillery Place...'

And then, Erredge gives two extracts from his manuscript by the (anonymous) diarist.

17 August 1805

On the 17th of August, 1805, soon after 12 o'clock, a shot was discharged from this battery by the Sea Fencibles, at a cask moored purposely in the offing, and it fell very close to the object: a second shot was also fired, of 42 pounds weight, merely to ascertain to what a distance the gun would throw it. From the time of the explosion until it struck the water, there was a lapse of 27 seconds; the ball consequently, ere it was received by the liquid element, must have traversed to a distance of three miles. The weight of the cartridge used was 14 pounds.

13 June 1807

The Volunteers this morning, for the first time this year, were practised at the Fort, in discharging the forty-two-pounders at a cask, moored, and floating on the water, at about three quarters of a league distant from the shore. Twelve rounds were fired; and though some of the balls immediately struck the object, they generally dropped so close to it, that a moderate sized fishing-boat would scarcely have escaped being injured by either of them. Many elegant spectators were on the Cliff during the exercise.

Erredge concludes the chapter: 'The west battery was removed in 1859. A flagstaff within a railed space, marks its last site; as, twice after its original construction, it was removed with the sanction of Government, to admit of widening the King's Road at that spot, to accommodate the increased traffic. The battery house and the other buildings in connexion with the Battery, were disposed of by auction by Mr P R Wilkinson, on Monday, September 9th, 1861, and by the 28th of that month the space was entirely cleared for the erection of an hotel. Government having disposed of the ground to the Brighton Hotel Company. The remnant of the battery platform, marked by the flagstaff, belongs to the town, the Corporation having purchased it of Government to prevent any other purchaser placing buildings upon it. Brighton thus, wholly depends upon such means of defence as the emergency of the occasion may require to be brought into operation, by means of the railway, the facility of transit offering the full assurance that every materiel would be at hand for the ready service of our Volunteers, should an enemy have the temerity to invade our shores and put to the proof every Englishman's motto, *Pro aris et focis*.'

The Steine and its Tributaries

'No part of Brighton has undergone so many changes during the last century as the Steine,' Erredge says, 'which was at first the drying-ground for fishermen's nets and the 'laying-up' place for such boats as were not in use at particular fishing seasons of the year. The term Steine is of Flemish origin, and is derived from *Ein*, *Stein*, or *Steen*, a rock, as at the time when the town received its Flemish colony, the southern extremity of the valley in which Brighton lay was edged and protected from the sea by a ledge of chalk rocks, and from these the name Steine, or rocky, was given to the field or meadow, which was called the Steine Field. [. . .] In 1779, according to a map of that date, the only building on the east side of the Steine, was Thomas's Library; just to the northwest of which, on the grass, was a slight erection much after the style of the judge's stand at races. This structure was the orchestra, in which the town band, of three performers, discoursed their music under their leader, Mr Anthony Crook, whose instrument was the trombone. [. . .]

The Steine at that period was of much larger dimensions at present. [. . . It] then was entirely open, and was a country walk for visitors. That is to say, in the Spring, Summer, and Autumn; as in Winter time, from its then lying very hollow, the southern part was generally flooded, and in severe weather the sheet of ice which was there formed was a general rendezvous for sliding and skating. When fashion made the Steine a place of public resort, attention was paid by the town authorities, to make it in some degree, attractive. The ground was made level, and verdure was encouraged to ornament it. On it the old Duke of Cumberland, of Fontenoy, delighted to turn out the stag and hunt the bounding deer, as the place was entirely open to the full extent of the Downs; and the inhabitants were gratified with repeated spectacles of the kind, sometimes as often as twice or thrice in a season.'

Erredge then writes about 'sports of a less aristocratic character' (donkey rides) sometimes taking place, and of 'Jenkinses of the Press' who watched 'with keen eye the doings of royalty, and of the nobility', before supplying the following extracts from his 'private diary' manuscript.

Little French milliners

4 August 1805
The Cliff Parade, from the South end of the Steine to the unfinished Crescent, displayed much genteel company this afternoon. The Cyprian Corps [courtesans] have much increased in number within the last two or three days. We have now *little French Milliners* in every part of the town.

27 August 1805
Townshend and Sayers, two Bow Street officers, arrived here this morning, in quest of an individual who has been guilty of a burglary in the metropolis. They had been here but a short time when the object they were in search of, in a laced livery, was descried by them in the act of crossing the Steine. They took him into custody, and having ornamented his wrists with a pair of iron ruffles, they bore him off in triumph to London.

19 September 1805
About half-past one o'clock the Prince of Wales returned from a walk to the west of the Steine, to the Pavilion. His Royal Highness, who was habited in a black coat and waistcoat, and nankeen pantaloons, appeared rather lame from the recent hurt he had received in his ankle. He walked with a stick, of sufficient dimensions occasionally to bear his weight.

26 September 1805
The Duke of Clarence was to-day, for a short time, on the Steine. Some of His Highness's sons are at this time here, and were under the military instructions of a sergeant of the South Gloucester Militia this morning on the Pavilion lawn.

'The Steine was first partially enclosed with common hurdles,' Erredge concludes, 'then it was partly paved and railed in. At last the present massive iron railings were erected. But not as they at present stand. They surrounded a much larger area, and the lamp-posts were the main standards, the rails being fastened in them. At that period the paving around the Steine, under the then Town Surveyor, Mr Thomas Harman, was considered a masterpiece of the art of paving in brick. Previous to this improvement, there was no carriage road completely round the Steine.'

Assemblies – an opportunity for a carouse or a spree

In the same chapter on the Steine, Erredge provides some details about the so-called assemblies. 'In the season, from August to March, Assemblies were held every Monday. These were under the management of Masters of the Ceremonies, the first of whom were, in 1805, Mr Yart at the Old Ship, and Mr William Wade at the Castle. [. . .] The duties of the Masters of the Ceremonies consisted in watching minutely the arrival of the nobility and gentry. For this purpose he attended the Libraries and Hotels regularly once or more a-day to copy the lists of the latest visitors, at whose addresses he then called and left his card, a hint that they should enter their names in his book, which lay at the principal places of fashionable resort, and with each entry deposit a guinea with the custodian of the M C's book, who received a per centage for his trouble and attention. The payment of the fee ensured a mutual recognition upon all occasions of meeting between the giver and the receiver during that visit of the donor at Brighton, and, on the occasions of balls and assemblies, he was expected to make all the necessary arrangements, and for dances provide all unprovided ladies and gentlemen with partners. Masters of the Ceremonies originated at a period when balls and routs terminated at ten o'clock in the evening, when "We won't go home till morning," had not come into vogue, but the sedan chair of "my lady" was in punctual attendance, and the fair burden was wafted home to admit of repose before midnight, and to give the sterner sex an opportunity for a carouse or a spree.'
Erredge then quotes a diary extract.

30 July 1805
This evening, at nine o'clock, the first assembly of the season, the Grand Rose Ball, was held at the Castle Inn, under the patronage of the Prince of Wales. The

Ball Room is large, lofty, and noble, and commands a full view of the Steyne; looks, also, into the Pavilion Gardens, the beautiful shrubberies of which are worthy of the Royal resident. The ceiling forms an arch, and is painted to represent the rising sun. Every part of the room is ornamented with various masterly paintings of classical antiquity. It was lighted up in a superior style, suited to the dignity of the guests, with three cut-glass chandeliers, 100 lights, and forty lustres and side-lights. The Prince entered the room at half-past nine, and at ten o'clock the Ball opened.

'When George IV,' Erredge adds, 'expressed a desire of converting the Castle Assembly Room into a Chapel to be attached to the Royal Pavilion, the fee simple of it was transferred to his Majesty, and as a tavern attached to a place of divine worship would be a great incongruity, the transfer of the license of the Castle was made to premises in Steine Place, the Royal York Hotel, so designated in reference to the Royal Duke, Frederick, whose permission for the name was applied for and obtained from his Royal Highness.'

Virulent pastimes – trinket auctions and the game of Loo

Here is Erredge writing about the developing pastimes on the Steine: '[The library under Marine Parade], and the original two on the Steine, were not merely the resort of visitors for the purpose of literary pursuits, as their name legitimately implies, but after eight o'clock in the evening, during the Summer season, that portion of the business in connexion with books ceased, and holland blinds being drawn down to cover over the whole of the books and book-shelves, a saloon was formed that nightly attracted hundreds of tonish idlers to the vocal and instrumental music that was discoursed, and to join in the raffles, similar to those that were going on at Raggett's subscription room.'

Erredge then quotes from Phillips (Bew!) about 'every trinket of luxury' (see Chapter 2), before recording that, in August 1805, a man named Fisher established a new Auction Mart in St James's Street, that was open morning and night. The following extracts from 'a private diary', Erredge says, 'will in some degree explain the rage which was on at those periods for this and similar virulent pastimes.'

2 August 1792

But little company stirred out to-day, on account of the intense heat of the weather. Sporting men of fashion, dashers, and blacklegs certainly assembled on the Steine, to make their bets for to-morrow's Lewes Races, where much excellent sport is expected. The other part of the day was spent mostly in Raggett's Subscription House, at Billiards, Dice, &c. *On dit.* Lady Lade is returning from Brighton in much dudgeon, because, forsooth, Lady Jersey, she says, made *vulgar* mouths at her yesterday on the race-ground!

Wilks's Pic-nic Auction

23 July 1805

A very select and elegant assemblage of nobility last night paraded the Steine until a late hour. Donaldson's library, also, was very fashionably filled; and Wilks's Pic-nic Auction exhibited a blaze of rank and beauty.

23 August 1805

Wilks's bargains were in fashionable request last night, and the knock-down blows of Fisher were directed with his usual ability and effect. Fisher's New Auction Lounge was again well filled with rank and beauty this morning. A monster of the finny tribe has been exhibited in a marquee, pitched purposely for the occasion, on the Steine to-day. It is called a *Star Fish*, and is so worthy the attention of the curious that it has divided the attention of the public with *Fisher*.

27 August 1805

Wilks's Auction Lounge, last night, was immensely crowded until a late hour: nor has the magnetical hammer of Fisher, at his new room, been less attractive this morning.

Mr Cartwright on the musical glasses

21 September 1807

Donaldson's and Pollard's libraries have had crowded assemblages, and the game of Loo has had more than its usual number of votaries. This evening Mr Cartwright will perform at Fisher's Lounge, on the musical glasses, under the patronage of Mrs Orby Hunter.

8 October 1807

Pam still possesses his original attraction, and the Belles are nightly *looed* in his presence. Rather a bad *pun* that, eh?

9 May 1810

Donaldson's and Walker's spacious and airy Steine and Marine Lounges have not been so interestingly decorated with rank and beauty as they have to-day appeared for many preceding months, though the amusements of one card loo, &c., are not yet there introduced. The diversion of raffling has not been permitted at either for some years past, nor will it again be allowed, so long as the Little-go Bill remains unrepealed; we may therefore conclude that the rattle of the dice will never be heard at either again.

The Loo Sweepstakes

More from Erredge by way of explaining some of the terms above: 'Trinket Auctions were established when an Act of Parliament, called Mr Vansittart's Little-go Bill, was passed, that did away with raffling at all places of public resort, as the profits to the librarians at the watering places generally, arose from these diversions, rather than from the high literary character of the books upon their shelves, or the erudite position of the persons whose names were in their subscription books because fashion ruled it so. The novelty of Trinket Auctions soon wore off, and then another pastime, under the name of Loo, was introduced.

The game was very diverting in its progress, and afforded an occasion for many agreeable sallies of wit, according to the talent of the conductor of it and the disposition to replications of those about him. The Loo Sweepstakes, as they were termed, were limited to eight subscribers, and the individual stake, one shilling. The full number being obtained, a certain quantity of cards, amongst which was a Knave of Clubs, or Pam, were shuffled, cut, and separately dealt and turned: the numbers were called in rotation during the process, and that against which Pam appeared was pronounced the winner.'

In September 1810, an attempt was made to outlaw the game of Loo, and the case was heard in Lewes before a full bench of Magistrates. The case was thrown out, and, according to Erredge, 'Pam, the good genius of Loo, continued to hold sway at the libraries till 1817, when the magistrates took an antipathy towards him, owing to the unbounded patronage which he received from the ladies in general. They considered him an unwelcome resident; so, by their mandate, supported by an obsolete Act of Henry VIII, he was excommunicated from all the libraries.'

6

Lord Glenbervie, umbrage and an eyesore statue of the Prince

'These Journals were sold, unclassified, together with other papers among the Sheffield and Gibbon documents recently disposed of at auction. I acquired them from a well-known bookseller who had bought them, and after perusing their contents, I found them to be the work of Sylvester Douglas, in 1800 created Lord Glenbervie of the Irish peerage. Lord Glenbervie, though certainly no genius, was in many respects a notable man, who filled high offices, gained, from ordinary beginnings, such a place in society that he married one of Lord North's daughters (a rather plain daughter, it must be confessed), and knew or was brought into contact with many of the conspicuous personages of his day.'

This is Walter Sichel, an eminent biographer and lawyer, introducing *The Glenbervie Journals*, published by Constable in 1910. The first of the two diaries he owned covers only three months at the end of 1793, and the second a period from April 1811 to February 1814. Sichel describes them as a 'kaleidoscope rather than panorama', but 'a kaleidoscope of vignettes'. Here and there, Sichel says, Lord Glenbervie seems proud of his stiff manners, circumlocution, and eruptions into accentless Greek and superfluous French. He loves moralisation, too, though he was often shrewd and observant. Sichel makes an interesting comparison between Lord Glenbervie, who shows himself like Polonius, from *Hamlet*, and Thomas Creevey (see Chapter 7), who was more like Paul Pry, a comical and mischievous character in a play of the same name by John Poole.

Although Sichel thought Glenbervie's other journals must have been lost or destroyed, they soon turned up and were edited by Francis Bickley and published, again by Constable in two volumes in 1928 – *The Diaries of Sylvester Douglas*. Sichel's two volumes, it transpired, were but the first and tenth of thirteen written between 1793 and 1819.

Sylvester Douglas – king's attorney

Sylvester Douglas was born into a land-owning family in Aberdeenshire in 1743. He studied at school and university in Aberdeen, but left college without a degree in

1760. After his father's death he moved to Edinburgh, then London, and took a medical degree at Leiden in 1766. After touring in Europe, he returned to London, took up law and moved in Whig circles. He also reported on elections and important legal decisions. His report on the disputed parliamentary elections to the 1774 House of Commons, for example, was published in four volumes. Moreover, he wrote *A Treatise on the Provincial Dialect of Scotland*.

In 1789, Douglas married advantageously, to Catherine Anne North, the eldest daughter of Frederick North, the former Prime Minister. They had one son, Frederick Sylvester, who also became an MP. However, he died very young, when only 28 years old.

For a decade, to 1794, Sylvester Douglas was king's attorney. Thereafter, he was MP for a series of different constituencies, and held various government posts. In 1800, he was made Baron Glenbervie, of Kincardine, in the Irish peerage. Towards the end of his career he was intermittently appointed as Surveyor General of Woods, Forests, Parks, and Chases and was one of the First Commissioners of Woods and Forests. He was also a trustee of the British Museum, and rector of Aberdeen University.

Here then is Lord Glenbervie in Brighton, taking the sea air and tepid sea baths, telling the odd amusing anecdote, gadding about, and, above all, hobnobbing.

A neat and plentiful market

1 September 1801
Barnes, Fred, and I are going to set out on a journey to Eastbourne and Brighthelmstone this morning for two or three days.

10 September 1801
Sheffield Place
Barnes and I in my open chaise and Weyland and Fred in Weyland's curricle set out yesterday morning at six on an excursion to Brighthelmstone, arrived at nine, stayed three hours and returned here [Eastbourne] to dinner, with a cargo of shell and other fish which I had myself bought in the market there. The purchase was quite a new transaction for me, and, as it is a neat and plentiful market, very entertaining.

There are great additions to Brighthelmstone since I was there in 1794, and the Prince is now adding two large bulges or bow-window rooms to each end of the house fronting the Steine, and also throwing out two bows in the back between the side perpendicular wings and the portico. They say the bow which fronts the south is to be a dining room and that fronting the north a greenhouse. At present he lives in a small house next to the library formerly kept by Crawford. Mrs Fitzherbert lives in one near this. The chief inmates of his own are MacMahon (whose father Ogilvy, whom I met in one of the libraries, was a footman in Dublin and has often waited behind his chair) and Trevis the Jew. I understand (from the same authority) that Mrs Fitzherbert is scarcely visited or taken notice of by the few people of fashion now there.

In Donaldson's library I met Fielding, and was glad to point out to Fred the son of the immortal author of 'Tom Jones'.

The Prince cancels his birthday party

8 August 1811
Brighton
We have been here since the 15th of July, and I find my health, sleep, and appetite much improved by the sea air on this elevated situation and the warm sea-bath.

16 August 1811
Brighton
The Regent had made great preparations for a splendid Fete at his Pavilion here on the 12th inst. when he entered into his fiftieth year. All the Cabinet were to come to it, and to sleep during their stay at Lord Chichester's at Stanmer. But some days before, H.R.H. sent notice that he did not mean, considering his father's present most lamentable situation, to celebrate his birthday here or anywhere else. That resolution has been generally applauded by all thinking people. It seems, indeed, an odd thing in H.R.H. and his brothers, the Dukes of York and Clarence, that of late years they have always given great entertainments on their own birthdays. I used for several years to dine with my neighbour, the Duke of Clarence, on his. For the last two years before this he had dropped the custom, but only on the ground of economy. There seems to us a good deal of wit in the following epigram, which the Dean of Battle brought us the other day. He could not tell us the author.

> When Theseus from the fair he ruined fled,
> The nymph adopted Bacchus in his stead,
> Which Allegory, in my humble thinking,
> Means that deserted ladies take to drinking.

Of blindness and of shade

I am going to dine to-day at Mr Philip Metcalfe's, a gentleman of large fortune, who has travelled a great deal, and possesses a fine collection of pictures in his house in Hill Street, and has a taste to judge of them and enjoy them. He is now old and has been blind several years, but still likes and enjoys society, and his fortune (though it arises from being out of the head of a great distillery) and accomplishments have enabled him to live always on the best.

Mr Metcalfe's blindness has reminded me of what Lord North said to Colonel Barre, on their meeting on the Pantiles at Tunbridge soon after they had both lost their sight. Lady Glenbervie, who was walking with her father, having named them to one another, Lord North said, "Colonel Barre, I am very glad to meet you. We have been long political enemies, and yet, I believe, there are no two men in England who would be now more happy to see one another."

The total want of trees and shade at this place gave rise to a joke of Jekyll's, which I never heard till the other day. Somebody was expressing great dislike to the place on that account, when he said, "Well, I did not think that anybody could take umbrage at Brighton."This is something like what Count and General Lally said of his Council, soon after he took possession of his Government of Pondicherry:"Je vois bien qu'on est directement sous le soleil ici, car on n'y trouve pas l'ombre d'un honnete homme." [I see that it is directly under the sun here, because we do not find the shadow of an honest man.]

An eyesore statue of the Prince

10 **September** 1811
Sheffield Place
We left Brighton yesterday at 4 pm, having been there ever since the 15th of July.

My health and spirits are, thank God, in a great degree restored by the air, exercise, and tepid sea-baths. I mean to return there about the 9th or 10th of October, when Lady Glenbervie will go into waiting and join me there or meet me at this place towards the middle of November. We had in general very fine weather, and for that season a house delightfully situated, No 6, near the center of the Crescent, from whose windows we had a full view of one of the noblest objects in nature, the open sea, often covered with ships and light, nautilus-like pleasure and fishing boats sailing and rowing in all directions and of one of the ugliest and most ridiculous productions of Art, a full length statue of the Prince of Wales, of a buff colour, in the complete uniform of his Hussar regiment, with a round hat surcharged with feathers, and an enormous quantity of hair turned up under his hat in the manner of that part of the costume of ladies about thirty or forty years ago, which they called a "Chignon".

The person who built the Crescent on speculation, a Mr Otto, a West Indian, had this frightful thing cast at Coades's, the manufacturer of artificial stone, and erected it on a high pedestal in the center, in order, as was said, to flatter H.R.H., and obtain admission to the parties at the Pavilion. But the Prince's taste was too good for such a bribe, and the effect was so different from what the foolish man expected, that the Prince never yet can hear his name mentioned with patience, and will not even permit Lord Chichester to present the son to him, a deserving young man now in the Sussex Militia.

All we inhabitants of the Crescent would willingly have subscribed any reasonable sum for the removal of the eye-sore, or even have contrived to have it clandestinely demolished in the night. All but one, Mr Perkins, the rich brewer, who has a permanent residence there, and, 'such and so various are the tastes of men,' is said to have bought it to secure its permanency as the chief ornament of his marine villa. The statue, however, has had one of its arms broken off, which produced a ridiculous mistake of Montie Lewis one day when he came into the Crescent to call on Lady Glenbervie. We saw him examining the sculpture at great length and in great detail, with his glass at his eye, being very short-sighted, before he came up-stairs to us, and soon after he joined us, he said that was a singular sort of compliment to Lord Nelson to have his statue erected there to represent him without the arm he had lost.

MERRY MAKING on the REGENTS BIRTH DAY 1812.

Society at Brighton

Our society at Brighton was mixed, and shifting, but not numerous, and very good. Mr and Mrs Steele; Lady Theodora Viner, her son and daughter; Colonel Murphy, Irish, Spanish, and English, a well-informed and cheerful military merchant, partner with William Gordon, nephew to the late Lord Aberdeen, his nephew Mr Menville, Mr George and Miss Jonstone, whose dinners, balls, and music were frequent and very good; Lord and Lady Charles Somerset and three daughters (than all of whom nothing can be conceived more disagreeable, nor, I believe, in essentials less respectable); the Baron and Baronne de Montalembert, he natural son to the late Baron, she the daughter of a Mr Forbes, an East Indian, who wrote the 'Picture of Verdun', both great walzers, and insufferable coxcombs; Philip Metcalfe, now blind and seventy-nine, but both cheerful and hospitable, with an excellent cook, an excelling cellar, and a good house, and two nieces, pleasant, sensible, unaffected women, and both great readers with happy memories; Lord Dundas, whose regiment of Militia, the North York, are in quarters at Brighton; William Frankland, his Lieut. –Colonel, and formerly my fellow-barrister – a man so abounding in paradoxes that his conversation consists of nothing else, and which he maintains with great apparent seriousness, but with perfect good humour, rather inviting than resisting contradiction. He amused Lady Glenbervie very much.

[And so on for several more pages!]

Postcript: Glenbervie and Creevey

Although Thomas Creevey (see Chapter 7) never mentions Lord Glenbervie in his diaries, Glenbervie does mention Creevey – and not very favourably.

16 June 1812
Whitehall Place.

But what has affected me most in this intervening space was the gross and igno-rant and ill-founded attack on my conduct in the proposed improvements of the Cr[own] Revenue in the case of Marybone [Marylebone] Park. This viru-lent and unjustifiable attack was made by that accusateur officieux, Mr Creevey and though afterwards refuted with spirit, truth and full success in the House of Commons by Mr Wharton, one of the Secretaries to the Treasury, remained unanswered for a week or fortnight. [...] Creevey has tried to obtain eminence (unsuccessful attempt!) by personalities in the absence of the parties concerned. He accused Fred North of inhumanity. He attempted to charge Fred North's brother-in-law with corrupt administration of the Cr[own] Revenue. Perceval [the Prime Minister] answered him on the ground of the absurdity of the facts alleged by him. But this was late at night in a thin and tired House. Next day Creevey's speech appeared in all the papers (sent no doubt by himself) without a word of Perceval's answer. Before a new opportunity occurred poor Perceval was murdered [the only Prime Minister, in fact, ever to have been assassinated].

7

Thomas Creevey dines at the Pavilion

It is still 1811, and a few months after Lord Glenbervie's visit, Thomas Creevey arrives in Brighton, and seems to do little more than dine every night with the Prince Regent – yet he then then falls out with him.

Creevey, the son of a merchant sea captain involved in the slave trade, was born in Liverpool in 1768. His father died soon after the birth and his mother married again. He studied at Queens' College, Cambridge, and then trained as a lawyer, but rose rapidly in the exclusive society of the Whig Party. In 1802, he married Eleanor Ord, a relation of Charles Grey, the future Prime Minister, and a rich widow with five children. The same year, he became a Whig MP in the House of Commons, and within a few years had been appointed Secretary to the Board of Control.

When, in 1811, the Prince of Wales became Prince Regent, the Whigs, including Creevey, were expecting him to favour them with government positions, but were much disappointed when he chose to retain the Tories appointed by his father. Creevey, who had been an enthusiastic visitor to the Prince's table in Brighton, then ceased to be an intimate of the Royal – the diary entries below capture this moment in his life. Increasingly, also, Creevey found himself at odds with the Whig leadership. When he stood as an MP for his home city Liverpool in 1812, he lost the election. To make matters worse, he was found guilty in a libel case, and consequently suffered heavy legal debts when trying to appeal.

The Creeveys moved to Brussels for five years, between 1814 and 1819, where Thomas came to know Arthur Wellesley, the first Duke of Wellington, and became the first civilian to interview him after the Battle of Waterloo in June 1815. It was Creevey who recorded the Duke's famous quote about the battle – 'It has been a damned nice thing – the nearest run thing you ever saw in your life'. He wrote about that interview, as follows.

A *damned nice thing*

'As I approached, I saw people collected in the street about the house; and when I got amongst them, the first thing I saw was the Duke upstairs alone at his window. Upon his recognising me, he immediately beckoned to me with his finger to come up. I met Lord Arthur Hill in the ante-room below, who, after shaking hands and congratulation, told me I could not go up to the Duke, as he was then occupied in writing his dispatch; but as I had been invited, I of course proceeded. The first thing I did, of course, was to put out my hand and congratulate him upon his victory. He made a variety of observations in his short, natural, blunt way, but with the greatest gravity all the time, and without the least approach to anything like triumph or joy. "It has been a damned serious business," he said. "Blucher and I have lost 30,000 men. It has been a damned nice thing – the nearest run thing you ever saw in your life. Blucher lost 14,000 on Friday night, and got so damnably licked I could not find him on Saturday morning; so I was obliged to fall back to keep up my communications with him." Then, as he walked about, he praised greatly those Guards who kept the farm (meaning Hugomont) against the repeated attacks of the French; and then he praised all our troops, uttering repeated expressions of astonishment at our men's courage. He repeated so often its being *so nice a thing – so nearly run a thing*, that I asked him if the French had fought better than he had ever seen them do before. "No," he said, "they have always fought the same since I first saw them at Vimeira." Then he said: "By God! I don't think it would have done if I had not been there." '

In 1818, Creevey's wife Eleanor died, and soon afterwards he returned to England with his stepdaughters. He served in Parliament again, as MP for Appleby in the first half of the 1820s, but became less interested in political affairs, and more concerned with society and gossip. Prime Minister Grey, though, made him Treasurer of the Ordnance in 1830, and then Lord Melbourne made him treasurer of Greenwich

Hospital in 1834. He died in 1838, having had no children of his own, and having lived the last decades of his life a relatively poor man.

The Creevey Papers

Charles Cavendish Greville, one of the best nineteenth-century diarists (see Chapter 10), wrote of him thus in 1829: 'Old Creevey is rather an extraordinary character. [...] He possesses nothing but his clothes; no property of any sort; he leads a vagrant life, visiting a number of people who are delighted to have him, and sometimes roving about to various places, as fancy happens to direct, and staying till he has spent what money he has in his pocket. He has no servant, no home, no creditors; he buys everything as he wants it at the place he is at; he has no ties upon him, and has his time entirely at his own disposal and that of his friends. He is certainly a living proof that a man may be perfectly happy and exceedingly poor, or rather without riches, for he suffers none of the privations of poverty and enjoys many of the advantages of wealth. I think he is the only man I know in society who possesses nothing.'

Creevey is mostly remembered today for his letters and to a lesser extent his diary which provide a colourful and accurate source of information about politicians and royalty of the day. They were collected and edited by Sir Herbert Maxwell and published in 1903 by John Murray as *The Creevey Papers – A Selection from the Correspondence & Diaries of the Late Thomas Creevey, MP*. The book is said (by an old edition of *Encyclopaedia Britannica*) to be 'a useful addition and correction' to *The Croker Papers*, written by John Wilson Croker from a Tory point of view (Chapter 8), and to be characterised by an almost Pepysian outspokenness. Creevey had 'an acute eye for absurdity', says the *Oxford Dictionary of National Biography*, and is very good at describing the surface of events and places. However, it adds, he is incurious about the underlying processes shaping them; and it is a cartoonist's talent, he has, sharp, but not deep or lasting.

Unfortunately, most of Creevey's extensive diary was lost, possibly destroyed by his friends wanting to suppress the contents. Greville, again, explains how after Creevey's death, some thought the publication of the journal and letters would be 'painful and embarrassing to many people now alive, and make very inconvenient and premature revelations upon private and confidential matters'. Thus, though there are diary entries in *The Creevey Papers*, the bulk of the book is made up of Creevey's letters and Maxwell's biographical commentary.

Mrs Fitzherbert, I wish you would call upon Mrs Creevey

There are also some reminiscences written by Creevey about his past. This is one, largely about Mrs Fitzherbert – the first woman with whom the future George IV undertook a wedding ceremony, though it was later judged invalid. She remained his companion for a large part of his adult life.

'At the beginning of September, 1805, Mrs Creevey and myself with her daughters went to Brighton to spend the autumn there, the Prince then living at the Pavilion. I think it was the first, or at furthest the second, day after our arrival, when my two eldest daughters and myself were walking on the Steyne, and the Prince, who was sitting talking to old Lady Clermont, having perceived me, left her and came up to speak to me, when I presented my daughters to him. He was very gracious to us all and hoped he should see me shortly at dinner. In two or three days from this time I received an invitation to dine at the Pavilion...

Mrs Fitzherbert, whom I had never been in a room with before, sat on one side of the Prince, and the Duke of Clarence on the other... In the course of the evening the Prince took me up to the card table where Mrs Fitzherbert was playing, and said "Mrs Fitzherbert, I wish you would call upon Mrs Creevey, and say from me I shall be happy to see her here." Mrs. Fitzherbert did call accordingly, and altho' she and Mrs Creevey had never seen each other before, an acquaintance began that soon grew into a very sincere and agreeable friendship, which lasted the remainder of Mrs Creevey's life.

Immediately after this first visit from Mrs Fitzherbert, Mrs Creevey and her daughters became invited with myself to the Prince's parties at the Pavilion, and till the first week in January – a space of about four months – except a few days when the Prince went to see the King at Weymouth, and a short time that I was in London in November, there was not a day we were not at the Pavilion, I dining there always once or twice a week, Mrs Creevey frequently dining with me likewise, but in the evening we were always there.

During these four months the Prince behaved with the greatest good humour as well as kindness to us all. He was always merry and full of his jokes, and any one would have said he was really a very happy man. Indeed I have heard him say repeatedly during that time that he never should be so happy when King, as he was then.

I suppose the Courts or houses of Princes are all alike in one thing, viz., that in attending them you lose your liberty. After one month was gone by, you fell naturally and of course into the ranks, and had to reserve your observations till you were asked for them. These royal invitations are by no means calculated to reconcile one to a Court. To be sent for half an hour before dinner, or perhaps in the middle of one's own, was a little too humiliating to be very agreeable.'

The Chicken and John Gully prize fight

Another Creevey reminiscence: 'Having mentioned a dinner I had at Johnstone's in Brighton in 1805, I can't help adverting to what took place that day. The late King (George IV) and the present one (William IV) both dined there, and it so happened that there was a great fight on the same day between the Chicken [Henry Pearce, the champion of England] and [John] Gully [son of a butcher and publican who later became informally recognised as champion of England]. The Duke of Clarence was present at it, and as the battle, from the interference of Magistrates, was fought at a greater distance from Brighton than was intended, the Duke was very late, and did not arrive till dinner was nearly over.

I mention the case on account of the change that has since taken place as to these parties. Gully was then a professional prize-fighter from the ranks, and fighting for money. Since that time, the Duke of Clarence has become Sovereign of the country, and Gully has become one of its representatives in parliament. As Gully always attends at Court, as well as in the House of Commons, it would be curious to know whether the King, with his accurate recollection of all the events of his life, and his passion for adverting to them, has ever given to Gully any hint of that day's proceedings.

There is, to be sure, one reason why he should not, for Gully was beaten that day by the Chicken, as I have reason to remember; for Lord Thurlow and myself being the two first to arrive before dinner, he asked if I had heard any account of the fight. I repeated what I had heard in the streets, viz. that Gully had given the Chicken so tremendous a knock-down blow at starting, that the latter had never answered to him; so when the Duke of Clarence came and told us that Gully was beat, old Thurlow growled out from his end of the table: "Mr Creevey, I think an action would lie against you by the Chicken for taking away his character.'"

Here, finally, are a few of Creevey's actual diary entries.

At the Pavilion, and talk of a rocket corps

30 October 1811
Brighton
The Prince Regent came here last night with the Duke of Cumberland and Lord Yarmouth. Everybody has been writing their names at the Pavilion this morning, but I don't hear of anybody dining there to-day... I presume we shall be asked there, altho' I went to town on purpose to vote against his appointment of his brother the Duke of York to the Commandership-in-Chief of the Army.

31 October 1811
We have got an invitation from the Regent for to-night and are going. I learn from Sir Philip Francis, who dined there yesterday, the Prince was very gay... There were twenty at dinner – no politicks – but still Francis says he thinks, from the language of the equerries and understrappers, that the campaign in Portugal and Lord Wellington begin to be out of fashion with the Regent. I think so too, from a conversation I had with one of the *Gyps* to-day – [Sit William] Congreve, author of the *rocketts*, and who is going, they say, to have a Rockett Corps. He affects to sneer rather at Wellington's military talents. The said Congreve was at the same school with me at Hackney, and afterwards at Cambridge with me; after that, a brother lawyer with me at Gray's Inn. Then he became an editor of a newspaper ... written in favour of Lord Sidmouth's administration, till he had a libel in his paper against Admiral Berkeley, for which he was prosecuted and fined £1,000. Then he took to inventing rocketts for the more effectual destruction of mankind, for which he became patronised by the Prince of Wales, and here he is – a perfect Field Marshall in appearance. About 12 years ago he wrote to me to enquire the character of a mistress who had lived with me some time before, which said mistress he took upon my rec-ommendation, and she lives with him now, and was, when I knew her, cleverer than all the equerries and their Master put together.

Ornamental monkeys in their red breeches

1 November 1811
We were at the Pavilion last night – Mrs Creevey's three daughters and myself – and had a very pleasant evening. We found there Lord and Lady Charlemont, Marchioness of Downshire and old Lady Sefton. About half-past nine, which

might be a quarter of an hour after we arrived, the Prince came out of the dining-room. He was in his best humour, bowed and spoke to all of us, and looked uncommonly well, tho' very fat. He was in his full Field Marshal's uniform. He remained quite as cheerful and full of fun to the last – half-past twelve – asked after Mrs Creevey's health, and nodded and spoke when he passed us. The Duke of Cumberland was in the regimentals of his own Hussars, looked really hideous, everybody trying to be rude to him – not standing when he came near them. The officers of the Prince's regiment had all dined with him, and looked very ornamental monkeys in their red breeches with gold fringe and yellow boots. The Prince's band played as usual all the time in the dining-room till 12, when the pages and footmen brought about iced champagne punch, lemonade and sandwiches. I found more distinctly than before, from conversation with the Gyps, that Wellington and Portugal are going down.

The Prince looked much happier and more unembarrassed by care than I have seen him since this time six years. This time five years ago, when he was first in love with Lady Hertford, I have seen the tears run down his cheeks at dinner, and he has been dumb for hours, but now that he has the weight of the empire upon him, he is quite alive... I had a very good conversation with Lord Charlemont about Ireland, and liked him much. He thinks the Prince has already nearly ruined himself in Irish estimation by his conduct to the Catholics.

The prince singing a lot, and occasionally considering army matters

2 November 1811

We were again at the Pavilion last night...The Regent sat in the Musick Room almost all the time between Viotti, the famous violin player, and Lady Jane Houston, and he went on for hours beating his thighs the proper time for the band, and singing out aloud, and looking about for accompaniment from Viotti and Lady Jane. It was curious sight to see a Regent thus employed, but he seemed in high good humour.

3 November 1811

I have heard of no one observation the Regent has made yet out of the commonest slip-slop, till to-day Baron Montalembert told me this morning that, when he dined there on Friday with the staff of this district, the Prince said he had been looking over the returns of the Army in Portugal that morning, and that there were of British 16,500 sick in Hospitals in Lisbon, and 4,500 sick in the field – in all, 21,000. It might be indiscreet in the Prince to make this statement from official papers, but he must have been struck with it, and I hope rightly, so as to make him think of peace.

5 November 1811

We were at the Prince's both last night and the night before (Sunday)...The Regent was again all night in the Musick Room, and not content with presiding over the Band, but actually singing, and very loud too. Last night we were reduced to a smaller party than ever, and Mrs Creevey was well enough to go with me and her daughters for the first time. Nothing could be kinder than the

Prince's manner to her. When he first saw her upon coming into the drawing-room, he went up and took hold of both her hands, shook them heartily, made her sit down directly, asked her all about her health, and expressed his pleasure at seeing her look so much better than he expected. Upon her saying she was glad to see him looking so well, he said gravely he was getting old and blind. When she said she was glad on account of his health that he kept his rooms cooler than he used to do, he said he was quite altered in that respect – that he used to be always chilly, and was now never so – that he never had a fire even in his bedroom, and slept with one blanket and sheet only.

6 November 1811

We were again at the Pavilion last night... the party being still smaller than ever, and the Prince, according to his custom, being entirely occupied with his musick.

Sitting opposite, and opposing, the Prince Regent

9 November 1811

Yesterday was the last day of the Prince's stay at this place, and, contrary to my expectation, I was invited to dinner. We did not sit down till half-past seven, tho' I went a little past six. [. . .] We were about sixteen altogether. The Prince was very merry and seemed very well. He began to me with saying very loud that he had sent for Mrs Creevey's physic to London. . . At dinner I sat opposite to him, next to Ossulston, and we were the only persons there at all marked by opposition to his appointment of his brother the Duke of York, or to the Government generally, since he has been Regent. [. . .] We did not drink a great deal, and were in the drawing-room by half-past nine or a little after; no more state, I think, than formerly – ten men out of livery of one kind or other, and four or five footmen. At night everybody was there and the whole closed about one, and so ended the Regent's visit to Brighton.

The editor of *The Creevey Papers*, Sir Herbert Maxwell, concludes this section of diary entries with a short comment: 'And so, it may be added, ended Creevey's intimacy with the Regent. Henceforward he acted in constant opposition to his future monarch's schemes.'

8

John Croker tries not to dine at the Pavilion

And so from Creevey to Croker, and from *The Creevey Papers* to *The Croker Papers*, both of which only mention Brighton a few times, and with little to say other than about the Prince Regent, his Pavilion or the society around him. Although Creevey's diary was published first, the only significant comments about Brighton are dated half a decade later than Croker's similarly brief descriptions.

Born in Galway, Ireland, in 1780, John Wilson Croker spent some years being schooled by French refugees in Cork, which may have led to his passionate early interest in the French Revolution. He studied at Trinity College, Dublin, and then at Lincoln's Inn, London, before being called to the Irish bar. Back in Dublin, he published, anonymously, several books poking fun at the theatre scene, and these proved enormously popular. More serious works followed, including a pamphlet, entitled *A Sketch of Ireland, Past and Present*, in which he advocated that the stability of Ireland required Catholic emancipation.

In 1806, Croker married Rosamund Carrington Pennell. They had two children, both of whom died very young, and then they adopted the daughter of a relative. In 1807, Croker was elected an MP for Downpatrick. His writings on Ireland brought him to the attention of Sir Arthur Wellesley (later the Duke of Wellington), who had just been given command of the army in Portugal, and who appointed him to deputise as his chief secretary. By late 1809, he had been made secretary to the Admiralty, a job he was to hold, against even his own expectations, until 1830, when he retired from active political service. Throughout that time, he remained involved in Parliamentary affairs, thereafter he focused more on his writing activities. He died in 1857.

The Croker Papers

Croker was generally admired for his administrative abilities, and his ability to grasp complex issues. He was said to be clever and amusing and to give clear-headed and practical advice. Which is perhaps why he was also a favourite of George IV, and a valued guest at the houses of leading Tory politicians. Nevertheless, his lack of political ambition meant he never rose to ministerial status. He did write a lot, though, on political and literary subjects, and he continued to compose the kind of light verse he first published anonymously in Dublin. Between 1809 and 1854, he wrote or co-wrote nearly 300 articles for the *Quarterly Review* (which is still around today). He also wrote many, many letters, and kept a diary intermittently. *The Croker Papers*, which combine both diaries and letters, was first edited by Louis J. Jennings and published in three volumes by John Murray, London, in 1884-1885.

The Duchess's life is an odd one

7 December 1818

Left Munster House on horseback at 9 for Cobham, where I was to meet Lord Yarmouth at 11 and thence to Brighton. A little beyond Kingston it came on to rain, and as I happened to overtake a stage coach I sent back my horse and got into it; in two minutes after I got to Cobham, Lord Yarmouth drove up and we set off and arrived at Brighton a little before 4. It rained the whole way, but the roads were so good that we had not a jolt for fifty miles. Passed through Leatherhead, Dorking, Horsham, and Henfield. Lord Yarmouth had come from Oatlands, where he had been for two days, and where the Duke of York [the Prince Regent's brother and second in line to the thrown] had assembled a parliament of dandies. The Duchess's life is an odd one; she seldom has a female companion, she is read to all night and falls asleep towards morning, and rises about 3; feeds her dozens of dogs and her flocks of birds, &c., comes down two minutes before dinner, and so round again. She sometimes walks a little, and does some local charities. She is now preparing her Christmas presents – the habitués of Oatlands give her *étrennes* and receive them in return from her

Poor (not so) old Mrs Fitzherbert

The Prince certainly married Mrs Fitzherbert with the left hand [a Morganatic marriage] – the ceremony was performed by parson Johns, who is still about town. The Prince had seen her in her carriage in the Park and was greatly struck with her – inquired who she was – heard the widow Fitzherbert, contrived to make her acquaintance and was really *mad* for love. The lady felt or affected reluctance and scruples, which the left-hand marriage and some vague promises of conversion to Popery and resignation of all hopes of royalty silenced. I cannot but wonder at her living here and bearding the Prince in a way so indelicate, vis-a-vis the public, and I should have thought so embarrassing to herself. To her presence is attributed the Prince's never going abroad at Brighton. I have known H.R.H. here seven or eight years, and never saw or heard of his being on foot out of the limits of the Pavilion, and in general he avoids even riding through the principal streets. I cannot conceive how poor old Mrs Fitzherbert (she is now near 70 [she was actually 62]) can cause him any uneasiness. Mr Horace Seymour and his lady met us as we were going to the warm baths before dinner, and he called in on us while we were at dinner. They are staying at Mrs Fitzherbert's. It was about his sister Mimi that there arose such a piece of work some time ago. Mrs Fitzherbert was dotingly fond of her, and when the Seymour family attempted to remove her from Mrs Fitzherbert's care, she induced the Prince to solicit the interest of Lord Hertford as the head of the family. This brought about the acquaintance with Lady Hertford, and Mrs Fitzherbert kept the child and lost the Prince.

Beau Brummell is going, or says he is going, to publish an English Journal at Calais, which alarms some great folks, and it is said the French police have been requested to look to it. I hardly think he can dare make such an attempt – he only wants to be bought off, but surely no one will buy him off. I had heard some time ago that he was writing memoirs of his own life; this is likely enough and may have given rise to the other report.

We came to the Castle Inn; the Prince was good enough to offer us lodgings in the Pavilion, but as he is to be down himself to-morrow in the strict incognito of grief, we felt we should be *de trop* there, and have come hither to "take our ease in our inn".

A ruin in a half a century or sooner

Before we went to ride, we went to look at the Pavilion. It is not so much changed as I had been told, and affords me a new proof how inaccurate people are. I had heard from Bicknell, who had just returned from it, that it was all altered, and even the "round room", which I especially asked about, thinking it unlikely to have been destroyed, he insisted was pulled down. On the contrary, none of the rooms which the Prince ordinarily uses are altered, that is to say, the low south room (which was the hall, and two sitting-rooms of the original Pavilion, thrown into one many years since), the dome or round room, and the Chinese gallery, are all unchanged. But in the place of the two rooms which stood at angles of 45° with the rest of the building – one of which I remember, a dining-room and which was also a kind of music-room, and the other, next the Castle Inn, a Chinese drawing-room, which was hardly ever opened – have been erected two immense rooms, sixty feet by forty; one for a music-room and the other for a dining-room. They both have domes; an immense dragon suspends the lustre of one of them. The music-room is most splendid, but I think the other handsomer. They are both too handsome for Brighton, and in an excessive degree too fine for the extent of His Royal Highness's premises. It is a great pity that the whole of this suite of rooms was not solidly built in or near London. The outside is said to be taken from the Kremlin at Moscow; it seems to me to be copied from its own stables, which perhaps were borrowed from the Kremlin. It is, I think, an absurd waste of money, and will be a ruin in half a century or sooner.

The RIVAL QUEENS.
or A POLITICAL HEAT for REGE & GREGE,

Mighty foolish all this

8 December 1818

The Prince not yet come, nor any reason why not. I hope he has not got the gout. A miserable rainy day but for a couple of dry hours before dinner; walked about, and bought some toys for my children – little darlings!

One reason why Mrs Fitzherbert may like this place is that she is treated as queen, at least of Brighton. They don't quite *Highness* her in her domestic circle, but they *Madam* her prodigiously, and stand up longer for her arrival than for ordinary folks, and in short go as near to acknowledging her for *Princess* as they can, without actually giving her the title. When she dines out she expects to be led out to dinner before princesses – mighty foolish all this. The Duke of York still keeps up a correspondence with her, for Seymour mentioned that she had had a letter from his Royal Highness this morning. I dare say the Prince would not be much pleased if he knew this.

10 December 1818

Returned to Minister House [Croker's residence in Fulham].

13 December 1818

Rode to Cobham again and met Lord Yarmouth who had come from Oatlands and arrived at Brighton at 6. We were afraid of being obliged to dine at the Pavilion, so we loitered on the road, and came into Brighton, and dined quietly and slept at the Castle.

The Pavilion kitchens and larders

14 December 1818

After breakfast Blomfield called to scold us for not going to the Pavilion at once, and to command us on the part of his Royal Highness to come there. We went there and walked through the rooms again and visited the offices. The kitchen and larders are admirable – such contrivances for roasting, boiling, baking, stewing, frying, steaming, and heating; hot plates, hot closets, hot air, and hot hearths, with all manner of cocks for hot water and cold water, and warm water and steam, and twenty saucepans all ticketed and labelled, placed up to their necks in a vapour bath.

Dined with his Royal Highness, eighteen at table. [. . .] We dined in the room which was once the hall and two rooms of the original Pavilion, and the one dining-table filled what was once the Prince's whole house. The Prince was in good spirits – he said, "Lord St Vincent is gone abroad only to marry Miss Knight, and to avoid the ridicule of marrying her at home. He has disposed of all his landed and much of his other property to his relations in the way one might expect, but he has kept a large sum for himself, which he intends to leave to this intended wife. She is sixty past, and he past eighty."

In the evening the new music-room was lighted and the band played, both magnificent – the band rather bruyant, and the music better heard from the next room in my opinion.

There was a fine boar's head at the side table at dinner. The Prince pressed Lord Hertford to eat some of it. He refused, and the Prince said it was the only kind of bore that Lord Hertford was not fond of; this is good, because Lord Hertford has a real passion for persons whom everybody else considers as bores. Got to our bed-rooms at half-past 12.

Etiquette at dinner

15 December 1818

Rode to Rottingdean, a poor little village, with a couple of good summer lodging-houses. Our dinner party, twenty, [. . .] The dinners are dull enough, they are too large for society and not quite crowded enough for freedom, so that one is on a sort of tiresome good behaviour. How much pleasanter it used to be with a dozen at a circular table in the old dining-room. His Royal Highness not looking well to-day. The fineness of the weather does not tempt him abroad; his great size and weight make him nervous, and he is afraid to ride. I am not surprised at it. I begin to fear that he never will ride again. He says, "Why should I? I never had better spirits, appetite, and health than when I stay within, and I am not so well when I go abroad." He seems as kind and gracious as usual to everybody.

The etiquette is, that before dinner when he comes in, he *finds* all the men standing, and the women rise; he speaks to everybody, shakes hands with new comers or particular friends, then desires the ladies to be seated. When dinner is announced, he leads out a lady of the highest rank or when the ranks are nearly equal, or when the nominal rank interferes a little with the real rank, as yesterday, with Lady Liddell and Mrs Pelham, he took one on each arm.

After dinner the new dining-room was lighted and he took the ladies to see it. It is really beautiful, and I like it better than the other, if I can venture to say that I prefer either. Everybody was comparing them, and the praise of one was always, as is usual in such cases, expressed by its superiority over the other. I ventured to say that this was not a fair way of judging of them; that though different they were, perhaps, both equally beautiful in their respective kinds, like a "handsome man and a handsome woman". This poor little phrase had great success. The ceilings of both the rooms are spherical and yet there is no echo. [John] Nash [the architect] says that he has avoided it by some new theory of sound, which he endeavoured to explain, and which I did not understand, nor I believe he neither. The rooms are as full of lamps as Hancock's shop.

In the evening His Royal Highness got the plans of the house to show Lady Hertford; she made a few criticisms, and I think the Prince was ready enough to have restored the old entrance if her ladyship had persisted in her opinion to that effect, but she retracted *hautement*, when she saw a tendency to additional expense. I think the tone between his Royal Highness and her ladyship was somewhat *aigre-doux*. She was against all additional expense.

Damn the king

16 December 1818

Before dinner His Royal Highness told me he had been reading Walter Scott's edition of Swift, which, and particularly the correspondence, greatly amused him; and above all he was surprised to find Dr Sheridan's character to be so exactly that of poor Sheridan. He said he thought the best letters were Lord Bolingbroke's. I ventured to mention Lady Betty Germain. "Oh yes," said the Prince, "excellent, and the Duchess of Queensberry's very natural." [...]

After dinner there was music as usual, and H.R.H. made me sit down near him and he repeated to me all that passed in Council on the subject of the men executed yesterday for forgery, in which Lord Liverpool's opinion prevailed (against the new Chief Justice) to pardon two, and to execute the law on the three unfortunates, who died yesterday. The Chief Justice seemed to think the whole equally guilty.

The supper is only a tray with sandwiches, and wine and water handed about. The Prince played a hand or two at Patience, and I was rather amused to hear him exclaim loudly when one of the kings had turned up vexatiously, "Damn the king."

9

Gideon Mantell,
surgeon and fossil hunter

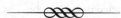

Although Gideon Algernon Mantell was almost 50 by the time Victoria became Queen, when reading his lively and interesting diaries from the first half of the nineteenth century, one has the sense of someone already living in the heart of the Victorian age. He held advanced views on science and medicine; he lived his life in the most energetic and industrious way; and he had a keen intellectual ambition married with a strong sense of social duty. However, although outwardly successful, Mantell was a man never fulfilled, never quite happy. Having moved, for example, from Lewes to the centre of Brighton to extend his medical practice to those attending the King's court there, he soon became very frustrated for being the centre of too much attention, not due to his surgical skills but because of his remarkable collection of fossils.

Mantell was born in the historic market town of Lewes in 1790, the son of a shoemaker. Partly educated by an uncle, at age 15 he was apprenticed to a Lewes surgeon, James Moore. Following six months training at St Bartholomew's Hospital, London, he joined Moore's practice as a partner, and eventually took it over. In 1816, he married Mary Ann Woodhouse, and soon after acquired a house in Castle Place. They had four children who survived into adulthood.

Discovering dinosaurs in the Weald

Apart from his medical practice, Mantell spent much time exploring the Weald of Sussex, studying its geology and looking for fossils. In 1822, he published *The Fossils of the South Downs* (with lithography by his wife), the first of a dozen or so books he was to write on geology and palaeontology. In the mid-1820s, he announced the discovery of *Iguanodon*, an extinct gigantic herbivorous reptile, a genus of, what later would be commonly called, dinosaurs. The fossils were proudly exhibited in a museum housed in his own home. A few years later he discovered a second kind of dinosaur, and confirmed they were land, not amphibian, reptiles.

Notwithstanding his growing fame as a palaeontologist, Mantell was constantly seeking to be and to be seen as a successful doctor. And for this reason, he wanted to move his practice to Brighton, where he could find higher class patients among the constant flow of aristocrats to King George IV's court at the Pavilion. However, for several years he prevaricated fearing the disruption to his family. Bolstered by a large gift of money from an aristocratic patron, he finally made the move towards the end of 1833, and took up a fashionable residence at 20 The Steine. Bizarrely, or so it must have seemed to him, his geological and scientific knowledge became far more in demand than his surgeon's skill. He could barely cope with the influx of visitors, and before long the house was turned into a public museum; and then in 1838 the collection was bought by the British Museum. That same year he bought a practice in Clapham Common, which soon became a success and allowed him frequent trips to London to attend institutional meetings. He moved again in 1844 to Pimlico, where he remained to his death in 1852.

Mantell's diaries

For most of his adult life, from 1818 until his death, Mantell kept a diary. The manuscripts, however, went with his son Walter to New Zealand, where they were given to the Alexander Turnbull Library in Wellington. Many years later, a typescript copy was acquired by the archaeologist Dr Eliot Curwen (who lived on St Aubyns, Hove) which is now held by the Sussex Archaeological Society. Curwen's son E. Cecil Curwen edited the typescript copy, and Oxford University Press published *The Journal of Gideon Mantell, Surgeon and Geologist* in 1940.

In his introduction, Curwen says of Mantell: '[He was] a man of abundant restless energy, fired with an ambition to become immortal in the realms of science; all obstacles were to him irritating frustrations which he bore down with the weight of his dominating personality, and even his domestic happiness was sacrificed to his ambition...The journal, however, reveals how the realisation of his ambitions brought neither joy nor peace nor any real satisfaction, for as time went on he became more and more disappointed and embittered...And yet Mantell was not in other respects a selfish man. He was a keen surgeon, with a great sense of fairness and a deep sympathy with the poor and down-trodden, and he would often put himself to much trouble to alleviate suffering or to right a wrong.'

Links to Charles II, and to Cromwell

15 October 1819
Rode to Brighton with my pupil Mr Lashmar – walked under the Cliffs from Brighton to Rottingdean and returned by the road. Inspected strata. Called on my friend Chassereau, and on Mr Brown in Ship Street. Penderell, who has lately taken the White Horse Inn in St Mary's Street, is a lineal descendant of Richd. Penderell, who concealed Charles II in the Oak, and still receives an annuity from the Crown, for the services of his ancestor: he has changed the sign to the Royal Oak.

14 December 1822
Drove to Brighton: called at Stanmer Park in my way, and left a medallion of Oliver Cromwell as a present to the Earl of Chichester. Drank tea with my friend

Chassereau. On my return found my dear boy Walter in a very dangerous state from inflammation of the lungs; applied three leeches which bled till he fainted.

The awful grandeur of the sea

16 August 1823
Drove to Brighton; the sea very rough and magnificent. I walked along to the beach and seated myself on a rock, viewing with delight the tempestuous foaming of the billows around me: the hull of a vessel wrecked the preceding night was lying near me, and was hurled to and fro by the impetuosity of the waves. The foam from the surges dashing through the piles of the pier was fine and imposing.

6 September 1823
Mrs Mantell accompanied me to Brighton; we went to the end of the Chain Pier, and returned late in the evening. [The Chain Pier was still under construction and was not formally opened until November.]

23 November 1824
A severe hurricane and occurring at the spring tide, the low tracts along the coast were inundated and considerable damage occasioned thereby. I drove to Brighton and arrived there between one and two, at the time the sea was raging with the greatest violence, the surf dashed over the pier and occasionally hid it from our view. So soon as the water was retired so as to allow of walking on the esplanade, we went to the Pier, which was much damaged by the waves; the railing in many places washed away, and the platform destroyed, so as to render access to the Pier-head difficult and dangerous: however we ventured to the farthest end although every now and then a sea dashed over us, and completely drenched us, but the awful grandeur of the scene more than compensated for the inconvenience of our situation.

Crowds on London Road

30 August 1830
Drove my friend W Lee to Brighton, whither Mrs M and Ellen and Hannah had preceded us in a fly; met them at Chassereau's and after taking some refreshments proceeded with them to the London Road and got them seats in a very convenient platform to see the entrée of the King and Queen. Mr Lee and I then walked thro' the dense crowd as far as Preston Turnpike Gate; the road was lined with rows of carriages and vehicles of all descriptions, and upwards of 60 thousand persons were supposed to be present. After waiting till past six (nearly four hours) the King and Queen arrived in a close carriage drawn by four horses, to the great disappointment of the people but few whom could obtain sight of them. I had stationed myself opposite the triumphal arch, and had a good view of their Majesties. In the evening there was a most splendid illumination, a grand display of fireworks. We left Brighton at half past eleven and reached home at midnight.

Jack-of-all-trades

6 September 1830

Every day last week at Brighton, visiting Miss Langham. On Friday a public dinner to 4,000 children on the Steine. The King and Queen visited them: a very gratifying sight. Mrs Mantell accompanied me and saw the Royal Family.

Called on a smuggler and dealer in vertu on the East Cliffe. Bought a magnificent Cabinet drawers of Buhl and tortoiseshell; formerly belonged to Napoleon – quite a bijou – cost me £25. 15s; purchased also a beautiful little statue of a child sleeping; said to be the King of Rome. This evening wrote addresses to the King and Queen; resolutions etc. for the town meeting. I am indeed jack-of-all-trades – more fool I, for I get neither profit, credit, nor thanks! still there is pleasure in moving the public mind and guiding it unseen.

18 September 1830

To Brighton every day. Miss Langham still very ill. [. . .] Last week performed the operation of trephining, or rather with Hey's saw removed several portions of skull that had been forced into the brain – a boy 16 years old crushed by a horse, died the next morning.

Moving to Brighton

5 October 1833

Drove to Brighton and called on Lord Egremont, who spoke to me on the subject of my removal to Brighton, and munificently offered me a thousand pounds to assist me in the removal!

21 December 1833

My family and all my servants etc. take up their abode in 20 Steyne – farewell for ever to Castle Place [Lewes].

1 May 1834

Brighton

Four months have passed since I took up my residence here, and yet so eternally have I been engaged with visits and visitings, and journeys to London and Lewes, and all the etc. etcs. of winding up an affair like that of mine at Lewes, that I have scarcely had breathing time, and not one moment of quiet that I could devote to the solitude of my own thoughts. [. . .] My reception in this town has certainly been very flattering so far as visitors and visitings have been concerned but my professional prospects are not encouraging [. . .] I gave two lectures soon after my arrival here – one for the benefit of the County Hospital, at the Old Ship, the other for All Souls' Church, at the National Schools – both very well attended, and affording a clear profit of 50 guineas. My museum [of fossils in his own house] has been visited by nearly a thousand persons.

The body in the bath

18 September 1834

Soon after tea was sent for to near Kemp Town to a young man who had just been drowned: an hour had elapsed from the time of the accident till my arrival: I inflated the lungs and assisted in removing the body to the hospital – where the surgeon put it in a warm bath for a few minutes then took it out again and placed it before a fire – *then* inflated the lungs! and after waiting there nearly two hours I left the place and returned home at near one o'clock very much fatigued.

9 October 1834

As usual murdering my time – hosts of visitors but no patients! Rambled on the Chain Pier in the evening – very beautiful weather.

Planet and comet gazing on the pier

6 July 1835

Had a beautiful view of the moon, Saturn and some double stars, through the telescope of a man who is a resident here and takes his station on suitable evenings on the Pier or Steyne, that persons may look at any celestial object by paying a small gratuity.

11 October 1835

Very unwell from a cold: saw the Comet (Halley's) last night with the naked eye: I had seen it through a telescope on Tuesday: how solemn is the thought that when this body of light next appears in its present situation almost every eye that now gazes on it will have closed for ever!

1 February 1836

For the last fortnight, scarcely a day has passed without my time being engrossed by meetings concerning the project [Sussex] Scientific Institution [and Mantellian Museum] – I am already tired of the eternal changes of opinion which the gentlemen engaged in it, are constantly evincing. I see but too surely that I shall be made a mere stepping stone for the accomplishment of the principal object with most of them – a gossiping club.

Cold-blooded creatures

25 April 1836

My family removed to Southover and I to lodgings on the Steyne. My collection to be arranged for public exhibition for two and three-quarter years – but I am sick of the cold-blooded creatures I am surrounded by – a change of circumstances with me is but a change of troubles – I will not record them! [From this point on, and at the cost of his home life, Mantell's house on The Steine was given over to the Institution and museum entirely.]

16 August 1836

Lady Byron (the widow of the noble poet) accompanied by a lady, came to the Museum, and spent nearly two hours in examining the chalk fishes etc. [...] She is a woman of a delicate form, rather palid, mild and very lady-like in her manners and conversation – she appeared deeply interested in the subjects of our conversation which was confined to geology and antiquity.

Violent oscillations on the pier

29 October 1836

A dreadful hurricane from the SSW at about eleven AM it was terrific – houses unroofed – trees torn up by the roots: chimney-pots and chimneys blown in every direction – sea mountains high. Went to the Pier, and was present when violent oscillations began to be produced by the hurricane: the whole lines of platforms and chains were thrown into undulations, and the suspension bridges appeared like an enormous serpent writing in agony – at length one of the bridges gave way, and planks, beams, iron rods – all were hurled instantaneously into the boiling surge! The tension of the bridge being thus set at liberty, the remaining bridges gradually became motionless; the damage done to this beautiful structure cannot be much less than £1,000. Some persons were killed by the falling of chimneys and lead blown off the houses.

1 July 1837

Negociating with the Council for the purchase of my Museum! and thus it is – vanity – vanity – vanity – oh! there must be some other state of existence where all the aspirations of the soul will be realised!

Streams of living light

24 July 1837

To the Devil's Dyke – arrived there at seven – the most glorious sight imaginable – the sun breaking through a mass of clouds poured streams of living light on the landscape – the distant downs, by Steyning and to the far west were crested with mist, and the reflection of the sun's rays, gave them a magical effect which is seen on the snow-clad Alps. This gorgeous scene continued about ten minutes and then all was wrapped in gloom. Broke the spring of my carriage – obliged to walk home.

4 March 1839

My Museum purchased by Government [British Museum] for £4,000.

10

Charles Greville, chronicler of histories

Of all the nineteenth-century diarists who recorded public and political events, Charles Cavendish Fulke Greville, is probably the most important. Arthur Ponsonby, who wrote two learned reviews of English diaries in the 1920s, says that as a commentator on contemporary events he 'holds a unique position', for 'he wrote history as it was in the making'. Other political and social diaries of the time 'fade into insignificance when compared with his very full and detailed chronicle'. Indeed his early diaries, when published a decade after his death for the first time, caused an uproar. The Prime Minister at the time, Benjamin Disraeli, called them an outrage, and Queen Victoria, taking her cue from him, was indeed outraged – at the things written about her uncles many decades earlier.

Greville was born in 1794 into a branch of the family of the Earls of Warwick. Educated at Eton and Christ Church, Oxford, he paged for King George III for a short while before working as a private secretary to Earl Bathurst. Then, for more than thirty-five years, he was Clerk to the Privy Council, a job which brought him into contact with many important people of the time. He was much liked, and maintained good relations with both Whigs and Tories, often being employed as a negotiator during ministerial changes. His interests extended from horse racing (he owned horses and managed the Duke of York's stables for some years) to literature. In 1859, he resigned the clerkship of the council, and in 1865 he died.

Sympathetic and kind, grumpy and vain

Described as sympathetic, generous and a delightful companion, he was also said to bustle with kindness. Smooth and urbane, Greville's features were marked by a long, pointed chin and a strong nose which led to him being given the nickname of 'Punch'; though he was also known as the 'Gruncher', on account of being grumpy when troubled by an attack of gout or his growing deafness. He could be vain too. Benjamin Disraeli, writing to a friend in 1874, said: 'I knew him intimately. He was the vainest being – I don't limit myself to man – that ever existed; and I don't forget Cicero and Lytton Bulwer [Edward Bulwer-Lytton – a very popular writer of the day, he who coined the epigram, 'the pen is mightier than the sword']. Although he never married, one of his mistresses bore him a son who died as a young man journeying back from India.

Well known and well liked as he was while alive, Greville's eminence today is entirely thanks to his diaries. Having always intended them for publication, Greville gave them to Henry Reeve, a Privy Council colleague. 'The author of these Journals,' Reeve says, 'requested me, in January 1865, a few days before his death, to take charge of them with a view to publication at some future time. He left that time to my discretion, merely remarking that Memoirs of this kind ought not, in his opinion, to be locked up until they had lost their principal interest by the death of all those who had taken any part in the events they describe.'

The first three volumes of *The Greville Memoirs – A Journal of the Reigns of King George IV and King William IV* were published by Longmans, Green in 1874. They caused a scandal. In Disraeli's letter (the same one as mentioned above), he writes: 'I have not seen Chas. Greville's book, but have read a good deal of it. It is a social outrage. And committed by one who was always talking of what he called 'perfect gentlemen.' I don't think he can figure now in that category.' According to Queen Victoria's biographer, Christopher Hibbbert, she wrote that she was 'horrified and indignant at this dreadful and really scandalous book. Mr Greville's indiscretion, indelicacy, ingratitude, betrayal of confidence and shameful disloyalty towards his Sovereign make it very important that the book should be severely censored and discredited,' she wrote indignantly.

Five more volumes followed, in the 1880s, entitled *The Greville Memoirs: A Journal of the Reign of Queen Victoria*.

The gaudy splendour of the Pavilion

18 December 1821

I have not written anything for months. 'Quante cose mi sono accadute!' My progress was as follows, not very interesting: To Newmarket, Whersted, Eiddlesworth, Sprotborough, Euston, Elveden, Welbeck, Caversham, Nun Appleton, Welbeck, Burghley, and London. Nothing worth mentioning occurred at any of these places. Sprotborough was agreeable enough. The Grevilles, Montagu, Wilmot, and the Wortleys were there. I came to town, went to Brighton yesterday se'nnight for a Council.

I was lodged in the Pavilion and dined with the King. The gaudy splendour of the place amused me for a little and then bored me. The dinner was cold and the evening dull beyond all dulness. They say the King is anxious that form and ceremony should be banished, and if so it only proves how impossible it is that form and ceremony should not always inhabit a palace. The rooms are not furnished for society, and, in fact, society cannot flourish without ease; and who can feel at ease who is under the eternal constraint which etiquette and respect impose?

The King was in good looks and good spirits, and after dinner cut his jokes with all the coarse merriment which is his characteristic. Lord Wellesley did not seem to like it, but of course he bowed and smiled like the rest. I saw nothing very particular in the King's manner to Lady Conyngham. He sat by her on the couch almost the whole evening, playing at patience, and he took her in to dinner; but Madame de Lieven and Lady Cowper were there, and he seemed equally civil to all of them. I was curious to see the Pavilion and the life they lead there, and I now only hope I may never go there again, for the novelty is past, and I should be exposed to the whole weight of the bore of it without the stimulus of curiosity.

The King's bathing habits

19 August 1822

I went to Brighton on Saturday to see the Duke [of York – George IV's brother and heir presumptive at the time]; returned to-day. The Pavilion is finished. The King has had a subterranean passage made from the house to the stables, which is said to have cost 3,000*l* or 5,000*l*; I forget which. There is also a bath in his apartment, with pipes to conduct water from the sea; these pipes cost 600*l*. The King has not taken a sea bath for sixteen years.

I shot 376 rabbits

16 September 1829

Went to Brighton on Saturday last to pay Lady Jersey a visit and shoot at Firle. Jersey and I shot 376 rabbits, the greatest number that had ever been killed on the hills. The scenery is very fine – a range of downs looking on one side over the sea, and on the other over a wide extent of rich flat country. It is said that Firle is the oldest park in England. It belongs to Lord Gage.

Heard at Brighton

I heard at Brighton for the first time of the Duke of Wellington's prosecution of the 'Morning Journal,' which was announced by the paper itself in a paragraph quite as scurrilous as those for which it is attacked. It seems that he has long made up his mind to this measure, and that he thinks it is a duty incumbent on him, which I do not see, and it appears to me to be an act of great folly. He stands much too high, has performed too great actions, and the attacks on him were too vulgar and vague to be under the necessity of any such retaliatory measure as this, and he lowers his dignity by entering into a conflict with such an infamous paper, and appearing to care about its abuse. I think the Chancellor was right, and that he is wrong.

[In December 1829, the editors and proprietor of 'Morning Journal' were found guilty of libel on ministers and parliament and sentenced to a year in Newgate. The paper closed a few months later.]

There is a report that the King insists upon the Duke of Cumberland [another of George IV's brothers] being Commander-in-Chief, and it is extraordinary how many people think that he will succeed in turning out the Duke. Lord Harrington died while I was at Brighton, and it is supposed that the Duke of

Cumberland will try and get the Round Tower [part of Windsor Castle], but probably the King will not like to establish him so near himself.

The King has nearly lost his eyesight, and is to be couched as soon as his eyes are in a proper state for the operation. He is in a great fright with his father's fate before him, and indeed nothing is more probable than that he will become blind and mad too; he is already a little of both. It is now a question of appointing a Private Secretary, and [Sir William] Knighton, it is supposed, would be the man; but if he is to abstain from all business, there would seem to be no necessity for the appointment, as he will be as little able to do business with his Private Secretary as with his Minister.

With tagrag and bobtail about him

19 January 1831

G[eorge] Lamb [politician and writer] said that the King [William IV] is supposed to be in a bad state of health, and this was confirmed to me by Keate the surgeon, who gave me to understand that he was going the way of both his brothers [George IV etc.]. He will be a great loss in these times; he knows his business, lets his Ministers do as they please, but expects to be informed of everything. He lives a strange life at Brighton, with tagrag and bobtail about him, and always open house. The Queen is a prude, and will not let the ladies come *décolletées* to her parties. George IV, who liked ample expanses of that sort, would not let them be covered.

King, Queen, Princes, Princesses, bastards, and attendants

14 December 1832
Brighton
Came here last Wednesday week; Council on the Monday for the dissolution [of Parliament]; place very full, bustling, gay, and amusing. I am staying in De Ros's house with Alvanley; Chesterfields, Howes, Lievens, Cowpers, all at Brighton, and plenty of occupation in visiting, gossiping, dawdling, riding, and driving; a very idle life, and impossible to do anything. The Court very active, vulgar, and hospitable; King, Queen, Princes, Princesses, bastards, and attendants constantly trotting about in every direction: the election noisy and dull – the Court candidate beaten and two Radicals elected. Everybody talking of the siege of Antwerp and the elections. So, with plenty of animation, and discussion, and curiosity, I like it very well. Lord Howe is devoted to the Queen, and never away from her. She receives his attentions, but demonstrates nothing in return; he is like a boy in love with this frightful spotted Majesty, while his delightful wife is laid up (with a sprained ancle and dislocated joint) on her couch.

The prize-fighter John Gully comes good

17 December 1832
Brighton
On Sunday I heard Anderson preach. He does not write his sermons, but preaches from notes; very eloquent, voice and manner perfect, one of the best I ever heard, both preacher and reader.

The borough elections are nearly over, and have satisfied the Government. They do not seem to be bad on the whole; the metropolitans have sent good men enough, and there was no tumult in the town. At Hertford Buncombe was routed by Salisbury's long purse. He hired such a numerous mob besides that he carried all before him. Some very bad characters have been returned; among the worst, Faithful here [George Faithful – a Nonconformist preacher and attorney – was one of the first two MPs returned for Brighton after it was created a Parliamentary Constituency]; Gronow at Stafford; Gully, Pontefract; [...]

Gully's [John Gully – see also Chapter 7] history is extraordinary. He was taken out of prison twenty-five or thirty years ago by Hellish to fight Pierce, surnamed the 'Game Chicken,' being then a butcher's apprentice; he fought him and was beaten. He afterwards fought Belcher (I believe), and Gresson twice, and left the prizering with the reputation of being the best man in it. He then took to the turf, was successful, established himself at Newmarket, where he kept a hell, and began a system of corruption of trainers, jockeys, and boys, which put the secrets of all Newmarket at his disposal, and in a few years made him rich.

At the same time he connected himself with Mr Watt in the north, by betting for him, and this being at the time when Watt's stable was very successful, he won large sums of money by his horses. Having become rich he embarked in a great coal speculation, which answered beyond his hopes, and his shares soon yielded immense profits. His wife, who was a coarse, vulgar woman, in the meantime died, and he afterwards married the daughter of an innkeeper, who proved as gentlewomanlike as the other had been the reverse, and who is very pretty besides. He now gradually withdrew from the betting ring as a regular blackleg, still keeping horses, and betting occasionally in large sums, and about a year or two ago, having previously sold the Hare Park to Sir Mark Wood, where he lived for two or three years, he bought a property near Pontefract, and settled down (at Ackworth Park) as John Gully, Esq., a gentleman of fortune. [...]

When Parliament was about to be dissolved, he was again invited to stand for Pontefract by a numerous deputation; he again hesitated, but finally accepted; Lord Mexborough withdrew, and he was elected without opposition. In person he is tall and finely formed, full of strength and grace, with delicate hands and feet, his face coarse and with a bad expression, his head set well on his shoulders, and remarkably graceful and even dignified in his actions and manners; totally without education, he has strong sense, discretion, reserve, and a species of good taste which has prevented, in the height of his fortunes, his behaviour from ever transgressing the bounds of modesty and respect, and he has gradually separated himself from the rabble of bettors and blackguards of whom he was once the most conspicuous, and tacitly asserted his own independence and acquired gentility without ever presuming towards those whom he has been accustomed to regard with deference. His position is now more anomalous than ever, for a member of Parliament is a great man, though there appear no reasons why the suffrages of the blackguards of Pontefract should place him in different social relations towards us than those in which we mutually stood before.

6 August 1835
Yesterday to Brighton, to see my horse Dacre run for the Brighton stake, which he won, and back at night.

Mrs Fitzherbert and her papers

31 March 1837

Among the many old people who have been cut off by this severe weather, one of the most remarkable is Mrs Fitzherbert, who died at Brighton at above eighty years of age. She was not a clever woman, but of a very noble spirit, disinterested, generous, honest, and affectionate, greatly beloved by her friends and relations, popular in the world, and treated with uniform distinction and respect by the Royal Family. The late King, who was a despicable creature, grudged her the allowance he was bound to make her, and he was always afraid lest she should make use of some of the documents in her possession to annoy or injure him. This mean and selfish apprehension led him to make various efforts to obtain possession of those the appearance of which he most dreaded, and among others, one remarkable attempt was made by Sir William Knighton some years ago.

Although a stranger to Mrs Fitzherbert, he called one day at her house, when she was ill in bed, insisted upon seeing her, and forced his way into her bedroom. She contrived (I forget how) to get rid of him without his getting anything out of her, but this domiciliary visit determined her to make a final disposition of all the papers she possessed, that in the event of her death no advantage might be taken of them either against her own memory or the interests of any other person. She accordingly selected those papers which she resolved to preserve, and which are supposed to be the documents and correspondence relating to her marriage with George IV, and made a packet of them which was deposited at her banker's, and all other letters and papers she condemned to the flames. For this purpose she sent for the Duke of Wellington and Lord Albemarle, told them her determination, and in their presence had these papers burnt; she assured them, that everything was destroyed, and if after her death any pretended letters or documents were produced, they might give the most authoritative contradiction to their authenticity.

11

Henry Edward Fox
visits a watering-place

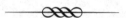

Henry Edward Fox, the third son of the third Baron Holland, was a fairly unremarkable aristocrat. Nevertheless, he was an interesting diarist, gossipy, observant and happily acerbic at times. He had no qualms, for example, in calling the King (George IV) a fool, or in describing the English countryside as being full of 'Lilliput ostentation'! But he liked Brighton, and was there for the opening of the Chain Pier which he described as 'a great ornament and convenience to the place'.

Fox was born in 1802 at Holland House in London. Lame from birth and of a delicate constitution, he was schooled privately, and studied at Christ Church, Oxford. He briefly held the parliamentary seat of Horsham before eschewing politics and joining the diplomatic service, taking posts in Italy and Austria. He married the daughter of the Earl of Coventry in 1833. Apart from a son who died at birth they had no children, though they did adopt a daughter in France, who later became Princess Liechenstein.

Fox succeeded to become (the fourth) Baron Holland in 1840 on the death of his father. On returning to England in 1846, he and his wife spent much money renovating and altering Holland House (Queen Victoria and Prince Albert attended parties there in 1849-1850). Thereafter, they spent part of each year in Paris and Naples. Fox's baronies expired with his death in 1859, and his estate passed to a cousin, the fifth Earl of Ilchester.

Diary writing – a family habit

Diary writing, it seems, was a family habit. The diaries of both Fox's parents were published, seventy years apart: *The Journal of Elizabeth Lady Holland* in 1908, and *The Holland House Diaries, 1831-1840* in 1977. This latter was based on the diaries of the third Baron Holland, but also included extracts from the diary of Dr John Allen, a physician and writer, and a significant figure brought into the Holland household by the third Baron.

The fourth Baron Holland's diaries – *The Journal of the Hon. Henry Edward Fox, afterwards fourth and last Baron Holland* – were published in 1923, after his mother's and before his father's, by Thornton Butterworth. Having been found among the manuscripts at Holland House, they were edited by the sixth Earl of Ilchester, and, somewhat bizarrely, cover a twelve-year-period chronologically earlier than *The Holland House Diaries* (i.e. those of his father).

Arthur Ponsonby says this about the fourth Baron's diaries: 'He has style, great facility of expression, terse and epigrammatic powers of portraiture and gives unreserved disclosure of candid opinions. So we get at the man through the gossip. This does not prevent the gossip of high society being very exhausting, nor does it prevent him from suffering from the common delusion that association with prominent people must necessarily mean gaining wide experience.'

Life in a watering-place

November 1823

We went back to Petworth for two days, and arrived at Brighton on the first of November. For the first three nights we slept in that wretched place, the York Hotel, and dined almost every day with Lady Affleck, who brought Mary from St Ann's. Our life at Brighton was just what all lives must be in a watering-place. Some agreable people were there, and latterly when Charles and Henry Webster came it was more agreable: Bedfords, Vernons, Cowpers, Ponsonbys, Duncannons, Hopes, Kings, Aberdeens. Our house was pleasantly situated immediately opposite the Chain Pier, which was twice the scene of gaieties. One night upon its' being publickly opened there were fireworks, and afterwards, in honor of King's arrival, illuminated. It is a delightful walk, and a great ornament and convenience to the place. Nothing very particular occurred in the world except that Ld Granville was appointed to The Hague as Ambassador, and that all London has been occupied with the murder of Mr Weare in Hertfordshire one of the most barbarous ever known; and the publicity of it and of all the proceedings has been so great that they thought it but fair to the prisoners to put off the trial, as they had been so much prejudged. [...]

The palaces of fairies

My father and I dined one day at the Pavilion. Nothing could be more civil than the King was to him, and the whole conversation after dinner was meant to be gracious to him, praising Holland House, General Fitzpatrick; and even what he did not address to him was meant as implied civility. To Lord Aberdeen he was almost rude. Lady Aberdeen fainted from the heat and looked quite lovely. Nothing could surpass the excellence of the dinner and the splendour of the whole establishment. The King after dinner talked about 'Junius', which he believes to have been written by Sir Philip Francis, and gave some strong corroborations of that suspicion. The rooms are splendid, and when lighted up look like the palaces of Fairies or Genii. After dinner the King played at écarté with the favorite and Lady Cowper, and all the rest of the company remained in the outer room. Afterwards there were several evening parties and a child's ball, to which I went. The music is so loud and the heat so overpowering, that they generally gave me a headache. Charles met Lady Errol for the first time one evening there. My father and mother went away on Xmas Day, but Charles and I staid on some time longer. Charles, however, got tired and left me.

One evening I was suddenly sent for to the Pavilion. My dismay was not small at finding myself ushered into a room where the King and [Gioachino] Rossini were alone. I found that I was the only person honored with an invitation to hear this great [Italian] composer's performances. A more unworthy object than I am could not have been selected. H.M. was not much pleased with his manner, which was careless and indifferent to all the civilities shown him. The King himself made a fool of himself by joining in the choruses and the Halelujah Anthem, stamping his foot and overpowering all with the loudness of his Royal voice.

Talk of Napoleon and Bourrienne's Memoires

29 November 1829
Old Steyne, Brighton

I was called a little after seven and got up immediately. The morning was foggy, damp and cold. I left London before 9 and stopped to hear how Miss Vernon [his great aunt] had passed the night at Little Holland House. I was happy to find that the new medicine and a blister had in some measure relieved her and given her a few hours' sleep. I cannot, however, help apprehending that all ultimate hopes of her recovery must be very faint. My journey was rapid and had no other merit. The country (indeed like almost all the country in this island) is tame and uninteresting; perpetual small country-houses with their mean trimness and Lilliput ostentation. There are few of those worst of all sights on this road – a vast green field, dotted with trees, surrounded by a wall, and damped by a variety of swampy ponds, which call themselves country seats.

I arrived at half past 2. My mother was on the pier. I sat with my father, who was, as he always is, very lively. He talked of the Grenvilles, and tho' he admitted all the faults which make them so unpopular in the world, he praised them for many merits, especially Tom Grenville for his disinterested generosity about Lord Carysfort's guardianship. I took a bath before dinner. Our guests were, The Lord Chancellor, Lady Lyndhurst, Duke of Devonshire, Sir James Mackintosh, Mr Whishaw, four selves. I never had met the Chancellor before; he is agreable in his manner and voice, and his language is choice and elegant. After dinner we talked of Napoleon and 'Bourrienne's Memoires' [Bourriene had been a private secretary to Napoleon Bonaparte, and the first volumes of his memoirs had just been published]. Sir James said that the conversation there given between the Emperor and Auguste de Stael (at that time only 17 years old), is quite correct. That he has seen Auguste's letter to his mother, detailing it just as it is told in 'Bourrienne'. He went to meet Napoleon on his return from Italy, in order to solicit for his mother to be allowed to go nearer Paris – but in vain. [. . .]

The room was hot and the evening fatiguing. It is very painful to see and be in the room with someone one wishes excessively to speak to, without the possibility of doing so without becoming the gaze of the whole party. I went to bed at 12.

Coarse language and shattered teeth

1 December 1829

A bright day. After my shower-bath I went with Mary to Mrs Cheney for the former to sit. Mrs Cheney has made two drawings of her; one is bad, the other tolerable.

I called on Lady Lyndhurst, and then joined her husband on the Chain Pier. He is agreable, but his language before his wife is distressingly coarse; he encourages and indeed forces her to talk as coarsely as himself. [. . .]

As soon as dinner was over Mary and I went to join Lady Jersey at the dancing-school ball at the Ship Inn. The room was very full and intolerably hot, and so ill-managed that I never contrived to sit down the whole evening. I stood by Lady H Baring, who is lively and clever, but unfeeling and loud. Her husband to-day has had a bad fall, which has shattered his teeth and obliges him to go to-morrow to London. She talked of it with great levity, and did not for a moment appear to think that her presence by his couch was more natural and proper than in a ball-room. The children seemed to dance prettily, but I could scarcely see them from the thickness of the crowd.

An embrace on the steps leading to the Chain Pier

2 December 1829

A cold, raw day. I got up late and took no bath. I called on Lady Webster and Miss Monson. The former is a fine, open-hearted, cheerful woman, perfectly good-humoured and devoid of any affectation. She has remains of very extraordinary beauty and is still very handsome. I then went to Lady L. The Chancellor is gone. Before he went she received another anonymous letter from London, threatening to expose her to him, and accusing her of an embrace with me on the steps leading to the Chain Pier on Saturday last, on which day I was in London and she was in her bed. This takes off any apprehension we might feel, for it proves the ignorance of our enemies. Great God! What a dreadful country this is to live in, and how much better for the peace of society and for the agré-mens of life is the despotism of one man to the inquisitive tyranny and insolent exactions of a whole nation. She very wisely instantly showed the letter to her husband, at the same time showing 'The Age' with a paragraph about her and Cradock, and desired him to direct her future conduct, which he has done in advising her to continue exactly as if she had never received such letters and not to allow the avarice of blackguards to harass and torment her. [. . .]

After dinner Mr [James] Kenney (the author of many comedies and farces) came and chatted very agreably. He is like the starved apothecary in 'Romeo and Juliet'. I went for two hours to the Brighton Almack's, rather a scanty ball. Lady L in low spirits. She had dined tete-a-tete with the D. of D., and he had used the privilege, or Gibbon would say abused the privilege, of a kind friend to tell her every disagreable truth and naming every painful possibility. I came home at 12.

12

Walter Scott, father and grandfather

Walter Scott – author of *Ivanhoe* and *Rob Roy* – is credited with writing the world's first real historical novels and the world's first best-sellers. Alas, he didn't start keeping diaries until the last years of his life, for they are beautifully written and always interesting. Some say they are a 'superb' work, and possibly his best. Alas, too, therefore that he didn't write about Brighton more, even though on one visit he called it 'a city of loiterers and invalids – a Vanity Fair for piping, dancing of bears, and for the feats of Mr Punch.'

Scott was born in Edinburgh, in 1771, and trained as a lawyer, like his father, but without much commitment. He did work in his father's office, but preferred to travel – exploring the highlands – and to read. In 1797, he married Margaret Charlotte Carpenter, from a French Royalist family, even though he knew very little about her. They lived happily to her death, a few years before his own, and had four children. Also in 1797, Scott first volunteered for the Royal Edinburgh Light Dragoons, and acted as its secretary and quartermaster. Although active, his health was never very good, and he had been left lame by polio in early childhood.

From 1806, a job as Principal Clerk to the Court of Session in Edinburgh allowed him a regular income without having to practise as an advocate. But it was a career in writing that was soon to take hold. He began by translating German Gothic romances, and then produced his own ballads, such as *The Lay of the Last Minstrel* and *The Lady of the Lake*, which proved immensely popular. Moreover, he worked on new editions of writings by Dryden and Swift. In the 1810s, Scott turned to novels, and found a new level of success with, what became known as, his Waverley novels, including *Rob Roy* and *Ivanhoe* among many others. All these novels, however, were published anonymously, and though reviewers were identifying him as the author from the first, he continued denying the fact until 1827.

From riches to ruin

Nevertheless, the income from these works gave him the wherewithal to build a huge mansion in the Scottish borders, 35 miles south-east of Edinburgh, which he called Abbotsford. Today the house is open to the public for much of the year, and is run by a charitable trust keen on celebrating Scott's life, and to develop Scottish literature. The trust says: 'Abbotsford is the exclusive creation of Scott... where Scotland's greatest son created a notion of Scotland that was more romantic perhaps, but also higher, more honourable, more noble than it had been in the past, and in consequence, raised Scotland's reputation in the world. Here he worked diligently and the result was the legend of a great man which exists for so many people across the world to the present day.'

By 1820, when he was knighted, Scott was a celebrity and important public figure. He organised the visit of King George IV to Scotland in 1822, turning it into a party with gentlemen wearing kilts, for example, and thus incidentally created a Scottish identity which still exists today. He helped created the Edinburgh Academy. He was chairman of the Edinburgh Oil Gas Company in 1824, was a governor of the Scottish Union, and an extraordinary director of the Edinburgh Life Assurance Company.

In 1826, though, his world collapsed with one of the worst financial crises of the century. Not only did he have the financial burden of Abbotsford, but the bankruptcies of his publisher and printer left Scott in financial ruin. Rather than declaring bankruptcy himself, he worked hard for the rest of his life to repay his debts – to the detriment, some say, of his later novels, which were, in modern parlance, churned out. He died in 1832, having cleared around three-quarters of his debt (the rest was partly repaid through the sale of his copyrights), and almost all the newspapers – according to his biographer J.G. Lockhart – 'had the signs of mourning usual on the demise of a king'.

John Gibson Lockhart

John Gibson Lockhart played more than a passing role in Scott's life. A gifted writer and editor, he came to Scott's notice in 1818 through working for the newly-launched *Blackwood's Magazine*. Scott and Lockhart became close friends, and in 1820 Lockhart married Scott's daughter Sophia. They moved to London in 1825, so Lockhart could take up a job as editor of the *Quarterly Review*, a position he held until near his death. They had three children: John, a sickly child who was taken to Brighton for his health but died aged 10; Walter, born in Brighton and named after his grandfather; and Charlotte.

Lockhart's most significant work, published in 1837-1838, was his seven-volume *Memoirs of the Life of Sir Walter Scott*, often considered second only to Boswell's *The Life of Samuel Johnson*.

Scott's literary remains

Lockhart was able to write this biographical masterpiece because he had the rights to all of Scott's literary remains, including a wealth of letters and two volumes of a diary which Scott had started writing in 1825, and kept up until his death. Lockhart noted, though, that writing so short a time after Scott's death, he could not use the diary as freely as he might have wished and 'by regard for the feelings of living persons' he had printed no chapter of the diary in full. This would have to wait half a century, until 1890, when it was published in two volumes by David Douglas as *The Journal of Sir Walter Scott, from the Original Manuscript at Abbotsford*. Here is the very first entry.

20 November 1825

I have all my life regretted that I did not keep a regular Journal. I have myself lost recollection of much that was interesting, and I have deprived my family and the public of some curious information, by not carrying this resolution into effect. I have bethought me, on seeing lately some volumes of Byron's notes, that he probably had hit upon the right way of keeping such a memorandum-book, by throwing aside all pretence to regularity and order, and marking down events just as they occurred to recollection. I will try this plan; and behold I have a handsome locked volume, such as might serve for a lady's album. *Nota bene*, John Lockhart, and Anne, and I are to raise a Society for the suppression of Albums. It is a most troublesome shape of mendicity. Sir, your autograph, a line of poetry, or a prose sentence! Among all the sprawling sonnets, and blotted trumpery that dishonours these miscellanies, a man must have a good stomach that can swallow this botheration as a compliment.

David Hewitt writing Scott's entry for the *Oxford Dictionary of National Biography* notes that only a month after starting his own journal, Scott published a review of Pepys's diaries in the *Quarterly Review*, by then being edited by his friend and son-in-law Lockhart. Hewitt explains how Scott is always aware of the way in which literary form tends to fix meaning, and that he therefore tries to ensure his diary is undistorted by method. Hewitt says: 'He is endlessly interesting; he records what he had been doing; he comments acutely on what goes on around him; he works out intellectual positions; he analyses himself; he lays himself out on the page. The Journal is a superb work, but its greatness is ultimately due to an accident of timing. It opens with Scott at the height of his fame and prosperity. Within six months he was ruined and his wife was dead. He undertook to repay all his debts, and the Journal records how a heroic decision to do right and to act well gradually destroyed him mentally and physically.'

That poor delicate child

2 December 1825

Rather a blank day for the *Gurnal*. Correcting proofs in the morning. Court from half-past ten till two; poor dear Colin Mackenzie, one of the wisest, kindest, and best men of his time, in the country, I fear with very indifferent health. From two till three transacting business [. . .]; all seems to go smoothly. Sophia dined with us alone, Lockhart being gone to the west to bid farewell to his father and brothers. Evening spent in talking with Sophia on their future prospects. God bless her, poor girl! she never gave me a moment's reason to complain of her. But, O my God! that poor delicate child, so clever, so ani-mated, yet holding by this earth with so fearfully slight a tenure. Never out of his mother's thoughts, almost never out of her father's arms when he has but a single moment to give to anything. *Deus providebit.*

17 March 1826
A letter from Lockhart, with one enclosed from Sophia, announces the medical people think the child is visibly losing strength, that its walking becomes more difficult, and, in short, that the spine seems visibly affected. They recommend tepid baths in sea-water, so Sophia has gone down to Brighton, leaving Lockhart in town, who is to visit her once a week. Here is my worst augury verified. The bitterness of this probably impending calamity is extreme. The child was almost too good for this world; beautiful in features; and, though spoiled by every one, having one of the sweetest tempers, as well as the quickest intellect I ever saw; a sense of humour quite extraordinary in a child, and, owing to the general notice which was taken of him, a great deal more information than suited his years. He was born in the eighth month, and such children are never strong, seldom long-lived. I look on this side and that, and see nothing but protracted misery, a crippled frame, and decayed constitution, occupying the attention of his parents for years, and dying at the end of that period, when their hearts were turned on him; or the poor child may die before Sophia's confinement, and that may again be a dangerous and bad affair; or she may, by increase of attention to him, injure her own health. In short, to trace into how many branches such a misery may flow is impossible. The poor dear love had so often a slow fever, that when it pressed its little lips to mine, I always foreboded to my own heart what all I fear are now aware of.

The child's name is Walter

24 April 1826
Good news from Brighton. Sophia is confined; both she and her baby are doing well, and the child's name is announced to be Walter, a favourite name in our family, and I trust of no bad omen. Yet it is no charm for life. Of my father's family I was the second Walter, if not the third. I am glad the name came my way, for it was borne by my father, great-grandfather, and great-great grandfather; also by the grandsire of that last–named venerable person who was the first laird of Raeburn.

20 May 1826
Sophia's baby was christened on Sunday, 14th May, at Brighton, by the name of Walter Scott. May God give him life and health to wear it with credit to himself and those belonging to him.

22 April 1828
Sophia left this to take down poor Johnnie to Brighton. I fear, I fear, but we must hope the best.

A *Vanity Fair* for the dancing of bears

20 May 1828

I set out for Brighton this morning in a light coach, which performed the distance in six hours otherwise the journey was uncomfortable. Three women, the very specimens of womankind – I mean trumpery; a child who was sick, but afterwards looked and smiled, and was the only thing like company. The road is pleasant enough till it gets into the Wealds of Sussex, a huge succession of green downs which sweep along the sea-coast for many miles. Brighton seems grown twice as large since 1815. It is a city of loiterers and invalids – a Vanity Fair for piping, dancing of bears, and for the feats of Mr Punch. I found all my family well excepting the poor pale Johnnie; and he is really a thing to break one's heart by looking at – yet he is better. The rest are in high kelter.

My old friend Will Rose dined with us, also a Doctor Yates and his wife – the Esculapius [Aesculapius – the god of medicine and healing in ancient Greece] of Brighton, who seems a sensible man. I was entertained with the empire he exerted over him as protector of his health. I was very happy to find myself at Sophia's quiet table, and am only sorry that I must quit her so soon.

The Devil's Ditch

21 May 1828

This being a fine day, we made some visits in the morning, in the course of which I waited on Mrs Dorset, sister of Mrs Charlotte Smith, and herself the author of the 'Peacock at Home', one of the prettiest and liveliest *jeux d'esprit* in our language. She is a fine stately old lady not a bit of a literary person, I mean having none of the affectation of it, but like a lady of considerable rank. I am glad I have seen her. Renewed my acquaintance with Lady Charlotte Hamilton, née Lady Charlotte Hume, and talked over some stories thirty years old at least. We then took a fly, as they call the light carriages, and drove as far as the Devil's Ditch. A rampart it is of great strength and depth, enclosing, I presume, the precincts of a British town that must have held 30,000 men at least. I could not discover where they got water.

We got home at four, and dined at five, and smoked cigars till eight. Will Rose came in with his man Hinvaes, who is as much a piece of Rose as Trim was of Uncle Toby. We laughed over tales 'both old and new' till ten o'clock came, and then broke up.

22 May 1828

Left Brighton this morning with a heavy heart. Poor Johnnie looks so very poorly that I cannot but regard his case as desperate, and then God help the child's parents! Amen!

13

Thomas Raikes reminisces on racing and duels

The Oxford Dictionary of National Biography introduces Thomas Raikes as 'dandy and diarist'. Born in 1777, he was educated at Eton where he became acquainted with Beau Brummel, another dandy-to-be, and other future friends. He visited the Continent with a private tutor to study languages, and then joined his father's firm, but liked the West End clubs better. He was an early member of the Carlton Club, and was nicknamed Apollo because he rose in the east (where his banking house was in the City) and set in the west (where the clubs were).

In 1802, he married Sophia Maria, daughter of Nathaniel Bayly, a proprietor in Jamaica. They had one son and three daughters. He was often abroad, in The Hague, Paris or in Russia, and moved permanently to France in 1833 to escape financial troubles. He returned to London in 1841, spending the next few years there or in Paris, before taking a house at Brighton, where he died in 1848. Less than ten years later, Longman, Brown, Green, and Longmans had published four volumes of his diary, entitled *A Portion of the Journal kept by Thomas Raikes, Esq, from 1831 to 1847 comprising reminiscences of Social and Political Life in London and Paris during that period.*

There are no diary entries written by Raikes in Brighton. However, while in Paris, and as part of his daily diary writing, he did reminisce about Brighton, and it is these entries (apart from the first) which are included here.

15 December 1832
The new borough of Brighton, under the very nose of the Court, has returned two most decided Radicals, Wigney and Faithful, who talk openly of reducing the allowance made to the King and Queen.

Race days, and betting on the Steyne

8 June 1836

Last week died Lord George Germaine, brother to the Duke of Dorset: they were both in their youth great friends to the late King when Prince of Wales, fond of the turf, and, with the late Delme Radcliffe, the three best gentlemen riders at the once famed Bibury races, which are now replaced by those at Heaton Park. They were all three little men, light weights, and, when dressed in their jackets and caps, would rival Buckle and Chiffney.

In those days, the Prince made Brighton and Lewes Races the gayest scene of the year in England. The Pavilion was full of guests; the Steyne was crowded with all the rank and fashion from London during that week; the best horses were brought from Newmarket and the North, to run at these races, on which immense sums were depending; and the course was graced by the handsomest equipages.

The 'legs' and betters, who had arrived in shoals, used all to assemble on the Steyne at an early hour to commence their operations on the first day, and the buzz was tremendous, till Lord Foley and Mellish, the two great confederates of that day, would approach the ring; and then a sudden silence ensued, to await the opening of their betting books. They would come on perhaps smiling, but mysterious, without making any demonstration; at last Mr Jerry Cloves would say, "Come, Mr Mellish, will you light the candle, and set us a-going?" Then, if the Master of Buckle would say, "I'll take three to one about 'Sir Solomon,'" the whole pack opened, and the air resounded with every shade of odds and betting.

About half an hour before the signal of departure for the hill, the Prince himself would his appearance in the crowd – I think I see him now, in a green jacket, a white hat, and tight nankeen pantaloons and shoes, distinguished by his high-bred manner and handsome person: he was generally accompanied by the late Duke of Bedford, Lord Jersey, Charles Wyndham, Shelley, Brummell, M Day, Churchill, and, oh, extraordinary anomaly! the little old Jew, Travis, who, like the dwarf of old, followed in the train of royalty.

The Downs were soon covered with every species of conveyance, and the Prince's German waggon and six bay horses (so were barouches called when first introduced at that time) – the coach-man on the box being replaced by Sir John Lade – issued out of the gates of the Pavilion, and, gliding up the green ascent, was stationed close to the great stand, where it remained the centre of attraction for the day. At dinner-time, the Pavilion was resplendent with lights, and a sumptuous banquet was served to a large party; while those who were not included in that invitation found a dinner with every luxury at the club-house on the Steyne, kept by Raggett, during the season, for the different members of White's and Brookes's who chose to frequent it, and where the cards and dice from St James's Street were not forgotten. Where are the actors in all those gay scenes now?

Minions for friends

4 November 1836

George IV never had any private friends: he selected his confidants from his minions. Macmahon was an Irishman of low birth and obsequious manners; he was a little man, his face red, covered with pimples, always dressed in the blue and buff uniform, with his hat on one side, copying the air of his master, to whom he was a prodigious foil, and ready to execute any commissions, which in those days were somewhat complicated.

Bloomfield was a handsome man, and owed his introduction at Court to his musical talents; he was a Lieutenant in the Artillery, and by chance quartered with his regiment at Brighton. The Prince, who was always fond of music, then gave frequent concerts at the Pavilion: some one happened to mention that a young officer of Artillery was a proficient on the violoncello; an invitation was sent, the Royal amateur was pleased, the visits became more frequent, a predilection ensued, and the fortune of the young Lieutenant was assured.

George Lee had also a long run of favouritism in those days, but his confidences were limited to the turf, and his influence never extended beyond the stable.

A French jeweller on his knees

The Prince was at one time a great supporter of Newmarket; an untoward event, which made great noise at the time, abated his ardour for that pursuit. His debts of all sorts were very great. Vulliamy's bill (a French jeweller in Pall Mall, who served the Court, and was employed by H.R.H.) amounted to a large sum, for which he could never obtain payment. In vain did he apply at Carlton House; he met with nothing but vague promises, which were never realised. At length the jeweller's affairs got so embarrassed, that he determined to make a personal application to the Prince, and went down to Brighton. The doors of the Pavilion, however, being locked against all intruders of that sort, he watched his opportunity when the Prince's carriage drove into the court, and, gliding in unobserved, hid himself behind one of the pillars of the colonnade. As the Prince came out, and had got one foot on the step, Vulliamy rushed forward, and, falling on his knees, cried out, "Sare, Your Royal Highness, pray stop one minute." The Prince looked round, and said, rather impatiently, "Vulliamy, what do you want?"'"Oh Sare, by God, if your Royal Highness not pay my bill, I shall be in your father's bench to-morrow." The Prince laughed and got into his carriage, but the debt was left unpaid till Parliament furnished the means.

Of the Earls of Barrymore, and why one fought a duel – naked

27 May 1837
At the beginning of this century the Barrymore family were conspicuous among the roués of the day in London; there were three brothers and one sister, dignified by the flattering *sobriquets* of Hellgate, Cripplegate, Newgate, and Billingsgate, to which might be added their tutor at college – Profligate.

The eldest, as Earl Barrymore, was foremost in every species of dissipation; he had a country house near Henley, on the river, which was the scene of various orgies, and where he gave private theatricals, which were much talked of. His career was short, and his death rather mysterious; he was escorting some French prisoners to Dover, with a party of his regiment, and was stepping into a whiskey with a fusee [flintlock rifle] in his hand loaded with ball, which, it was said, went off as he put it down, and wounded him so dangerously, that he died within half an hour.

He was succeeded by his brother, who was lame, and whose excesses and eccentricities were for many years afterwards the talk of the town. He was entertaining, and had a certain degree of talent; but, among other vices, was fond of low company; and from his want of principle, as well as his want of good taste, was generally avoided by those whom his rank might have entitled him to live with. This Lord Barrymore was very fond of mystifying people, and drawing them into discussions after dinner, when he was himself generally drunk, and never failed to end by some mischievous trick, which was very annoying to the victim.

On one of these occasions he was dining with a party at Windsor, when the conversation turned on the practicability of taking Windsor Castle by an armed force, and Colonel Cowper, a very quiet, inoffensive man, was drawn by Barrymore into a discussion of the means which he would use, as a military man, to effect this object. Each began to draw his plans of attack and defence by marks of wine on the table, as Ovid would say, *Pingis et exiguo Pergama tota mero*; but Barrymore was little of a tactician, and the Colonel drew up his forces with such skill, that he proved undoubtedly to the company the superiority by which his combinations must ensure his getting possession of the Castle. The Earl being thus foiled, became mischievous, and after a little reflection, cried out, "Your plan is faulty, you have forgotten the river Thames;" and taking up a tumbler of water, which stood near him, instead of deluging the works of his adversary, threw the contents directly in the Colonel's face. Great confusion of course ensued, but the plea of ebriety was allowed as an excuse. [...]

I remember his fighting a duel with Humphry Howarth, MP for Evesham, who was a *farceur* like himself, that was treated more as an object of ridicule than anything serious. It arose out of a quarrel after dinner at the Castle Inn, at Brighton, during the race week, and they adjourned to the course early in the morning to settle the difference. The seconds and a few friends who went to see the show, were soon convulsed with laughter when they saw Howarth, who was a fat old man, deliberately take off his clothes and present himself naked (except his drawers) to the murderous weapon of his adversary. The fact was, he had been a surgeon in the Company's army in India, and knowing professionally that gun-shot wounds were often aggravated by parts of the clothing being driven by the ball into the orifice, he had determined to avoid at least this risk, by divesting himself of all incumbrances. The precaution, however, was needless, as no blood was spilt, and the matter arranged by a random shot from each party.

14

The servant and wretched bad writer, William Tayler

In contrast to almost all the literary upper-class diarists encountered so far, William Tayler was a servant, a footman, and therefore his observations, keen and interesting as they were, on Brighton are all the more precious. His spelling is appalling, but his meaning is always clear.

Born in 1807, Tayler grew up with many siblings on a farm in Grafton, Oxfordshire. He was the first of his family to go into gentlemen's service, initially for a local squire, and then for a wealthy widow in London, a Mrs Prinsep who lived in Marylebone. Also in the household was the widow's daughter (at least forty years of age, says Tayler, and therefore deserving of the title 'old maid'), and three maidservants – he was the only manservant. Mrs Prinsep died in 1850, and William moved his employment several times thereafter, rising to butler, and eventually being able to afford to rent a whole house in Paddington.

At the beginning of 1837, Tayler decided to keep a diary, to practise his writing.

1 January 1837

As I am a wretched bad writer, many of my friends have advised me to practise more, to do which I have made many attempts but allways forgot or got tired so that it was never atended to. I am now about to write a sort of journal, to note down some of the chief things that come under my observation each day. This, I hope, will induce me to make use of my pen every day a little. My account of each subject will be very short – a sort of *multo in parvo* – as my book is very small and my time not very large.

And for the rest of the year, almost every day, he wrote short entries. The manuscript was first edited by Dorothy Wise and published – with the title *Diary of William Tayler, Footman, 1837* – by the St Marylebone Society in 1962, but has been reprinted several times since then. In her brief introduction referring to the social history of the time, Wise argues that Tayler was one of the many people being displaced from rural society and migrating to towns, particularly London.

In the summer of 1837, Mrs Prinsep decided to take a long vacation in Brighton, and the enterprising William Tayler used all his spare time to explore the seaside town.

Something like London but not so big

7 July 1837
We've been very buisy preparing to go to Brighton tomorrow. Plenty of packing up and running about.

8 July 1837
Got up very early and of course very buisy loading the carriage and one thing and the other. We started at half past ten with post horses, traveled on very pleasently through Surry. The whole road is a complete mass of hills, which make the road very pleasent and butifull views from the hills. We stopt about two o'clock at one of the places where we change horses and had some dinner of cold roas beef and pickles and goosberrys tart. I made no small hole in it and the other servant did the same.

I should think this part of the country produces the worst sheep in England. Sussex is worse than Surry. Some of the half starved creatures apears to be hardly able to stand. We arrived at Brighton at six o'clock, tired enough as the sun was enough to scorch us as we set outsid the carriage. Brighton is a very pleasent place something like London but not so big. We have a butifull view of the sea which comes allmost up to the houses. We have a very nice house and very pleasently situated.

A great many bed bugs

9 July 1837
This is Sunday. Had a very bad night's rest last night. I slept downstairs in a little room but, when I came to lay down, I found the bed covered with bugs. I began to kill them but they were so numerous that I found it impossible to kill all. Therefore I shook the bedding and layed it on the floor. There a great many of them found me, so that I could get but little rest.

10 July 1837
Had a walk before breakfast. The sea air gives me an exolent apatite.

11 July 1837
Have been this morning and had a bathe in the sea for the first time in my life. I like it very much. Have been walking about townd to make discoverys.

The large waves jumping

12 July 1837
I go to the sea side two or three times a day and amuses myself by seeing the pleasure boats or seeing the fishermen come in with their vessils of fish, or sometimes I stand and watch the large waves jump over the small ones.

13 July 1837

Been walking about seeing all I could. Here are many things to be seen here. Brighton is a very pleasent place. The townd lays two miles along by the sea side and the shore is verey smothe and gravely and lays full south which causes this place to be very warm in the summer. The back or north part of the tound is surrounded by a rang of hills called the Brighton downs or South Downs, where the South Down sheep come from.

14 July 1837

This day I have been seeing some of the most grandist sights that can be seen. That is some large ships going past here in full sail going out to India.

15 July 1837

Have been looking about Brighton Market today. A very exalent market, well supplied with fruit, vegitables, meat &c &c. A very fine building.

A great curiosity hung on chains

16 July 1837

Went to church but it was so full that I could not get inside the door, therefore I took a walk and called at a Methadist Chapple. There I stayed but a very short time. From there, I went to another Chapple but on looking at a board on the door, I found I must pay a shilling if I went in and that would not do.

18 July 1837

Went on the pier. This is a kind of bridge brojecting into the sea a quarter of a mile. It's a great curiosity as it's hung on chains. People can get from that into the boats without going into the water at low water.

19 July 1837

I get up every morning at half past six and goes out on the beach looking at the boys catching crabs and eels and looking at the people batheing. There are numbers of old wimen have little wooden houses on wheels, and into these houses people goe that want to bathe, and then the house is pushed into the water and when the person has undressed, they get into the water and bathe, and then get into the wooden house again and dress themselves, then the house is drawn on shore again.

24 July 1837

Had a very pleasant rowe on the water for an houre. I wished it longer but I was treated, therefore I could not chose.

Election day – bands of music, and women dancing

25 July 1837

I have been to here the candidates nominated at the tound hall. Heared them make their speeches and so on. The election take place tomorrow.

26 July 1837

This is the day of the Election. The town is alive with bands of musick and colours flying, men, boys and wimen hallowing. The old fishermen and wimen have got their boats mounted on wheels and trimed up with lawrels and flags. I saw a number of old wimen danceing before one of the candidates' houses. They pulled off their bonnets and twirled about us they hallowed. One old woman unfortunately had no bonet, therefore she pulled off her cap [a close fitting cap worn under bonnets]. The town is full of such seens as this. Carriages of all description cuting about in every direction, from the stage coach to the dog cart. Two members are returned for this borough and here has been four trying for it.

27 July 1837

Today the successfull candidates have been round the town in prosession with their musick and carriages and some on horseback. There was so many that it lasted them half an houre to pass our house. These three days I have spent as much time in the streets as I have in the house. I like to see all I can at such times.

Women with petticoats over their heads

29 July 1837

This has been a tremendious rough day. I never saw anything half so grand as the sea looked. Indeed, there cannot be a grander sight than a rough sea. It looked like a large hilly plain, moor than like a piece of water. The waves rolled mountains high, and when two of these waves met, sometimes it was with such violence that the water flew into the air out of sight, foaming and frothing like a boiling furnace, and the wind blows a mist from the waves that regularly pickle the streets, houses and everybody and everything from the salt water. It's ruination to clothes. My hat is as white as though I had rolled it in the salt tub. The fishermen nor no one elce dare got out with boats such weather. Many of the people were obliged to put up their shutters for fear of haveing their windows broke by the wind blowing the stones and gravel about. I have seen many wimen with their peticoats over their heads. Most of them keep at home, and it would be as well if they was all to do so such a day as this.

5 August 1837

The water very rough. A man rideing his horse in to wash it, the waves came and knocked them man and horse both down in the water. They both scrambled up again and got out, but the man lost his money.

Dragoons playing at St Peter's

6 August 1837

Went to the new church [St Peter's, nearly 10 years old by this time but still called the new church] which is a very handsome building in the cathedral stile with very butifull painted windows. The rigiment of Dragoons are here. They go to church and play their band there and away again.

7 August 1837

Went out with the intention of batheing but found the water to low. Have been this morning on the pier. Have been and saw the Camera Obscura. Its machienery, fixed in a house, by which they can bring the shadow of everything for miles round in at a hole of the house, on to a table. So that if a person was commiting a theft half a mile away and thinking no one was looking at him, any person mite see him if they was in the Camera Obscura and looking on the tables.

8 August 1837

This evening I looked through a very large telescope to see the planet Saturne. It appeared about as large as a smallish pumpkin. It has a ring round it. This is the only planet that has a ring round it. I saw the moon at the same time which was a very curious sight.

At the races: whores and rogues in abundance

10 August 1837

It's Brighton Races today. Have been on the race course all the afternoon. I never felt the heat so much before in my life. There were whores and rogues in abundance and gambleing tables plenty and everything elce that is jeneraly at races. The town is very full on account of it.

12 August 1837

Went by the water's side and saw some fishermen bring a very curious fish ashore. They called it a sea monster. It was as big as a donkey and about eight feet long and a mouthfull of teeth like a lion. They erected a tent and showed it for a trifle each person. They often catch some of these creatures which are of no use other than make a show of, as long as they can keep them fresh.

Betting on a grand cricket match

14 August 1837

Here is a grand cricket match between the Marleybone Club in London and the Royal Sussex Club. These two clubs are considered to be the best players in England. The match will last two days. I have been to see it today. People come from many miles of to see it. There is a great deal of better on both sides. I have layd a shilling the St Marylebone set will beat as I comes from that parish.

15 August 1837

The cricket match is over and the Londoners have beat and I have won a shilling.

18 August 1837

Have been round Brighton Park [now Queen's Park], a very pleasent place, and have been to the German Spaw, a place that people go to drink mineral waters. Those that fancy themselves ill go to it.

21 August 1837

Have been round the suberbs of Brighton for a ride. Saw no less than five cricket matches on our way round. The farmers are very buisy carreying their wheat. I saw one rick today, but it's just beginning to rain.

To be buried in such a nice place

27 August 1837

I went to a Methodist Chapple, but that was so full I could not sit down. From there, I went to the new Church, where I stayed to hear sermon, and after the sermon I stayed to hear the soldiers' band play. On my way home, I called at the Hanover Chapple. The service was over, therefore I satisfied myself by looking round the burieing ground, which is more like a garden than anything elce. The graves are all in rows from one side of the ground to the other, and between these rows there is a very nice flower border, and between each grave there is a row of flowers. At the head of every grave, there is a large choice flower. There are green houses and three gardners kept to keep it in order. I wonder some of the people don't wish themselves dead on purpose to be buried in such a nice place.

30 August 1837
Beginning to pack up ready to start to London.

31 August 1837
Very buisy getting in bills and paying of them and wishing all our new acquaintance farwell.

1 September 1837
Up very early getting ready to be off. Wished good by to Brighton and started of at ten o'clock for London.

15

Henry Crabb Robinson and the best preacher

Although never distinguishing himself in any particular field, Henry Crabb Robinson was a keen and useful diarist. He knew a lot of literary types, and was on very good terms with Wordsworth with whom he travelled often. He was one of the first to recognise the genius of William Blake; and the contemporary reports of the theatre he wrote are certainly valued. His connection with Brighton, though, was of a more religious bent. He fell – along with thousands of others – for the charismatic preacher Frederick William Robertson, based in Brighton, and after his death helped Lady Byron publicise the reverend's teachings. Intriguingly, it seems, Robertson himself kept a short and coded diary, which has revealed to modern researchers that he had an extra-marital affair.

Robinson was born in Bury St Edmunds in 1775 and articled to a lawyer in Colchester when 15, and subsequently to another in London. In 1796, he was left an inheritance which allowed him to travel to the Continent frequently. Between 1800 and 1805 he studied in Germany, meeting, among others, Goethe and Schiller. He operated as a war correspondent for *The Times* for a short while during the Peninsular War, and, on his return to London, finished his legal training and was called to the bar.

Through an old friend, Catherine, who had married the writer and abolitionist Thomas Clarkson, he was introduced into London literary society; and, in time, his own breakfast parties became famous. After retiring in 1828, he continued to take part in public affairs and to travel often. In 1828 he was one of the founding members of London University; and, in 1837, he revisited Italy on a tour with the poet William Wordsworth. He never married, but lived to an old age, dying in 1867.

Home diary and tour journals

Crabb left behind a large amount of papers including the following: brief journals covering the period to 1810, a much fuller home diary (begun in 1811, and continued to within five days of his death – thirty-five volumes), and a collection of thirty tour journals. The papers were edited by Thomas Sadler and published by Macmillan in 1869 in three volumes as *Diary, Reminiscences and Correspondence of Henry Crabb Robinson*.

And it is thanks largely to these volumes that Crabb is remembered today, for his diaries are full of important detail about the central figures of the English romantic movement, not only Wordsworth, but Coleridge, Charles Lamb, and William Blake. Of the latter, he was an early admirer, writing in his diary: 'Shall I call Blake artist, genius, mystic or madman? Probably he is all'.

While most of his diary-keeping predecessors were drawn to Brighton by the social glamour and glitter of the Royal Court, Robinson was drawn there by one of the most exciting and charismatic preachers of the day, Frederick William Robertson, or simply Robertson of Brighton.

Frederick William Robertson of Brighton

Although initially aiming for a military career, Robertson was ordained in 1840, and after several other appointments moved to Brighton in 1847, where he took up ministry at Trinity Chapel (Ship Street). His sermons soon attracted crowds, including the wealthy and literary, not least Charles Dickens, who said he was one of the greatest masters of elocution he had ever heard. With a large and accurate knowledge of the Bible, he had a dazzling ability to communicate spiritual ideas in a strong but contemporary way, combining liberal theology with religious feeling, though he is not considered to have developed any particular new theology.

He died while still young, in his 30s, from what was called at the time 'brain fever', a brain haemorrhage. The hearse at his funeral is said to have been followed by 1,500 mourners, with thousands more lining the streets.

Robertson married Helen Denys in 1841, and they had two children. However, it is assumed that the marriage was unhappy, at least in the later years, since Robertson indulged feelings, and indeed passion, for other women. He had a very close friendship with Lady Byron, but the recent discovery and decoding of a diary he kept in 1849 reveals this intensely religious man had an affair with a married woman, Augusta Fitzpatrick. The climax of the affair, according to Christina Beardsley, in *Unutterable Love: The Passionate Life and Preaching of F. W. Robertson*, is disclosed in an entry for 1 October, 'Four hours in bed with Augusta.'

So it is Robertson who is the main focus of Crabb's Brighton diary entries. Indeed after Robertson's death, Crabb with Lady Byron and Robertson's family were foremost in trying to keep alive Robertson's teaching by publishing his sermons. Once printed, they proved immensely popular, and widened his fame.

Here, then, are some of Crabb's diary entries.

Paginini wins over a vulgar ear

7 December 1831
Brighton
Accompanied [John James] Masquerier [a British painter] to a concert, which afforded me really a great pleasure. I heard Paganini [Niccolò Paganini, an Italian musician and composer]. Having scarcely any sensibility to music, I

could not expect great enjoyment from any music, however fine; and, after all, I felt more surprise at the performance than enjoyment. The professional men, I understand, universally think more highly of Paganini than the public do. He is really an object of wonder. His appearance announces something extraordinary. His figure and face amount to caricature. He is a tall slim figure, with limbs which remind one of a spider; his face very thin, his forehead broad, his eyes grey and piercing, with bushy eyebrows; his nose thin and long, his cheeks hollow, and his chin sharp and narrow. His face forms a sort of triangle. His hands the oddest imaginable, fingers of enormous length, and thumbs bending backwards.

It is, perhaps, in a great measure from the length of finger and thumb that his fiddle is also a sort of lute. He came forward and played, from notes, his own compositions. Of the music, as such, I know nothing. The sounds were wonderful. He produced high notes very faint, which resembled the chirruping of birds, and then in an instant, with a startling change, rich and melodious notes, approaching those of the bass viol. It was difficult to believe that this great variety of sounds proceeded from one instrument. The effect was heightened by his extravagant gesticulation and whimsical attitudes. He sometimes played with his fingers, as on a harp, and sometimes struck the cords with his bow, as if it were a drum-stick, sometimes sticking his elbow into his chest, and sometimes flourishing his bow. Oftentimes the sounds were sharp, like those of musical glasses, and only now and then really delicious to my vulgar ear, which is gratified merely by the flute and other melodious instruments, and has little sense of harmony.

Snow stops the ordinary mails

26 December 1836
Brighton
This was a remarkable day. So much snow fell, that not a coach either set out for or arrived from London – an incident almost unheard of in this place. Parties were put off and engagements broken without complaint. The Masqueriers, with whom I am staying, expected friends to dinner, but they could not come. Nevertheless, we had here Mr Edmonds, the worthy Scotch schoolmaster, Mr and Mrs Dill, and a Miss Robinson; and, with the assistance of whist, the afternoon went off comfortably enough. Of course, during a part of the day, I was occupied in reading.

28 December 1836
The papers to-day are full of the snow-storm. The ordinary mails were stopped in every part of the country.

The cordial Revd Robertson

30 October 1848
Brighton
I called on Robertson, Senr., [a lawyer who had made his fortune in the West Indies] and Miss Levesque, and I had a long and very agreeable walk with Rev F. Robertson. We talked to-day on religion; he spoke of the happiness he felt in

being able freely to be a member of the Church of England, which implies a harmonious consent to all its doctrines. How he can be this, and yet entertain such liberal opinions and, what is much better, liberal feelings, I cannot comprehend; but this is not, perhaps, of much moment. He was as cordial as ever, and seemed not at all offended by the freedom of my expressions.

3 May 1850

I read early a speech by Robertson to the Brighton Working Class Association, in which infidelity of a very dangerous kind had sprung up. His speech shows great practical ability. He managed a difficult subject very ably, but it will not be satisfactory either to the orthodox or the ultra-liberal.

I went to Mr Cookson, who is one of the executors of Mr Wordsworth, and with whom I had an interesting conversation about Wordsworth's arrangements for the publication of his poems. He has commissioned Dr Christopher Wordsworth to write his Life, a brief Memoir merely illustrative of his poems. And in a paper given to the Doctor, he wrote that his sons, son-in-law, his dear friend Miss Fenwick, Mr Carter, and Mr Robinson, who had travelled with him, "would gladly contribute their aid by communicating any facts within their knowledge."

Notions on Papal aggression

15 February 1851
Brighton

I had a three hours' chat with Robertson. A very interesting talk of course. He said: "I feel myself more comfortable in the Church of England than I did. I feel I have a *mission*, and that, if I live a few years, it will not be in vain. That mission is, to impress on minds of a certain class of intellect, that there is a mass of substantial truth in the Church of England, which will remain when the vulgar orthodox Church perishes, as probably it soon will." He used expressions very like those of Donaldson, and I have no doubt he is with perfect sincerity, and without any constraint, a firm believer in the doctrines he professes. It is true that he understands almost every orthodox doctrine in a refined sense, and such as would shock the mass of ordinary Christians. I told him of my notions on Papal aggression, and he so far agrees that he thinks the Government does right in resisting the assumption of titles.

One of the most remarkable men of the day

18 February 1851
At Masquerier's, Brighton

We had calls soon after breakfast. The one to be mentioned was that of [Michael] Faraday, one of the most remarkable men of the day, the very greatest of our discoverers in chemistry, a perfect lecturer in the unaffected simplicity and intelligent clearness of his statement; so that the learned are instructed and the ignorant charmed. His personal character is admirable. When he was young, poor, and altogether unknown, Masquerier was kind to him; and now that he is a great man he does not forget his old friend.

We had a dinner-party, and an agreeable evening; Dr King, Dr Williams, Miss Mackintosh, &c. The interesting man of the party was Ross, the Presbyterian minister, with whom I had much talk on theology, more, indeed, than would seem right; but I am told that we interested the company. Ross is learned in German theology, and a great admirer, as well as friend, of Julius Hare. Therefore liberal beyond the ordinary measure allowed to the ministers of the Scotch Church.

The unsettling of men's minds

30 November 1851
Brighton

Heard Robertson preach an extraordinary sermon, reconciling philosophy with piety in a remarkable way, [. . .] His subject was the resemblance between the revelation that had already appeared, and that which is to appear. In the course of the sermon, he uttered a number of valuable philosophical truths, which I cannot reconcile with Church doctrines, though I have no doubt he does so with perfect good faith. He spoke of a divine system of education, in the same way as [Gotthold Ephraim] Lessing speaks in his work on 'The Education of the Human Race.' And his definition of inspiration and prophecy is precisely such as is contained in the 'Prospective Review', in an article by J J Tayler. I know not when I have heard a discourse so full of admirable matter; and this was the impression of others apparently. Yet he was full of Scripture allusions.

I have been walking with him to-day. He is greatly improved in health, as his sermon showed, and does not appear to be materially altered in his notions. He acknowledges that he is surprised at being so long permitted to preach: he is aware how much he must be the object of distrust.

21 November 1852
Brighton

I heard a sermon from Robertson, marked by his usual peculiarities, he speaking of imputed righteousness as the righteousness to be obtained in an advanced state of excellence, and of man being reconciled to God, and therefore God reconciled to man. Samuel Sharpe told me that people here complain that he unsettles men's minds. Of course, no one can be awakened out of a deep sleep without being unsettled. An eloquent eulogy of the Duke, as exhibiting a perfect devotion to duty. He concluded with the declaration that he was proud of being an Englishman.

28 November 1852

The wet weather continued, and kept me within to a great degree. I was at Robertson's, and heard a sermon full of striking thoughts, on the relation of Christianity to Judaism being abolition by expansion, as the Judaic Sabbath is abrogated when every day is devoted to the Lord.

Lady Byron, and the death of Robertson

29 November 1852
I went to Robertson's, and had two hours of interesting chat with him on his position here in the pulpit; also about Lady Byron. He speaks of her as the noblest woman he ever knew.

17 August 1853
Dr King wrote to me, informing me of the death of Robertson, of Brighton. Take him for all in all, the best preacher I ever saw in a pulpit; that is, uniting the greatest number of excellences, originality, piety, freedom of thought, and warmth of love. His style colloquial and very scriptural. He combined light of the intellect with warmth of the affections in a pre-eminent degree.

13 September 1853
Brighton
Dr King called, and in the evening I called by desire on Lady Byron – a call

which I enjoyed, and which may have consequences. Recollecting her history, as the widow of the most famous, though not the greatest, poet of England in our day, I felt an interest in going to her; and that interest was greatly heightened when I left her. From all I have heard of her, I consider her one of the best women of the day. Her means and her good will both great. "She lives to do good," says Dr. King, and I believe this to be true. She wanted my opinion as to the mode of doing justice to Robertson's memory. She spoke of him as having a better head on matters of business than any one else she ever knew. She said, "I have consulted lawyers on matters of difficulty, but Robertson seemed better able to give me advice. He unravelled everything and explained everything at once as no one else did."

Robinson's last visit to Brighton

1–13 August 1866

The first two weeks of this month were spent at Brighton, very pleasantly. I was the guest of Mrs Fisher, a very kind and considerate friend. There are few persons with whom I talk so agreeably. Sarah, with her sister and nieces, were also at Brighton. During this visit I had a letter from S Sharpe, stating that James Martineau had not been elected at the Council-meeting at University College, but that no one else was elected, and he might be appointed at a future meeting. *Nous verrons*. Several days I did not quit the house. The great victory of the Prussians over the Austrians [in the Austro-Prussian War] was the subject of general interest.

16

Xue Fucheng does
as Londoners do

By the late nineteenth century, Imperial China and the Qing Dynasty, which had been ruling it since the mid-seventeenth century, was in trouble, under all kinds of pressure internally from rebellions, as well as from the West and from Japan. It would eventually collapse and give way in 1912 to the Republic of China. All of which doesn't have a lot to with Brighton, except that in an effort to understand the West a little better, the Qing Dynasty started sending ambassadors to Europe. The second of these was Xue Fucheng who lived in London for a while, and, keen to experience local ways, as so many travellers are today, he followed the fashion of taking summer holidays by the sea.

Born in 1838 in Wuxi, up the Yangzi River from Shanghai, Xue Fucheng was a civil servant all his life, and a prolific scholar. His published works include more than thirty volumes of essays, papers, and notes. As a middle-aged man, he took on what would be his last job, a long diplomatic mission to Europe. For decades, the Qing Dynasty had found itself increasingly out of a kilter with a fast-changing world. Not only was it having to deal with internal pressures from rebellions all over the country, but international pressure was increasingly forcing it to make territorial and trade concessions. One response was to send Xue Fucheng to Europe to collect information and act as an ambassador to the main European governments.

He stayed four years, much of it in London, and kept a diary of his activities. This was partly to fulfil his ambassadorial obligations of providing information for the imperial court, which often paid to have such diaries printed as public documents, but was also a personal record of his travels to very foreign places and within very foreign cultures. Six volumes of the diaries were published in 1892 while he was still in Europe. He died only days after returning to Shanghai in 1894, and another ten volumes were published posthumously.

A great granddaughter translator

A century would pass before Xue's great granddaughter, Helen Hsieh Chien, translated some of the diary texts into English for publication by St Martin's Press in 1993 as *The European Diary of Hsieh Fucheng: Envoy Extraordinary of Imperial China*. It has been calculated that the sixteen published volumes of his diary in Chinese would amount to around 3,000 pages in English, but this one tome contains only 200 of them, with an introduction by Douglas Howland.

There is a rather sweet note, in the preface, by the translator: 'I also would like to express my deepest gratitude to my grandfather, Hsieh Tze Ming. Without his diligent work and devotion, some of my great-grandfather's overseas writings would never have been published. I sincerely hope that he may heave a sigh of relief in heaven that his astronomical chart in 1929 for his unborn grandchild was correct: a granddaughter can be as effective as a grandson to carry out one's wishes.'

A vacation at the seaside

13 July 1892
People in London are in the habit of taking a vacation at the seaside in the early summer, spending two or three months there. This summer I followed this tradition and rented a house at Brighton. At four o'clock this afternoon I took my family and Interpreter Wang, boarded the train at Victoria Station and arrived at Brighton two hours later.

14 July 1892

I toured the city of Brighton with Interpreter Wang in a carriage and stopped at the old pier. It cost two pence to be admitted to an open-air concert where the seating capacity could be extended to fit several hundred people. Across from the river there is a new pier, and between these two piers there is another one under construction.

15 July 1892

I went to the new pier with Wang to enjoy the cool breeze. The new pier is made of wood planks, and I feel more secure walking on it. We also visited the aquarium by the seashore, which exhibits a large assortment of unique sea creatures. It appears to me that this aquarium possesses more specimens from the sea than the one in London.

The mighty influence of China

28 July 1892

I took my family to Brighton for the summer holiday. Interpreter Wang and Military Attaché Wang both came along with us.

2 August 1892

This afternoon I went to visit the palace of William IV, who was the former king of England and the uncle of the present queen. The palace was constructed sixty years ago, and the architecture is visibly different from that of contemporary times. It appears to me to be similar to that of China; the wall murals in the palace are filled with drawings of Chinese figures. This proves that the mighty influence of China had already arrived during that period and had obviously aroused the admiration of the people of England.

This afternoon I strolled along the boardwalk of the old pier and watched women and children swimming in the sea.

A flea pulling a cart

4 August 1892

I went down to the new pier and watched men and women swimming in the sea. Later, I watched a performance of a flea circus and marvelled at a flea pulling a cart around.

10 August 1892

A letter from China reported uncontrollable floods brought on by incessant rain from the Yangzi Valley to the Yellow River basin. The countryside in China has been devastated by this disaster.

12 August 1892

The total construction cost of both the old pier and the new pier in Brighton was £30,000.

Xue Fucheng's last diary entry

28 May 1894

The rain stopped momentarily in the early morning, and the ship began to sail again. Another rainstorm developed a few hours later, and the ship had to make another stop. The rain finally ceased around noon, and the ship entered the harbour of Wusong. There was a steamboat provided by my family waiting there; I went aboard and reached Shanghai in the evening.

17

Henry Peerless, Brightonian and holiday-maker

Henry Peerless was born in Brighton in 1866 into a middle-class family, and entered the family timber business when only 14. The business and Peerless were reasonably prosperous, in part because Brighton itself was prosperous, a booming town thanks to the railway and holiday-makers flocking to the seaside. Peerless married Amelia (Millie) Garrett in 1891, and they had four children. The oldest, though, died during active service in the last year of the First World War. Peerless himself died in 1930, at his home in St James's Avenue.

There is nothing out of the ordinary in this brief biography, and yet Peerless had a passion, or two passions that seem to have destined him for a little posthumous attention. One of these was for holidays, and the other for writing a diary about them. For thirty years, from 1891 to 1920 Peerless took a holiday every year (even during the First World War), going all round the British Isles and beyond, by horse-drawn carriage, steam train, steam ship, bicycle and motor car. And on every holiday, he kept a journal. He completed twenty-seven notebooks, which were inherited by his son, and then his grandson, before being sold to a dealer and then purchased by Edward Fenton, a publisher specialising in diaries.

Fenton edited the diaries to produce *A Brief Jolly Change*, published by Day Books in 2003. It gives, what Day Books calls, 'a lively travelogue from a vanished world'. But more than that, Fenton sees the diaries as providing a real insight into the rise of mass tourism, one of the most important social trends emerging out of the Victorian era, with a larger middle class not only having more money, but more leisure time too. Because he wrote his diary over so many years and so methodically, Fenton believes that it 'amounts to one of the fullest pictures that we have of a whole class of people seeking diversion, at a time of unprecedented and – ultimately – cataclysmic change.'

Unfortunately for this collection, Peerless gives his home town far less attention than any of his holiday destinations. It's only on leaving Brighton or on returning, or when comparing it to some other seaside resort, that he deigns to mention his home town and favourite place.

A bomb in Preston Park

5 August 1895

At Brighton the station is literally choked with people, and elbowing our way through we gain a cab and are off on the home stretch. We draw up at our door and find all well, and Lily waiting to receive us.

I regret to add that we had about reached home when a terrific explosion of a bomb and mortar took place during a display a fireworks at a Foresters' Fete in Preston Park, injuring nearly twenty people, several of whom have since died. We were of course ignorant of its happening until the next morning and I have only entered it here now, because if I or anyone else should happen to read this years hence it will serve to localise the date in one's mind.

17 June 1907

As Brightonians I think we feel sorry to see so much evidence of prosperity in Bournemouth and neighbourhood, when we at home are certainly passing through a dull and trying time.

Of course Bournemouth is new compared to Brighton, and their houses are more modern, and it has natural beauties that have been conserved and made the most of, but as I say, our greatest asset still is that only 52 miles separates us from the great metropolis.

Brighton's fair beach

6 September 1909
[Lynton]
The bathing place is a narrow strip where the rocks have been cleared away.
On either side are cruel rough jagged black rocks – not at all a cheerful spot to
one accustomed to Brighton's fair beach. However, I found the sea was wet and
much like ours at home, only not so clear.

5 June 1911
[Ramsgate]
[We] go down to the sands east of the harbour and find crowds of bathers
besieging the bathing-machines. After a struggle we secure machines belonging
to Mr Mumford and have a dip in the briny ocean. Water was very nice, but too
shallow for a swimmer who knows the pleasure of taking a header off the West
Pier, Brighton, which I should pronounce to be one of the best bathing places
in England.

Brighton full of soldiers

23 June 1915
For over ten months now, we have lived in a world of war. The piping days of
peace seem a faraway dream of the past. All over England are soldiers training,
and we have raised an army of probably three million men.

Brighton has been full of soldiers. The Pavilion has been transformed into a
hospital for wounded Indians. The Workhouse and York Place School have been
acquired for the same purpose. For hospitals for our own soldiers, we have the
New Grammar School and St Mark's School. Camps have sprung up all over
England. Life is changed and we all have War on our minds.

Hitherto, I am thankful to say, England has not suffered depredations to any
extent, except bombardment at Scarborough and Whitby, and occasional zep-
pelin air-raids on east coast, Southend and Ramsgate.

The Germans have developed a submarine warfare against our shipping, and the
biggest blot on any nation's record she made by sinking the *Lusitania* off Ireland,
when quite 1,400 innocent men, women and children met their death. The world
was shocked by this senseless crime, and characterised it as an act of murder.

I, hitherto a peaceful citizen, was on 31 August 1914 sworn in as a special constable of the Brighton Borough Police, and am now Special Constable no. 111 of
the A Division: and, in company of a colleague, patrol the streets three evenings in
succession, and worry the citizens, principally about obscuring their lights.

Also I have become an amateur soldier, having enrolled early in September in
the Home Protection Brigade, 1st Battalion Sussex, and have been drilling and
route-marching two or three times a week ever since. We now have uniforms
and look like soldiers, and in case of invasion shall expect to do our bit.

London people escaping the air-raids

8 June 1918

To Brighton Station. [. . .] We take our seats with quite half an hour to spare, which we considered wise, as trains being now considerably curtailed are generally overcrowded. Brighton has been invaded by a large number of London people, who have come to escape 'air-raids', and journey daily to town, thus putting a severe strain on the carrying capacity of the London, Brighton & South Coast Railway.

18

Arnold Bennett at work
on Clayhanger

'The putting-on of brakes took her unawares. The train was in Brighton, sliding over the outskirts of the town... Hilda saw steep streets of houses that sprawled on the hilly mounds of the great town like ladders: reminiscent of certain streets of her native district, yet quite different, a physiognomy utterly foreign to her. This, then, was Brighton. That which had been a postmark became suddenly a reality, shattering her preconceptions of it, and disappointing her she knew not why. She glanced forward, through the window, and saw the cavern of the station...

Her first disappointment changed slowly into expectant and hopeful curiosity. The quaint irregularities of the architecture, and the vastness of the thronged perspectives, made promises to her romantic sense. The town seemed to be endless as London. There were hotels, churches, chapels, libraries, and music-shops on every hand. The more ordinary features of main streets – the marts of jewellery, drapery, and tobacco – had an air of grandiose respectability; while the narrow alleys that curved enigmatically away between the lofty buildings of these fine thoroughfares beckoned darkly to the fancy. The multiplicity of beggars, louts, and organ-grinders was alone a proof of Brighton's success in the world; the organ-grinders, often a man and a woman yoked together, were extraordinarily English, genteel, and prosperous as they trudged in their neat, middle-class raiment through the gritty mud of the macadam, stolidly ignoring the menace of high-stepping horses and disdainful glittering wheels. Brighton was evidently a city apart....

Then the carriage rounded into King's Road, and suddenly she saw the incredible frontage of hotels, and pensions, and apartments, and she saw the broad and boundless promenade alive with all its processions of pleasure, and she saw the ocean.'

The above is not a diary entry, for a change, but a fictional account of Hilda Lessways' arrival in Brighton, as written by Arnold Bennett in his novel of the same name. That novel was the second of the so-called Clayhanger series, largely set – as most of Bennett's novels – in the Midlands. It was written and published in 1911, a year after Bennett had spent a few winter months in Brighton writing the first book of the series, *Clayhanger*.

A man from the Midlands

Bennett was born in Hanley, Staffordshire, in 1867, the eldest of nine children, three of whom died in infancy. His father, having been a master potter, inherited some money which he used to train and qualify as a solicitor, but money problems were never far away during Arnold's childhood. Aged 16, he left school to work for his father, encumbered with various tasks including rent-collecting. In 1889, he escaped to London where he found employment as a solicitor's clerk. Within a few years, an interest in journalism had led him to become an editor, and then editor-in-chief, of a magazine called *Woman*.

Bennett's debut novel – *A Man from the North* – was published in 1898, and gave him sufficient confidence, a couple of years later, to give up his day job and become a full-time writer. *Anna of the Five Towns*, the first of his stories about life in the Potteries, appeared in 1902. From the outset, he adopted an unmistakable style, aligned to the French realists, aiming to depict a real – rather than romantic – view of life, with all its everyday and banal activities, not least when connected with poor social conditions.

Bennett's allegiance to this style came about, biographers suggest, because he had acquired a love of the French language from an early schoolteacher, and because he had liked or been influenced by works of the writer George Augustus Moore, himself a follower of realists such as Zola and Balzac. At the turn of the century, Bennett moved to Paris, then buzzing with literary and artistic talent, where he stayed for the best part of a decade. During this time he met and married Marie Marguerite Soulié. He also wrote *The Old Wives' Tale* which brought him fame throughout the English-speaking world, and money.

Back in England, Bennett's authorial skills were put to use during the war, by the end of which he was in charge of propaganda in France. He separated from his wife in 1921, and the following year became involved with Dorothy Cheston, an actress, who bore him a daughter. Though he continued to pump out novels, their critical reputation declined during the 1920s, his literary style coming to be seen as old-fashioned. Nevertheless, his non-fiction was much sought after, and he was famously the highest paid literary journalist in England, with a weekly column in the *Evening Standard*. He caught typhoid on a trip to France and died in 1931.

Bennett began keeping a diary in 1896, and continued to the end of his life. The journals, which were inherited by Dorothy Cheston, are said to contain over a million words. They were edited by Newman Flower and published in three volumes by Cassell in 1932-1933, titled *The Journals of Arnold Bennett 1896-1928*. In his introduction, Flower says Bennett's diaries show him in the manner of a modern Pepys; elsewhere, though, they are considered to have been inspired by the famous French diaries of Edmond and Jules De Goncourt, themselves very influential in the realist/naturalist movement.

On their way back to Paris in early 1910, the Bennetts stayed for a few winter months in Brighton. Arnold had done all his research for a new book, to be called *Clayhanger*, and he used his time in Brighton to write most of it, averaging about 1,000 words a day. The novel was published before the end of the same year, and, by early 1911, he was writing a sequel, *Hilda Lessways*, part of which would be set in Brighton.

Comfort, luxury, ostentation, snobbishness

2 January 1910

We came down to Brighton by the 1:55 on Saturday, to the Royal York. In the afternoon I called at the Exeter to learn the terms there, as Farrar had recommended it. When I gave the landlord my card, he started back, let his hands fall, and said "My God! Is it you?" This is the first landlord of my acquaintance who had ever read anything, much less a book of mine. He seemed to know me pretty thoroughly. I gave him my card at the end of the interview, and then the interview had to begin all over again.

However, we didn't go to the Exeter, as when it came to the point, the celebrated Harry Preston of this celebrated hotel would not let me go. He agreed to my terms.

Our first stroll along the front impressed me very favourably, yesterday afternoon. But I am obsessed by the thought that all this comfort, luxury, ostentation, snobbishness and correctness, is founded on a vast injustice to the artisan-class. I can never get away from this. The furs, autos, fine food, attendance, and diamond rings of this hotel only impress it on me more.

This morning I worked genuinely for an hour on the construction of the first part of my novel.

3 January 1910

To-day I wrote a 'New Age' article, arranged the outline of an article for the 'Nation', and schemed out the first nine chapters of 'Clayhanger' which I hope to begin to write on Wednesday. This afternoon we moved into our new room on the fourth floor, and I arranged everything for my work. We walked on the pier, and I saw subjects for water-colours and pastels.

Mediocre music and first-rate fishes

5 January 1910

This morning at 9:45 I began to write 'Clayhanger'. I felt less nervous and self-conscious than usual in beginning a book. And never before have I made one-quarter so many preliminary notes and investigations. I went out for a little recess, and at 1:30 I had done 1,000 words, which was very good for a first day.

We went to the Aquarium after tea, and heard mediocre music, and saw first-rate fishes, etc., living long under highly artificial conditions. The seals and alligators seemed to be intensely bored and sick of life, but perhaps they weren't. Then I came back and wrote half an article for the 'Nation' about the Hanley music-hall.

Earlier in the afternoon I went out and viewed the shore, and the launching of fishing boats. All kinds of activity in progress, spoiling to be described. But now that I am on my novel I am tied up again for six months from anything really swagger in the way of description.

Weather misty. No visible round trace of the sun. The hotel is haunted by barrel organs. In fact in various ways Brighton seems to be what London was. Its architecture is old Belgravia and Tyburnian.

Seymour Hicks in Brighton

9 January 1910

Last week I wrote 4,500 words of 'Clayhanger' and two articles. So that it was a good beginning. Rickards [Edwin Rickards, the architect] came on Friday night. [. . .] Last night we went to the Hippodrome, a vast circular human sight. And he made a good caricature of Seymour Hicks who was in a stage box. Hicks is staying here. He wore a flannel shirt all day and all evening, but dined upstairs, probably to hide it. Drove off to the Hippodrome at 9, and there rolled about with laughter at the comic turns in the sight of all. I liked him for his frank enjoyment of the most mediocre things. He had a fine rich voice, and his unavailing but well-meant efforts to appear natural, and non-celebrated are our joy. [Seymour Hicks was an actor, playwright and theatre manager knighted in 1934.]

Sporting damned Tory colours

11 January 1910

Grand rolling weather. Foamy sea, boisterous wind, sun, pageant of clouds, and Brighton full of wealthy imperative persons dashing about in furs and cars. I walked with joy to and fro on this unequalled promenade. And yet, at this election time, when all wealth and all snobbery is leagued together against the poor, I could spit in the face of arrogant and unmerciful Brighton, sporting its damned Tory colours.

18 January 1910
Since Saturday night, when I stood out in the rain and wind 2¾ hours to see the election returns on the 'Daily News' lantern screen in the Old Steyne, I have been perfectly obsessed by politics, perhaps to my harm artistically. To-day I finished my 3,000 word article on 'The Forces behind the Elections' for the next issue of the 'English Review'. I don't think very much of it.

Sea-gulls and the Palace Pier

3 February 1910
The other morning I watched the sea-gulls helping the scavenger to scavenge the remains of the daily fish market on the beach. Rain. Strong wind. They could not alight. They had a lot of balancing and steering to do. They dived again and again for the same bit of offal, missing it, till they got it. Then each prize-winner sailed off against the wind with difficulty towards the Palace Pier, and out of my sight somewhere; but some seemed to swallow the piece *en route*. I was watching them alight in the water the other day; all did exactly the same; a planing descent, then, close on water, 2 or 3 half-flaps, a raising of the head, and they were afloat.

9 February 1910
On Monday morning, in the bedroom and in the drawing-room, I finished the 1st part of 'Clayhanger', 42,000 words instead of 40,000.

17 March 1910
Our stay here on the whole has been a very great success. We have both enjoyed it. I have written over 100,000 words, and Marguerite three short stories. But I doubt if the climate suits us now that it has duly braced us up. [The Bennetts moved next to Lausanne, Switzerland. The following year, in January 1911, Bennett would begin to write 'Hilda Lessways'.]

A Brighton newspaper man

29 April 1912
Left Paris and got to Newhaven yesterday. Drove car for the first time this morning round about Newhaven.

Went over to Brighton to see the Sharpes. Newspaper man in street [. . .]: "I wish I'd been in Paris yesterday. I could have made a bit o' money. When Crippen did it, I made £3 before 5 o'clock. Nobody got no change that day... Now they mucked up this *Titanic* disaster for us. They ought to have put 'hundreds drowned'. Then we should have made a bit." [Bonnot, a notorious Paris bandit, had been killed after a police siege the day before.]

19

Lady Cynthia Asquith flirts through the First World War

Lady Cynthia Asquith has been described as one of the most fascinatingly beautiful women of her time, and as the greatest flirt that ever lived. Yet, today, she is best
remembered for her diaries, only a few years of which during the First World War
have been published. These provide a startlingly open and self-absorbed account of
a life privileged on the surface – an aristocratic family and married to the Prime
Minster's son – but affected deeply and painfully by the pressures of marriage, children, war, and her own intense social needs. During the war, and the period of the
published diaries, Cynthia was often in Brighton, where she first took her children to
benefit from the sea air, and where she herself loved to bathe.

Cynthia Charteris was born at Clouds, her mother's family estate, in 1887, but
spent most of her childhood at Stanway House near Cheltenham, where she was
educated privately. In 1903, she was sent to Dresden, the then fashionable European
city for finishing young ladies, and there met Herbert Asquith. Since her family did
not approve of the match, they became engaged secretly in 1907. The couple married
in 1910, and found a home in Sussex Place, Regent's Park in London. Their first child,
John, born a year later, proved to have special needs and caused them much anxiety
and grief. In 1926, they put him in an institution far away, in Dumfries, where he
became increasingly apathetic and enfeebled, eventually dying in 1937. Two other
children were born, in 1914 (Michael) and 1919 (Simon).

The First World War

At the start of the First World War, Herbert enlisted in the Royal Field Artillery;
and Cynthia inherited, from her grandfather, the title Lady Cynthia, though there
was no money or property attached. The Sussex Place property was rented, and
her two sons, cared for by a nanny, were lodged at various times in Brighton and
Littlehampton. Cynthia herself moved around a lot, staying at Stanway, Downing
Street, where her husband's father was Prime Minister, and at friends – 'cuckooing',
as she called it. Visiting her children often, she also stayed in Brighton a fair amount
during these years, especially when Herbert happened to be stationed there. Much
of her life, during the war and after, was devoted to social activity, and attractive men

seemed a particular focus – Randolph Churchill called her the greatest flirt that ever lived.

The war took its toll, though, on Cynthia, especially when Raymond, her brother-in-law, was killed in 1916. Not till 1919, did the Asquiths reoccupy Sussex Place, Cynthia was by then subject to depression, and Herbert was suffering from shell shock.

During the 1920s, Cynthia began producing anthologies for children and for adults, which proved popular, and later she also wrote several novels. Also, for twenty years, starting in 1918, she was secretary (and more) to her friend, the writer J. M. Barrie. After his death, in 1937, the Asquiths moved to Sullington, Sussex, and in 1946 to Bath. Herbert died the following year. Cynthia moved back to London, where she invested money in a publishing venture launched by James Barrie, her friend's nephew, which, over the next decade or so, published several of Cynthia's memoirs, as well as her works on Tolstoy. She died in 1960.

A life insufficiently purple

Early on during the war, a friend of Cynthia's suggested she start a diary. Here, in her first entry, she explains the new resolution.

15 April 1915

I have always thought it would be unwholesome for me to attempt to write a diary. I'm sure it will make me think my life drab and strain after sensation to make copy for my autobiography. I shall become morbidly self-conscious and a valetudinarian about my career, so I shall try not to be un-introspective, and confine myself to events and diagnoses of other people. In any case I am entirely devoid of the gift of sincerity, and could never write as though I were really convinced no other eye would ever see what I wrote. I am incurably self-conscious. This impromptu resolution sprung from an absurd compact I made with Duff Cooper [a British politician and writer] that we would both begin a diary at the same moment, and bind each other over to keep it up. He has given me this lovely book – but instead of inspiring, it paralyses me and makes me feel my life will not be sufficiently purple.

Cynthia kept up the diary habit, writing several hundred words most mornings, until the end of her life. Only a selection of entries from the war years, though, have seen the light of day, and even these had to wait until 1968, when they were published by Hutchinson as *Lady Cynthia Asquith Diaries 1915-1918*. Her lifelong friend, L.P. Hartley, in the book's foreword says: 'Lady Cynthia was one of the most fascinatingly beautiful women of her time – painted for love by McEvoy, Sargent, and Augustus John – and her lively wit and sensitivity of intelligence made her the treasured confidante of such diverse characters as D.H. Lawrence and Sir James Barrie, but when she died in 1960 she left a new generation to discover yet another of her gifts – as a rarely talented diarist.'

Hartley gives three reasons for the 'value and fascination' of her diary: 'Familiar figures cross her pages, often in 'undress', and a pulsing cross-section of the society of her time is shown. . . Secondly, the diary is also the story of the end of an era... And, finally, it is the unconscious analysis of a family and a woman's identity – developing, maturing, changing, and almost completely breaking under the pressure of the most disastrous events that any generation had ever known.'

All glare and asphalt

10 May 1915
Went down to Brighton by 4:30. Long journey in taxi from station to Kemp Town and found lodgings recommended by Charlie Meade – disappointingly poky and not convenient in many ways. Beastly place Brighton seems – all glare and asphalt and pebbles instead of sand. I think I must go to the other part of town. Kemp Town is inconveniently far from the shops and so on, without any of the compensations of remoteness.

By the evening I was devoted

11 May 1915
A lovely day, and by the evening I was devoted to Brighton. [. . .] The D.H. Lawrences arrived at one o'clock and we went out on a bus and had lunch at a filthy little shop. They decided to stay the night and we engaged another little room in my lodgings. [. . .] I find them the most intoxicating company in the world. I never hoped to have such mental pleasure with anyone.

Beb gazetted and ordered to Brighton

23 June 1916
In the morning we had great excitement and revolution of the future. Beb [Herbert] has been waiting, momentarily expecting orders, ever since he saw the General at the W. O. who told him he would soon have instructions about going to Larkhill. He was gazetted [whereby appointments were announced in official public documents] last Saturday and we have had about twelve LAST-days. At length the orders came in, but instead of Larkhill, Brighton is his destination. It is a great let-off for him, as it will be much more comfortable, and of course it is much more convenient for me, only I think it spells financial ruin. Instead of being safely marooned in a tin hut on Salisbury Plain, he will now probably want to reside at the Grand Hotel! If I can find lodgings, I think I must transfer the children to Brighton.

25 June 1916
Travelled down to Littlehampton by 3:50. A minute after my arrival, to my astonishment, enter Beb! A typical War Office practical joke. The object of going to Brighton was, after all, only to see his C. O. – who was to instruct him as to his next steps – and the C. O. was away till Monday. There is no training course at Brighton, so I expect it will be Larkhill for five weeks or so, and then he will join a Brigade at Brighton.

In horror and misery

7 July 1916

Polly [Cynthia Asquith's maid] and I went down to Brighton by 3:10. Beb had taken rooms in the Royal York Hotel. A note came from him saying he couldn't get away from barracks till 12:30 next morning. Found hotel much too expensive and nosed around, deciding to move next morning to another hotel (commercial and family). Poor Beb won't be too pleased. I hope I plumbed the depth of human misery alone in this beastly hotel: dead tired – the first sort of excitement gone and succeeded by the dreary, dreary stage, with sense of desolation gradually soaking through and through. Every wounded soldier here, too, seems to have one and often both legs amputated – a perfect nightmare. Had breakfast-dinner in a café, and went to bed in horror and misery.

8 July 1916

Breakfasted downstairs by myself. When poor Beb arrived about 12:30 looking forward to the comfortable quarters he had chosen, he found me on the doorstep with all his luggage, just migrating to the new hotel. It is pretty dingy I must admit. What I really like about it is the advertisement for false teeth right across its front. We get bed and breakfast for five shillings each.

Beb is looking wonderfully better – quite different. We rested after lunch, which he insisted on having at the Royal York – our Paradise Lost. After tea we went out to the very nose of the pier.

In search of a bathing cap

20 July 1916

Back in Brighton. After I had written some letters, I went out in search of a bathing cap, thinking I should find a suitable one nearby, but I had to walk for miles and miles in grilling sun, but God forbid that I should complain of any ray of heat vouchsafed to us during this awful summer! It was delicious in the water – really warm and heavenly.

21 July 1916

The gentility of this establishment, the commercial hotel, beggars all description, and the landlady is the queen of snobs. I hear her talking about "her ladyship" with bated breath, and issuing stern injunctions to the poor parlourmaid to be sure and help me first, and to mind and open the door for me, and so on.

A creature of context

22 July 1916

I sat on the balcony reading Byron's letters. Partook of tea in the drawing room – a rather blood-curdling experience. We all sat around balancing cups of strong tea, and a few remarks about the weather were barked out. As I went upstairs, I heard the landlady rebuking the wretched parlourmaid for NOT having "opened the door for her ladyship". Beb and I dined at the Café Royal. Sat in the garden afterwards – lovely evening after a really hot day. These days are really resting me. I am so much a creature of context that I cannot really feel and realise deeply here – my mind only skims.

24 July 1916

I went in a tram to see Horatia Seymour and her mother. They live in Sussex Square – the 'aristocratic' part of Brighton. We had tea and then sat out in the little garden. How I LOVE making friends! The initial stage fascinates me – exploring their personality, or perhaps to be honest, exploring my own THROUGH them – seeing myself from another angle and feeling quite free and UNLABELLED.

As the Lido is to Venice

30 July 1916

Glittering, scorching day and the town teeming like an anthill. No signs of war, save for the poor, legless men whom Michael tried to encourage by saying, "Poor wounded soldiers – soon be better." There is no doubt that Brighton has a charm of its own, almost amounting to glamour. I am beginning to be quite patriotic about this end of the town – Kemp Town as it is called – in opposition to the parvenu Hove, which has less character and is to this rather what the Lido is to Venice.

We joined the children on the beach – painfully hot and glaring. We took them in a boat to try and get cooler. Beb and I bathed from the rather squalid bathing machines – perfect in the water, except for the quantity of foreign bodies.

Bathing off the pier

31 July 1916

Grilling hot again. [. . .] I boldly decided to bathe off the pier as the machines were all full. I shall never bathe from anywhere else again! It was the most delicious thing I have ever done – down a ladder straight into the bottomless green water. Apparently there is no risk of drowning as there is a man in a boat, a raft, a life-buoy, etc. There was a strong current taking one inwards, so I rowed out and swam back. Luxurious dressing rooms, too. It's a great discovery.

After dinner we sat on the pier, which was most delicious. Lovely lights on the water and in the twilight Brighton looked quite glamorous, and I like the teeming, happy crowds. Being here is strangely like being abroad.

7 August 1916

Reluctantly coming to the conclusion that I shall have to make my home at Brighton, I feel and look so incomparably better there.

A beach policeman

13 August 1916

Banged at Basil's door at seven [Lord Basil Blackwood who died attacking German trenches the following year]. We had agreed to bathe if awake. We just ran down to the beach with coats over our bathing clothes. A man, perhaps what they call a 'beach policeman', stopped me, saying it was only for men that station. I said, "Rubbish!" which, unfortunately, he overheard and was furious, threatening to send for the police and saying I must go to Kemp Town. My bathing dress was very wet from the day before and I didn't at all like the idea of going either to Kemp Town or the police station in it. However, we found the situation could be overcome by going through the technicality of taking a bathing machine and leaving one's coat. We had the most heavenly bathe – soft sand and delicious waves, exactly the right size.

A phrenologist, and a grouse

15 August 1916

Sat outside hotel reading Byron's letters till one, [. . .] Horatia took me to a phrenologist, a Professor Severn. I nearly had giggles. He spoke his patter too quickly to be convincing, but on the whole wasn't bad. [. . .]

I had a divine, very rough bathe in enormous breakers which boxed my ears. Beb and I dined in our own hotel – he had shot an excellent grouse which we eat. Went for a walk in Madeira Drive. Very contented mood.

16 August 1916

Lunched with [Horatia], the mother and Cynthia. [. . .] I told them about the grouse Beb said he had shot and – when I heard my own voice – for the first time realised the absurdity of such a cock-and-bull story, and what a gull I had been. Of COURSE there are no grouse in Sussex – he must have bought it at great expense from a shop. I shall buy a salmon and claim to have caught it bathing.

The art of swabs

1 November 1916

Conscience told me I must do some war work, so I went up to Sussex Square and Lady Seymour introduced me at the depot and I was instructed in the art of swabs, sitting between rather grim Brighton ladies in caps and aprons. It looks easy and is really very difficult, and I felt very humiliated by my clumsiness. I wasn't at all good: my instructress kept assuring me that the 'knack' would come to me. I hope it may.

1 December 1916

Cold and fine. [. . .] We were determined on a walk on the downs, so we went in the Dyke Road tram to its terminus and then took to our legs. We must have walked quite six miles altogether. It was very cold, but very delicious and it made me feel well and happy.

3 December 1916
We played the fool on the pier and went to the tourist's whole hog by being photographed with our heads through burlesques. I was the head of the woman sponging. [. . .] We dined at St James's – very amusing conversation. Have never seen Beb in such good form. We all made autobiographical confessions of past susceptibilities and, in inverted conjugal style I twitted and upbraided Beb with incurable faithfulness and single-heartedness. He tried desperately to prove his dogdom, but I dissolved his evidence.

Flirting with Freyberg

26 January 1917
Really miserable at leaving Brighton. I have loved the life there and feel the ground has been cut away from under my feet. I believe the air and so on has spoilt me for life anywhere else, and I don't know how to lead any sort of existence any longer.

1 December 1917
Went down to Brighton by 11:40 to spend the day with Freyberg [Bernard Cyril Freyberg – British-born New Zealander, the youngest general in the British Army during the First World and recipient of the Victoria Cross]. [. . .] He was looking better and had a fine appetite. With his youthful face and the insignia of his anomalous rank (his medals and preposterous number of gold stripes) he is very conspicuous and much stared at – obsequious deference from the waiters. I insisted on taking him to Professor Severn, the phrenologist, but he was hopelessly out about him, marking him LOW for self-esteem and concentration. Freyberg's contemptuous indignation was such that he threw his chart into the mud directly he got out of the house. Twice it was picked up and returned to him. We went to the Kitchener Hospital to have his wound dressed. [. . .]

We walked to dinner at the Metropole. He told me of his wonderful swimming exploit in Gallipoli, when he swam for four hours and landed naked and alone, and crawled quite close to the enemy's trenches and lit torches. His eyes shine and he becomes poeticised talking of military adventures, and I was touched to see his eyes fill with tears once when he was talking about his men. I find him very, very attractive.

20

Virginia Woolf and Harold Nicolson

'We went to Brighton today; & thus added a pounds worth of pleasure to life.' So wrote Virginia Woolf, one of the best literary diarists of the twentieth century, in September 1927. By then she'd been living with her husband Leonard at Monk's House in Rodmell, a small Sussex village, for the best part of a decade and was well accustomed to visiting nearby Brighton for shops or to see friends, or occasionally to attend a Labour Party Conference. She loved the second-hand bookshops, afternoon tea, and having 'a debauch' in some stationers. But the people sometimes distressed her, and she wasn't above writing about the women she saw as 'fat white slugs'. For much of her life she was on intimate terms with Vita Sackville-West, who was married to Harold Nicolson, and lived further east in Kent at Sissinghurst. Nicolson, too, was a diarist of the first rank, though he mentioned Brighton only a couple of times in his diary – notably when he came to dispose of his mother-in-law's ashes.

Virginia was the second daughter of Sir Leslie Stephen, the first editor of the *Dictionary of National Biography*. The family lived in Hyde Park Gate but had a country home at St Ives in Cornwall. Woolf's mother died when she was 13 and her father died ten years later. Both these losses precipitated mental breakdowns which left her psychologically fragile for the rest of her short life. She settled in Gordon Square with her sister Vanessa and her brother Adrian, and subsequently married Leonard Sidney Woolf. The Woolfs, along with their many literary friends, became known as the Bloomsbury Group.

In 1917, Virginia and Sydney launched the Hogarth Press, and, two years later, they bought Monks House in Rodmell, East Sussex, a small village three miles from Lewes and not much further from Brighton. It was at Rodmell that Virginia wrote most of her novels. *Mrs Dalloway* was published in 1925, and *To the Lighthouse* in 1927. The following year she published *Orlando*. This novel, which was written quickly and is seen as a kind of love letter to her friend Vita Sackville-West, sold much better than any of her earlier books. Two further, now-famous novels followed in the 1930s – *The Waves* and *The Years* – before severe distress about the war, and depression led to her committing suicide by drowning in the nearby Ouse River in 1941.

Woolf's thirty volumes of 'great' diaries

Woolf began jotting down notes about her life as a teenager, and intermittently continued until 1915 when the diary writing habit took hold permanently. From then until a few days before her death, she wrote regularly and in some detail about her daily life. Extracts were published for the first time in *A Writer's Diary* by the Hogarth Press in 1953. The extracts were chosen by Leonard Woolf specifically to reflect his wife's life as a writer.

After Leonard's death in 1969, some thirty or so volumes of his wife's diaries were deposited with the Albert A Berg Collection of English and American Literature at the New York Public Library. These were prepared for publication by Anne Olivier Bell, wife of Virginia's nephew and biographer Quentin Bell, to provide a much fuller (and more faithful – Leonard had made Virginia's prose more formal than it was) version of the diary. *The Diary of Virginia Woolf* was published in five volumes by the Hogarth Press during the late 1970s and early 1980s.

In his introduction Quentin Bell wrote: 'This is the last of Virginia Woolf's major works to be offered to the public. In calling it a major work I wish to imply not merely that it is a large work of major historical and biographical importance (which it certainly and obviously is) but also that, considered as a whole, it is a masterpiece... It is in fact one of the great diaries of the world.'

Indeed, the volumes were much acclaimed for being beautifully written, for giving a first-hand account of the revered Bloomsbury Group, and for providing an excellent insight into Woolf's creative processes.

Tea at Booth's, lunch at Mutton's

7 August 1917

Queer misty day. Sun not strong enough to come through. Went to Brighton after lunch. German prisoners working in the field by Dod's Hill, laughing with the soldier, & woman passing. Went to Pier; tea at Booth's [East Street]; horrible men at our table; staged at Lewes on way back. Bicycled back from Glynde. N & L [Nelly and Lottie – resident cook and housemaid] went to get mushrooms, & found several, also blackberries getting ripe, only have no sugar for jam.

3 September 1918

This is written on the return from our great Brighton treat. Everything succeeded. L[eonard] foretold a wet day by the light on our shutters, but on opening them we found a perfect September morning. The sun is thinner but very clear, & the air sparkling, now that we are past August. The colours are being burnished on the trees too. The shadows seem lighter & paler. [. . .] A perfect treat must include a visit to the 2nd hand bookshops. (I bought the life of Col. Hutchinson); sweets (we found chocolate unlimited) lunch at Mutton's; the band on the pier; some human grotesques; tea at Booth's; Buns at Cowley's; a trail past shops with many temptations to buy, for the most part resisted; & a debauch at some stationer; & so home, to find the downs & this house lovelier than ever. All these things we did; & we had too a feeling of lightness because of the villages won in France.

You're a back number

22 August 1922

But I always have to confess, when I write diary in the morning. It is only 11.30 to be honest, & I have left off Mrs Dalloway in Bond Street; & really why is it? I should very much like to account for my depression. Sydney Waterlow spent the week end here; & yesterday we had a days outing at Brighton. At Brighton I saw a lovely blue Victorian dress, which L advised me not to buy. Sydney reproduced in his heavy lifeless voice exactly the phrases in which Murry dismisses my writing "merely silly – one simply doesnt read it – youre a back number." Then Squire rejected Leonard's story; & perhaps I dont like seeing new houses built all about; & get edgy about our field. So now I have assembled my facts – to which I now add my spending 10/6 on photographs, which we developed in my dress cupboard last night; & they are all failures. Compliments, clothes, building, photography – it is for these reasons that I cannot write 'Mrs Dalloway'. Indeed it is fatal to have visitors, even like Clive for one day, in the middle of a story. I had just got up steam. All that agony now has to begin again.

A pounds worth of pleasure

5 September 1927

As a matter of fact, we are just in from Brighton, & my mind is agitated by having bought a jersey, which I like; & by having let Leonard bump the back of the car on the gate post. So, to soothe these whirlpools, I write here. We went to Brighton today; & thus added a pounds worth of pleasure to life. Monotony is avoided. Oh, & I thought – but the thought is already escaping – about the enormous activity of the human kind; his feverish runnings about; Brighton & the roads being nothing but a swarm & agitation of human flesh; & yet it is not despicable.

15 August 1929

We are back from Brighton where I bought a corner cupboard. And if I had time, I would here dissect a curious little spotted fruit: this melancholy. It comes with headache, of course. And I had come to the blind alley – the cul de-sac. Writing this compressed article, where every word is like a step cut in the rock – hard work, if ever writing was; & done largely for money; & whats money, compared with Nessa's children [Nessa – Virginia Woolf's sister, Vanessa Bell].

Baaing at the Labour Party Conference

2 October 1929

I am dazed with the Brighton [Labour Party] conference; hearing Henderson [Arthur Henderson, Foreign Secretary] orate & seeing him get red slowly like a lobster; we went on Monday too (how many days of reflection have dwindled! one must give it all up now) & heard a good, interesting, debate. The audience makes an extraordinary baaing noise; not talk, not footsteps – & I thought how politics was no longer an affair of great nobles & mystery & diplomacy, but of commonsense, issuing from ordinary men & women of business – not very exalted, but straight forward, like any other business affair.

2 October 1935

Yesterday we went to the L. P. meeting at Brighton, & of course, though I have refused to go again this morning, I am so thrown out of my stride that I cant hitch on to 'The Years' again. Why? The immersion in all that energy & all that striving for something that is quite oblivious of me; making me feel that I am oblivious of it. No, thats not got it. It was very dramatic: Bevin's attack on Lansbury. Tears came to my eyes as L spoke. And yet he was posing I felt – acting, unconsciously, the battered Christian man. Then Bevin too acted I suppose. He sank his head in his vast shoulders till he looked like a tortoise. Told L[eonard] not to go hawking his conscience around. [George Lansbury was then leader of the Labour Party and the attack was on his pacifism. It led to his resignation; and within a week, Clement Attlee had taken over the party leadership.]

To write a dream story

22 June 1937

So now to draw the blood off that brain to another part – according to H Nicolson's prescription, which is the right one. I wd like to write a dream story about the top of a mountain. Now why? About lying in the snow; about rings of colour; silence... & the solitude. I cant though. But shant I, one of these days, indulge myself in some short releases into that world? Short now for ever. No more long grinds: only sudden intensities. If I cd think out another adventure. Oddly enough I see it now ahead of me – in Charing X road yesterday – as to do with books some new combination. Brighton? A round room on the pier – & people shopping, missing each other – a story Angelica told in the summer. But how does this make up with criticism? I'm trying to get the 4 dimensions of the mind... life in connection with emotions from literature. A days walk – a mind's adventure: something like that. And its useless to repeat my old experiments: they must be new to be experiments.

A love-corner for slugs

26 February 1941

Yesterday in the ladies lavatory at the Sussex Grill at Brighton I heard: She's a little simpering thing. I don't like her. But then he never did care for big women. (So to Bert) His eyes are so blue. Like blue pools. So's Gert's. They have the same eyes, only her teeth part a little. He has wonderful white teeth. He always had. Its fun having the boys... If he dont look out he'll be court martialled.

They were powdering & painting, these common little tarts, while I sat, behind a thin door, p——ing as quietly as I could.

Then at Fuller's. A fat, smart woman, in red hunting cap, pearls, check skirt, consuming rich cakes. Her shabby dependant also stuffing. Hudson's van unloading biscuits opposite. The fat woman had a louche large white muffin face. T'other was slightly grilled. They ate & ate. Talked about Mary. But if she's very ill, you'll have to go to her. Youre the only one. . . But why should she be? ...I opened the marmalade but John doesnt like it – And we have two pounds of biscuits in the tin upstairs... Something scented, shoddy, parasitic about them. Then they totted up cakes. And passed the time o' day with the waitress. Where does the money come to feed these fat white slugs? Brighton a love-corner for slugs. The powdered the pampered the mildly improper. I invested them in a large house in Sussex Square.

We cycled. Irritated as usual by the blasphemy of Peacehaven.

Virginia's last days

8 March 1941

Just back from L's speech at Brighton. Like a foreign town: the first spring day. Women sitting on seats. A pretty hat in a teashop – how fashion revives the eye! And the shell encrusted old women, rouged, decked, cadaverous at the tea shop. The waitress in checked cotton.

24 March 1941

A curious sea side feeling in the air today. It reminds me of lodgings on a parade at Easter. Everyone leaning against the wind, nipped & silenced. All pulp removed.

This windy corner. And Nessa is in Brighton, & I am imagining how it wd be if we could infuse souls.

Octavia's story. Could I englobe it somehow? English youth in 1900.

Two long letters from Shena & O. I cant tackle them, yet enjoy having them.
L is doing the rhododendrons...

Editor's note: [...] LW, alarmed by her state of mind and health and the ominous
signs of breakdown, now persuaded her to see Octavia Wilberforce as a doctor
as well as a friend, and took her to Brighton for this purpose on Thursday 27
March. The following morning Virginia drowned herself in the tidal river Ouse;
Leonard found her stick on the bank near the swing bridge at Southease; her
body was found some three weeks later on the further side of the same stretch
of water. It was cremated on 21 April, and Leonard buried her ashes beneath
one of the great elms at the edge of the bowling lawn in Monks House garden.

Harold Nicolson, husband of Virginia's lover

Harold Nicolson was born in Tehran (Persia at the time) in 1886 and worked in the
British diplomatic service before becoming an MP in 1935. He married the writer
Victoria Sackville-West in 1913, and together they created the famous garden at
Sissinghurst, Kent. While not an especially remarkable politician in his own right,
Nicolson's skills lay in his talents as an observer, and as a journalist and writer. He is
also well remembered for the relationship with his wife, which was both very close
yet also open, in the sense that each partner allowed the other to have affairs, including with same-sex lovers. Anne Olivier Bell, in her introduction to Woolf's diaries
notes: 'Virginia's one serious infidelity is remarkable in that it exhibits clearly the
secure strength of her marriage; and if Leonard was discomposed by any of Virginia's
lovers it was not Vita.'

But Nicolson is best known for his brilliant diaries. These were edited by his son,
Nigel Nicolson, and published, with letters, in three volumes by Collins in the last
years of Harold's life (he died in 1968). Since then there have been many reprints
and reissues. Recently, Weidenfeld & Nicolson (now part of Orion, but originally
founded by Nigel Nicolson and George Weidenfeld in the 1940s) published a one-
volume edition – *The Harold Nicolson Diaries 1907-1963*. And most recently Faber
Finds has reprinted the original three volume set.

In advertising the reissued books, Faber Finds quoted a number of past reviews. Sir
Kenneth Clark, for example, said the diaries provide 'not only a brilliant picture of
English society in the 1930s, but a touching self-portrait of a highly intelligent and
civilized man driven by conscience and curiosity to enter politics'. And Michael Foot:
'One stops to marvel at the achievement. Honesty, decency, modesty magnanimity
are stamped on every page, as evident as the wit. These are not the normal virtues of
successful diarists or would-be politicians, but Harold Nicolson possesses them all.'

There are very few entries about Brighton in the three volumes, and those there
are record trips to see Vita's mother, Victoria Sackville-West, Baroness Sackville (BM
in the diaries), who lived at White Lodge, on the cliffs at Black Rock, to the east of
Brighton. Today the house is on the main road to Rottingdean and overlooks the
marina. Baroness Sackville died there in 1936.

Poor Vita, what a strain

23 April 1933

Over to Brighton. Find BM very weak. She abuses Nigel unjustly and then I lose my temper. I say I shall kill her if she hurts my children. I then ask for her forgiveness. She gives it. We part as friends, but it was hell. Poor Vita, what a strain for her.

30 January 1936

Dr Broadbent has telephoned to say BM cannot live through the day. Vita goes down by the 12 noon train and I promise to follow as soon as I have put off all my engagements. Reach Brighton at 2pm and go to White Lodge. Go straight up to BM's room and find that she had died some three minutes before, quite painlessly and without recovering consciousness. Take Vita into the other room. Rhind [Lady Sackville's secretary] is much upset but behaves well. The solicitor arrives and also the priest. The latter is disgusting and refuses to have a service over BM if she is to be cremated. She has left a pathetic little typewritten notice saying that she was to be cremated and the ashes flung into the sea. Vita is much harassed and shattered, but inwardly, I think, relieved.

A handful of dust in the sea

8 February 1936

Go down to Brighton. It is a bitter cold day with a strong east wind. I am met by Cecil Rhind and we lunch at the Metropole. We then go to the oyster-shop of Mr English where BM's ashes have preserved overnight. The reason for this strange procedure is that the Press had got hold of the story, and it was feared that they would picket the undertakers and take snapshots of us as we carried out the urn. The latter is placed at the back of the car by Mr English. He is anxious to come with us in the boat, but I am very firm on the point. "No, Mr English, we really should prefer to be by ourselves."

The boat is there on the shingle – a large open fishing-boat with two sailors and a petrol engine. We climb in, holding the little container in its neat brown-paper parcel. We are launched down the shingle in Homeric fashion and chug along the coast until we get opposite White Lodge. Cecil and I sit there huddled in our coats with a most inadequate rug over our knees, bending our heads from time to time as the spray lashes over us. Sun shining and an angry brown sea.

"We're two miles out," says the boatman, at which I undo the string of the parcel. The urn or container is of gun-metal, and one opens it by pressing up the lid with one's thumbs. I am terrified lest the ashes be caught by the wind and I keep the lid on. The two men stand up and take off their hats. So does Cecil. I kneel by the gunwale and spill the ashes over into the sea, saying "BM, all who love you are happy that you should now be at peace. We shall remember always your beauty, your courage and your charm." It is merely a handful of dust which slides out of the container into the waves.

21

Mass Observation and Olive Stammer in the Second World War

The social research organisation Mass Observation was launched in 1937 to record life in Britain, 'an anthropology of ourselves', according to the founders. With little funding, it relied on a panel of around 500 volunteers who either kept diaries or replied to open-ended questionnaires. Researchers also recorded, anonymously, people's conversations and behaviour at work, in public places, and sports and religious events. It operated throughout the Second World War producing thousands of reports and a series of published books. However, after the war, the emphasis shifted away from social issues towards consumer behaviour, and, in 1949, Mass Observation was registered as a limited company, and eventually incorporated into an advertising firm.

The Mass Observation Archive is held at the University of Sussex, and holds all the material generated between 1937 and 1949, with a few later additions, from the 1950s and 1960s. The project was re-launched in 1981, and today continues to collect information aimed at providing a structured programme through which 'ordinary' people can write directly about their lives, and at creating 'a resource of qualitative longitudinal social data'.

Box SxMOA 99/69

Given the location of the archive on the outskirts of Brighton, it is somewhat ironic that there is so little diary material about the city itself. However, there is one contribution which does stand out in this regard – box SxMOA 99/69. It was not collected as part of the Mass Observation project during the war, but was donated by Olive Wood Stammer in 1986. The box contains material written by herself and her brother George. Inside are the letters they sent to each other, twice a week, during the war. George's letters, in fact, were published by Olive in a slim white paperback volume as – *George 1940-1946:*

A Collection of Letters from George Stammer to his Sister, edited by Olive Wood Stammer. George served in the General Headquarters Liaison Regiment, Richmond, dubbed the 'Phantom Regiment' because of the classified secret work it undertook.

But box SxMOA 99/69 also contains two A4-sized volumes titled 'Boots Scribbling Diary', one is for 1940 and the other for 1941. The cover of each one also boasts 'British Manufacture throughout – Three Days on a Page – Interleaved with Blotting Paper'. They are both filled with Olive's daily diary notes. Throughout 1940, these notes are beautifully and densely written in block capitals; in the 1941 volume, however, Olive reverts to normal handwriting which packs the pages less fully.

There is no biographical information about Olive in the Mass Observation archive, other than that she worked in a shop. Local records, however, reveal she was born in 1907, and her brother George in 1910. Olive died in 1997, having lived almost all her life at 41 Crescent Road, which is high above Upper Lewes Road. She never married, nor, it seems, did her brother, who lived in Hove, and who neighbours remember carrying shopping up the hill for her.

Brighton men lost

In the first of the two diaries, some parallel lines have been ruled on the title page, and filled in with a summary of events for the last months of 1939. Here are a few of those notes.

1 September 1939
Last tram to run in Brighton leaves Aquarium at 2am on its final journey to the depot.

3 September 1939
Prime Minister's speech announcing state of war with Germany. Followed by first air raid warning throughout England.

14 October 1939
Several Brighton men lost in sinking of *Royal Oak* at Scapa Flow.

16 November 1939
Demonstration of Brighton's first 'producer' gas driven bus.

1 December 1939
2 Brighton men missing in sinking of *Rawalpindi* by German Deutschland

21 December 1939
Post office Brighton reports record Christmas. 2,110,910 outward letters.

28 December 1939
There can be little doubt that the extraordinary flashes of light that crossed the sky on Thursday evening Dec 28th at times ranging from 6:30 to 8pm were due to the aurora borealis. Scientific observers say colours arranged through blues & green & occasional orange.

A left-hand margin

In the diary proper, the sections of each day (three per page) are filled with news about the war, taken, presumably, from the newspaper or radio broadcasts. However, on every page Stammer has ruled off a left-hand margin, and in this she jots down personal and local news. Occasionally, however, there are also personal items in the main body of the diary too.

For Wednesday 10 January, for example, the main section includes: 'Fight between Messerschmidt and RAF planes over North seas'; 'Nazi planes bomb Danish ships'; and 'Airplane swooped into sea East of Palace Pier. Engine trouble. Pilot rescued.' And the following notes are in the left hand margin: 'Paid Fire Insurance'; 'George and Stan attend first Home Nursing Lecture. Both have passed their first aid'; and 'Mr G Steel died today, age 78.'

The following extracts are taken from both the main body of the diary and the left hand margins.

The great freeze up

28 January 1940
I fell heavily on back of head 3.30 pm. During the great freeze up today the S. C. Hospital were called upon to deal with 51 casualties.

2 February 1940
I went to Dr Lindeck who examined my head.

8 February 1940
Mine washed up at Hove. Traffic diverted.

10 March 1940
Meat is rationed from today.

Wounded and hospitals

7 May 1940
Saw about 20 motors crossing Race Hill and wondered if it was wounded returning from Norway. Saw some continuing down Elm Grove. (25 May – Learned it was not wounded for Bton Municipal Hospital.)

10 May 1940
N[eville] Chamberlain resigned tonight. W[inston] Churchill is new Prime Minister.

27 May 1940
Soldiers at Sussex County badly wounded & not expected to live. Many cases at 'Municipal'. A lot of mental & shock cases.

Fighters and steamers

30 May 1940
A lot of British planes passing over about 6 am today. Saw 15 fighters in formation.

5 June 1940
Pleasure steamers lost during the evacuation from Dunkirk. *Brighton Belle*, *Brighton Queen*, *Waverley* and *The Crested Eagle*.

Of blood and gangrene

6 June 1940
Dr Warden's son ~~killed~~ (July – now ~~missing~~ prisoner)
   T B opposite: B[ritish] E[xpeditionary] F[orce] says they have been up to their knees in blood.

8 June 1940
Gwen says B. E. F. in Sussex County Hospital are bad cases, some without legs, some without arms & others dying from gangrene.

10 June 1940
First strawberries from allotment today.

Rattling windows and seafront curfew

30 June 1940
12:20 am we heard 3 loud bursts of gunfire which seemed to come from Kemp Town District, saw 8 search lights & heard plane out to sea. About 12:40 heard more gunfire in distance to west of Bton. Windows rattled.

2 July 1940
An extension of the seafront curfew imposed yesterday from Black Rock, Brighton, to Worthing, has been made by the Local Military Commander. The beaches and promenades along the coastline, including that from Black Rock to Worthing, will now be closed to civilians as from 5 o'clock this afternoon for the whole 24 hours instead of from 5 pm to 5 am.

16 August 1940
Binoculars & field glasses wanted urgently in Bton for troops.

Red warnings and loud planes

Around August, the number of short entries in the left margin increases hugely, mostly these say 'red warning' with a time (but soon these are so frequent that Stammer simply uses 'R.W.'); there are also many other briefs like: 'loud planes', 'bomb dropped', 'heard bang'.

30 August 1940

Fights between planes over Bton, Hove & Patcham. Spitfire down in Portland Road. House tops damaged. Pilot killed. They could only find his hand.

31 August 1940

Plane circled over Bton from 8:30 pm Friday until nearly dawn. It dropped a few bombs at long intervals.

3 September 1940

Mrs Vine has piece of glass taken from G plane brought down at Steyning.

Digging out bodies

20 September 1940

No warning. 11:50 am.

1st 1,000lb bomb dropped in Lewes Road on public house, bottom of Franklin Road.

2nd 1,000lb bomb dropped on houses in Caledonian Rd, Upper Lewes Road end. E saw large cloud of smoke go up and pieces of buildings. Feathers blowing everywhere. Miss S saved herself by diving behind a counter. Uncle W and Pastor took urn of tea along for workmen, digging out bodies and injured. Salvation Army did good work with refreshments.

10 October 1940

This morning about 12:15 pm bombs dropped from a single plane at Patcham and then in line near Ditchling Road, in Sandgate Road, Dover Rd, 2 houses down and Hythe Road. Time bomb near Preston Drove. 50 families moved.

Saw soldier motor cyclist laying London Road this morning with broken leg, lorry cut out of Baker St on wrong side.

Crater outside Hanningtons

30 November 1940

Small crater in Pavilion, another one large enough to take a car in East Street Lyons. The inside of their shop badly damaged, a lot of glass out in East Street. Another crater outside Hanningtons in Castle Square, all their lower floor was damaged by blast & had to be strutted up to prevent upper floor from falling. Barfoots & Hopes damaged also Regent & Odeon. B Herald said 1 incendiary crashed through roof of cinema & fell in corner of auditorium, film was not interrupted. [. . .] 1 incendiary through roof of dance hall, on to ballroom floor. 1 incendiary outside another dance hall & outside a theatre. More in parks and open spaces. Another heavy in undertakers yard.

At the end of November 1940, Olive's writing changes from immaculate block letters, to more normal handwriting, and this continues in the 1941 diary. By the middle of 1941, the left hand margin notes have almost fallen away completely, and the main entries too have become much less detailed.

5 January 1941

George had his first leave from Aldershot today. He has a bad cold and cough.

Fire watching duty, and cat meat

15 February 1941

I booked up for fire watching.

15 March 1941

Brighton man stated to carry on a posh butchers business in Dyke Road & a cats meat shop at Lewes. Frank Saggers was fined £25 for possessing certain food intended for sale but unfit for human consumption.

Brighton children are to be evacuated. The government has decided to ban Brighton to visitors from March 25th.

22

A teenage Tony Simmonds experiences VE Day

While Olive Stammer documented the first years of the Second World War, a teenager called Tony Simmonds, who had only just moved to Brighton, wrote in his diary about the latter years of the war. In his diary, though, there are no reports about the national or international news, but simply raw responses to what is going on around him. 'People just went mad – dancing, singing, chanting, shouting – the crowd just surged this way and that,' he wrote about VE Day, 'fire crackers, flares and even pre-war 'jumpers' were thrown about the streets – even into busses – all policemen 'had their eyes shut'.'

Tony lived his early years in Winchester but then moved to Brighton in 1942. He left school in June 1944, and worked in the insurance industry until his retirement in the 1980s. He takes an active interest in local history, and cooperated on several books about wartime Brighton. Extracts of his diaries were first published in 1990 by QueenSpark in *Brighton Behind the Front*. Some of these extracts and others can be found on the My Brighton and Hove community website. The website also carries some material from an interview with Tony in 2005. One of his diaries is on display in Brighton Museum.

I was having geography and saw Jerry swoop

21 May 1943
Evening. Phew! Daddy, Denny [Tony's younger brother] and I put up the Morrison Shelter. What a job – my hat!

25 May 1943
At about 12.15 Brighton had its worst raid yet. 25 planes came over machine gunning and bombing. I was having Geography and had to get under the desk – I saw one Jerry swoop past our window. I was really scared. One boy went absolutely green. The house opposite was gunned. At home Mummy got very

scared and went under the shelter. Daddy, walking home, rushed inside a shop after seeing bombs fall out of several planes. Bombs were dropped at: top of Eaton Place, Chichester Place, the other side of the Hospital in Eastern Road (about 200 yards from here) which was the worst, Bennett Road, St Mark's School (near the gas works), the gas works, all our gas went, the flats at Black Rock (where we were on Sunday) and where a soldier on the roof was blown out to sea with his gun, the viaduct in London Road (1 span was destroyed) & that's about all – oh – Arundel Road caught it, and Hove was machine gunned. Evening. I toured around the damage – it was awful.

29 May 1943
Coming back on a 41 trolley bus we saw the funeral of the 2 children killed in Down Terrace, behind our school. And I saw 4 Jerry vapour trails.

6 June 1943
The family went for a tour of the bomb damage. Gosh! Those gas works are terrible; so are the flats.

Wailing Willy, Moaning Minny

7 October 1943
Just as the new series of Tommy Handley was beginning, Wailing Willy, or Moaning Minny went. We went in the shelter when we heard Jerry. Then about 9 o'clock he dived. There was terrific gun fire. Some bombs may have been dropped – I don't know. All Clear went at 11 o'clock. Wow! what a long siren. [Tommy Handley was a comedian known for his radio programme 'It's That Man Again' or ITMA.]

16 October 1943
We had another night of it tonight. The siren went at 7:30. The all clear went – the siren went again – the all clear went again and as there is gunfire now, I have reason to believe the siren's gone again.

Why don't they leave us alone

17 October 1943
Wow! I'm fed up. At 2 o'clock morning the W.W. went and we went down S. Then at 8 am another W.W. went and heavy gunfire.

22 October 1943
H[err] J[erry] came early tonight and 2 sirens went at different times in the evening. A good many J's came over and dropped a bomb in Bonchurch Road. Why don't they leave us alone?

Brighton and Hove Albion

23 April 1944

Yesterday Brighton and Hove Albion beat Luton Town 8-0 what a victory.

18 November 1944

I went in the 3/6d Stand to see Brighton (bottom of the Southern League) put up a super show against Chelsea (the top). At half time the score was 2-2. We scored the first goal in the second half giving us the lead – the cheer for that goal was terrific but then Chelsea piled on three more goals – one beauty by Hardwick – making the final score 5-3.

17 February 1945

Saw Brighton beat Millwall 6-2 this afternoon – it looks as if we are going to get in the semi-finals. The great Tommy Lawton played for the Lions too – he's a marvellous chap.

My bike has streamers on its handlebars

8 May 1945

VICTORY IN EUROPE DAY – I was at work – when I came back from
lunch at 2 pm I found everyone in a hustle and bustle. The Manager said we
were going to get out by 3.30. We did. Even then we had time to rush out to
hear Churchill's speech at 3 o'clock and a fine speech it was too.

We all knew something would happen in the evening and it did. It came right
up to my fullest expectations. I just can't describe the scene. I was alone most of
the time and spent almost five hours around the Clock Tower. People just went
mad – dancing, singing, chanting, shouting – the crowd just surged this way and
that – The Academy, the Odeon and the Regent were all floodlit for the first
time in almost six years – fire crackers, flares and even pre-war 'jumpers' were
thrown about the streets – even into busses – all policemen 'had their eyes shut'.

I left at just after 11 pm leaving behind me a riot going on outside the Regent
– where a drunken sailor was protesting against a charge of 10/6d for a dance in
the Regent Dance Hall. What a day – I shall never forget it for the rest of my life.

Our house is decorated up – four flags – a shield and red, white & blue
streamers. Even Mrs Guild next door has her standard flying. As for the town
itself – well I never knew there were so many flags manufactured. My bike has a
big rosette and streamers on its handlebars.

Never to be forgotten day

15 August 1945

[Victory in Japan Day]

THE GREATEST DAY THE WORLD HAS EVER KNOWN – Right up
to 8 am I was ready to go to work today – even though I had been informed
by Head Office that today was Victory Day no news had come through by the
time I went to bed on the 14th. Thus at 7.30 this morning I got up as usual
feeling a little disappointed and very tense – you never know there might be
something on the 8 o'clock news but I wasn't hoping for too much.

The music for 'This week's Composer' ceased at 5 to eight and the usual 'Lift up
your Hearts' programme came on the air. I can truthfully say that I nearly swal-
lowed my spoon when I heard a voice say "Lift up your Hearts in this morning
of final Victory."

"Did you hear that?" I shouted and we knew it was all over. The 8 o'clock
news confirmed that today was Victory Day and that today and tomorrow were
to be a national holiday. That was 8 o'clock – by ten past 8 we had our flags out
and the never to be forgotten day had started.

The one drawback in the morning was that it was raining – still Denny and I
braved the elements and went out. We came back soaking wet but with the news
that the flags were out everywhere – there wasn't much doing yet but still we
didn't expect it. The rain stopped in the afternoon and the family trooped out,
Denny and I with whistles in our pockets. Last time there was hardly anything

doing in the afternoon, but, this time, the crowds were almost as big as on V. E. evening. The centre of attraction was at the bottom of West Street where a score or more of Dominion troops surrounded by literally thousands of people, were leading in patriotic songs. We joined in.

We decided not to go out as early in the evening as we did on V. E. Day but at 7.15 we trooped out heading for the Clock Tower. Even by 8 o'clock the fun exceeded even that on V. E. Day. Where all the fireworks came from remains a mystery – never before have I seen so many people jammed together in two streets. It was impossible even to guess how many shouting, singing, dancing clapping uproariously happy people were there. Every bus or car daring to invade the area was banged and rocked and 'fireworked'. No bus left the area without its boards being missing – still they make a nice bonfire.

The fire was as high as buildings

The first big bonfire was lit in a patch of waste land near the Prudential – on this was dumped all the material used to begin a fire at the top of West Street – a fire soon put out by Police. I think I led the 'Boos' that followed this action. Still the other bonfire soon made up for it. Denny and I now went off again up to the Clock Tower giving repeated blasts in our whistles – what hooligans – but still, even old men were blowing whistles and shaking rattles and every old dear was waving a flag. Then about 11.30 the fun really began.

A huge bonfire was lit at the bottom of West Street, every moveable piece of wood in the area was dumped on this fire. The Sports Stadium, the Odeon, Sherrys and the Harris Grill were all stripped of their advertisement boards – time and time again. The police tried to stop it but they hadn't the slightest chance against such a crowd. Then the N[ational] F[ire] S[ervice] arrived. In course of ten minutes, every moveable article on the lorry was dumped onto the fire – from hose pipes to doors. As a retaliation one Fireman drenched the crowd with showers of water.

The fire was as high as the buildings when Denny and I left at 12.30. On the way home we saw other huge bonfires on the beach and smaller ones in almost every street – and around each bonfire danced hilariously happy people – men, women and children. That ended the most glorious evening of my life – the crowds weren't riotous – on the whole very little damage was done – but just supremely happy that the greatest of all wars was over.

23

Three 'Letter in the Attic' diarists

The 'Letter in the Attic' is a collection of nearly 800 letters, diaries, memoirs and other personal papers related to Brighton and Hove. It was created by a general appeal to the public from the community publisher QueenSpark in 2007-2008 'to show the historical value of everyday writings, such as letters and diaries'. East Sussex Record Office, the Mass-Observation Archive, and the Community website My Brighton and Hove were also involved. There are not many diaries in the collection, but here are samples from three of them.

Hinda Harris goes to the cinema

Hinda Harris was born in London, and her parents owned a sweet shop in Stoke Newington. In the 1930s, the family moved to Hove, but were evacuated during the Second World War to Swindon for a while, returning to Hove in 1941. It is believed that Hinda worked as a secretary and office assistant, and acted as a secretary to a local writers' circle. She never married or had children. The 'Letter in the Attic' (LIC) collection includes four diaries covering her life in 1941, 1943, 1965 and 1967. Hinda's niece, Sophie Harris, selected and transcribed the following entries (among others) for the LIC project.

13 January 1941
Further cleaning up. Surveyed town in afternoon. Fine weather. Plenty of people and blessed absence of uniforms. Ran into Margaret outside Wade and had a pow wow. Everything much as usual except absence of onions in Hove and general scarcity of meat.

15 January 1941
Snowed here first time since we got back, but no hills to climb so I don't care! To Lido to see 'Ghost Breakers', very funny and 'Miracles do Happen', quite amusing. Place almost empty.

24 January 1941
'The Great Dictator'. Grand comedy and great propaganda, if only someone would listen.

13 March 1941
Sudden call from Miss Simon to do a little typing job. 9 popular songs – 30 copies for a canteen. Earned enough to almost pay for grey skirt! Wish there were more 'jobs' of this variety!

10 May 1941
25! Quarter of a century old. So what? Grey gloves (one pair wool, one silk) posy, jumper and chocolates. 'Quiet Wedding' funniest film for weeks. 'Rumba' old but bearable. Wonder if I shall be 26?!!

1 June 1941
Clothes Rationed!! Biggest bombshell on the home front.

2 December 1941
To the Imperial for the first time. A nice theatre but badly heated and unorganised. The bill was very weak. Two good turns, one just bearable and the rest flat. The audience was 'cold' in more senses than one!

Jane Lucas, student at Sussex University

Jane Lucas was born in South London but moved to Brighton in the mid-1970s to study English at Sussex University. She lived in Shaftesbury Road, although spent much of her time with friends in Broad Street. After leaving Brighton in 1978, she returned to live in the town in 1989 with her two young daughters. The LIC collection includes a selection of Lucas's diary entries from 1977-1978, the last year of her degree studies. She told the LIC project that, on looking back at her diaries, she realised she had hit her 'stride as a Brighton girl' in that last year.

'Brighton was a quieter place then – a town rather than a city,' she said. 'We drank in ordinary pubs in town – the student bars and clubs were to be found on campus. The Crypt (next to Falmer Bar) holds the best memories. Some of the places we went have been renamed or moved – the Top Rank Suite and the original Concorde, for example. The extent to which I mention music in the entries surprises me and reminds me that in your student days, music isn't incidental, as it is now, but the soundtrack of your life.'

15 October 1977
Walked to Broad Street via sparkling, misty magic sea – Palace Pier arose out of it like a magic Eastern city. [...] Home and worked and meditated. Veg pie from Jill for dinner – decided too reclusive to go out. Enter Graham with new Bowie record. Listened to it with him and Anton and appropriate rapping.

Eventually, to Railway pub for Twix, crisps and ginger wine and mad bar billiards. Home to watch 'Kiss me Goodbye' film and 'So It Goes' [TV show with] Elvis Costello and Penetration. Positive day – am fitting much in recently. Must materialise more written work though. More push needed, though very well motivated.

27 November 1977
Wondered if George would come round. Read 'Spare Rib' and realised (a) how many things that seem personal hang-ups are general to role of women and (b) that women's movement isn't a sewn up thing, but a on-going experience, struggle. NB Kate Millet [an American feminist writer]. Thinking about sexuality and my attitude to – how much I act as I'm expected to.

26 May 1978
Worked through night to finish dissertation. Dad drove me down 7.00 am. Hung about waiting for office to open at 9.00. Coffee in Arts D common room. To no. 9 [Shaftesbury Avenue]. Dad crashes while I bathed.
    To campus, Final return of library books – £2.50. Sun. [. . .]
    To beach and met Pen and David. Hello Superman Paul – just broken finger from karate and bad taste comments about me struggling into bikini. Quell jerk.
    To Browns for delicious mushrooms. To King and Queen and cider drunk. Rap with David about responsible cinema going. Pen and David split.
    To Concorde [old Concorde behind Sea Life Centre] [. . .] Really good music. Looser than soul disco. Danced with Nigerian Tayo till my limbs started giving out. Walked home and CRASHED. C'est fini at last. Up and upper.

1 June 1978
Picnic on beach with Julia. Hot hot sun. Getting red and bit brown.
    To Mock Turtle for tea and cake. Real summer boogie. Keep feeling little panicky about what [to] do in short term summer period before settle down and work.

Sharon Forsdyke on the South Coast

Sharon Forsdyke was born in Leigh-on-Sea, Essex, in 1965. After graduating from Chester College, she worked in London. In the early 1990s, she spent some time travelling around the South Coast, including a visit to Brighton. The LIC project has a collection of scanned extracts from a travel journal she kept at the time, and of photographs she took.

25 September 1991
More rain – it was a good job I had not intended to do a lot of walking. I decided to go to the Royal Pavilion and got there just as it opened. I was rather disappointed as none of the exhibits were explained, without use of a guide book or a tour. And as I had neither, I had to wander round blindly with my free leaflet plan. Of course, the most impressive rooms are the Banqueting Room & the Music Room. I expect every guide ever written has used the words, grandiose, ostentatious, majestic. How like Neuschwanstein [Bavaria, Germany] this is!
    Funny that society considered both kings to be mad. Mad to spend money on creating a dream palace, mad to put such dreams to reality, mad to employ the best craftsmen of the day. They paid for their 'madness' but we should be thankful, for their creations have put both places on the map and given the local people something to be proud of.

The outside with ambrosia cream coloured minarets, turrets and domes do look out of place but it's such a lovely surprise. The colours inside reminded me of kaleidoscope patterns made in a tube etc. and the more you look at each room the more you like. I could understand why Queen Victoria was disappointed with no sea view. I have missed the sea when out of sight especially when you know it is not that far away.

Moons in the Lanes for dinner of fish and chips. Then back to the museum and art gallery – more students were drawing again. I think this could be rather compared to the British Museum with its vacuous rooms and voluminous windows. A school party shuffled through the corridor, excited voices echoing round the museum. It's a wonderful place to research things in. No luck in finding a print of the Seven Sisters for Mum.

Pier, bit battered not as nice as Eastbourne Pier. Past the Brighton Centre. 'Welcome to the 1991 Conference of the Labour Party', next to the Grand Hotel. Further on a very strong smell of salt washed up by the tide. The afternoon had brightened considerably and exposed a few more cracks on Brighton's front and brought the sun-worshippers out. The luminescent silver ball winked in the sunlight as it rotated on the dome of the Palace Pier.

I still prefer the ruin of the West Pier. A lady walked past wearing black ski pants, a black jacket and gold flecked plimsolls. It suddenly reminded me that an elderly man on the bus from Alfriston had been wearing pumps emblazoned with the Bart motif. I had smiled at the time as they had looked a little out of place on his feet. In a way Brighton's hotels look a bit like those on the Costa Del Sol. Sprouting at all different heights trying to out-expand one another.

24

Des Marshall, the Urban Robinson Crusoe

A 'tinsel town', a 'mad-house', and 'a crazy, unreal town that can take a well-adjusted person to the edge, and does', are just three of the ways Des Marshall describes Brighton in a journal he kept while living in the town during the mid-1990s. In the same journal he records his feeling that a book should be written on how to survive in the place, but also acknowledges that it's one of the most accepting of towns, and one of the least judgemental. Marshall, now an elderly man living in Camden, has lived a trouble life, never at ease in his own mind, and almost always at odds with society. Indeed, he sees himself as something of an urban Robinson Crusoe.

Marshall was born in 1941, in Bury St Edmunds, Suffolk, the son of a Russian Jew and a Welsh coalminer's daughter. He suffered so badly from asthma as a young child that he spent most of the first ten years of his life in an institution for sick children. He found life no less difficult as a young man in London in the 1960s, with depression – a family illness – rarely far away. He worked at many jobs, not least being a stand-up comedian in holiday camps; and he travelled widely, to Russia and India among other places.

But depression, which continued to trouble Marshall's life, led him to Dr Peter Chadwick, a psychologist, who had suffered from schizophrenia and written very sympathetically about mental illness. Indeed, in two publications, Chadwick used Marshall as a subject of his studies. In 1994, Marshall became a Quaker, and in the same year he began to write a journal. At the time he was living in Camden, but in February 1995 he moved to Brighton, and stayed for over two years. For the last six months of his stay in Brighton, Marshall became involved with a woman, and his journal was put aside, but after moving back to Camden in the summer of 1997 he resumed his jottings, and continued until 2001.

The following year, David Roberts, who runs Saxon Books, published the diary as *Journal of an Urban Robinson Crusoe*. 'Dear Reader,' Marshall says by way of introduction, 'I want to tell you the truth about this journal. I didn't write it. It was written by a man who called himself Urban Robinson Crusoe who, for some reason I don't understand, happened to look very much like me. I met him late in 1994, December, I think it was. He didn't look very well. Small, nervous, thin faced.'

Crusoe writes about life at street level

'Crusoe,' the publisher says, 'writes about the life he finds at street level – about the lost, the lonely, the loud, the great unknowns, the ordinary, the disconnected – a multitude of outsiders who exist everywhere in Britain's urban society. He writes about his interior existence, his lifelong search for answers to his sense of rejection, the meaning and purpose of love, the sickness of modern society, the mystery of human existence. He is fascinated by human behaviour and the workings of his own mind. *Journal of an Urban Robinson Crusoe* is a portrait of a troubled yet resilient and compassionate man and the people he meets in London and Brighton in the closing years of the twentieth century.'

Rob Whitley at the Institute of Psychiatry, King's College London, says the book is required reading for anyone, researcher, clinician or lay person trying to understand depression. Marshall is not a fictional character, he says, though the reader may sometimes forget that, as he or she becomes immersed in the subtle mixture of pathos, wit and beauty which characterises Des's writings.

In 2009, *Journal of an Urban Robinson Crusoe* was transformed into a drama at Pentameters Theatre, Hampstead, for a three-week run, with six actors playing different facets of Marshall's character. Marshall, who now lives in Primrose Hill, was interviewed by the local newspaper *Camden New Journal*, before the opening. 'When people come to the theatre tomorrow,' he said, 'I've got this fantasy about begging outside. I'll tell them, "Oh Crusoe, I knew him. Strange bloke. I think he's dead".'

I am a Brightonian now

15 February 1995

I suppose I am a Brightonian now. I still wander the streets but it's just so much more pleasant to do that here, and I see so many so-called Robinson Crusoes, who don't realise what they have become.

Brighton is a strange town of contrasting types of people jumbled up and thrown together: the very poor, the very rich, gangsters, day-trippers, the unemployed coming down for the summer from the cities, possibly to get work for the season, students from other countries to learn English, artists, writers, street performers. Well-off show-biz people live here, and there's a big gay scene.

Graham Greene, the writer, who lived in Brighton, called Brighton a fugitive town. There's a sort of truth in that; people are always coming and going, just like London.

There are mad people thrown out of the asylums that they are closing down. There is a big one at Haywards Heath, half way between London and Brighton. The inmates have a choice when they leave, London or Brighton. Most opt for Brighton, for reasons I would think are obvious. Anything you want in London you can get here.

An unreal town, and frivolous

21 April 1995

I believe Brighton has more disturbed people in relation to the size of the population, than any other town in the country. There's a sort of unreality about the town. It's too frivolous. People don't really listen to each other. They seem very excited and distracted. It is because it's a holiday town, with too many distractions – the sea, the beach, the pier, the pretty women (there seems so many of them here), the men on the prowl for women, the buskers, the beach cafes with their coloured sunshades and ice-cream adverts, a sense of permanent holidaying atmosphere. It distracts people, even if you live here. You get sort of sucked into the excitement and get distracted. [. . .] People wear such odd clothes that don't really match. Could be, sort of punk, with a bit of hippy thrown in, or mohair with greatcoat, or a collar and tie man, with shorts of different colours, possibly even with a bowler hat.

Paranoia City

29 April 1995

I am beginning to have negative feelings about this place called Brighton. I am becoming disturbed, angry and depressed. I have a feeling I would like to go into myself and not come out and say goodbye to the world. It sounds very attractive. I suppose many people do and don't come out. They go mad, and have to be committed. People might pity them but it might be their choice.

I am not blaming anybody else for my own inadequacy and hopelessness. Is it PARANOIA? I would call Brighton *Paranoia City*.

A friend of mine, Dr Peter Chadwick, sent me his new book that's just come out called 'Understanding Paranoia'. That's what made me come to this conclusion about Brighton. It's also made me aware of my own paranoia, at times in Brighton.

27 May 1995
I'm feeling very lonely and cut off here in Brighton. I would like to move back to London. I felt less paranoid there and I felt safer and less lonely. But moving back would be horrendous, the stress of moving is too much to face.

All sorts of activities

15 February 1996
There should be a book written on how to survive Brighton. One thing I have found out is that you don't take it, or even the people, too seriously. That might sound like a harsh thing to say, but that is the nature of the beast. What I mean is, it's a hello, goodbye, sort of town, tinsel town.

The people who live here, or have made their life here, probably live very varied lives, and are into all sorts of activities outside their own domesticities – things like dancing, singing, writing groups, yoga, t'ai chi, religious groups, psychology meetings, humanist groups, the state of the nation groups, psychic groups, political discussion groups, old age discussion groups, gender bender groups, gay groups, social issue groups, single people meeting groups, history of Brighton groups. [...]

There is a sort of warmth about Brighton, a sort of warm superficiality. It's probably one of the most accepting of towns, and one of the least judgemental. It's just that people who live here all the year round see so many different ideas of how people live, dress and look. Anything goes, [...] All this in about two or three miles radius, houses crammed together spilling over each other.

A body to work on

14 April 1996
I joined Brights, an organisation that swaps skills in a barter context, no money involved. Since joining, I have had three messages from a woman who advertised that she needed bodies to work on, so she got mine. The experience was wonderful. [...] A beautiful Polish woman. When she finishes, she always asks me what I am doing afterwards, and I say something of what I am doing. When she asks me, I always think that I have a chance with her. But I realise many people say this in Brighton, as a means of communication.

13 June 1996
I blamed myself unmercifully, blamed people, blamed Brighton, fell out with people. My feelings towards myself were undermining and unbalancing me. God, why do we do these things to ourselves?

Cafes in Whitehawk

1 August 1996

Where I live in the Whitehawk area there are two working men's cafes that I don't go into anymore. The first week I moved here I went to both of them, but I didn't like the people's attitude in them – very abrupt – and the atmosphere in the cafes was full of tension. Parts of where I live are very rough. It's known as a rough area, and people don't want to move to this particular area.

20 August 1996

This Brighton, this crazy unreal town can take a well-adjusted person to the edge, and does! A woman I was having a casual conversation with said she was attracted to a man she met who had just moved to Brighton, an accountant. What attracted her was his stability of nature, and even his conservative outlook. After two years of living together in Brighton, he changed from this straight guy to a hippie-type beatnik. He fixed himself up with an ear-ring, wore way out clothes, started smoking pot, grew a beard, let his hair grow. She said, she was sure it was Brighton that had affected him. Because of the way he had changed they split up.

Unable to escape the inmates

8 October 1996

Two young women were behind me on a number 44 bus going from Whitehawk down to Elm Grove, talking about their hen night with a male stripper. All their intimate details were there. I kept looking round so they were aware I could hear everything they were saying, hoping they would stop. Not a bit, they just went on talking, oblivious of anybody else. At the same time I had this young kid in front of me, staring right in my face, making faces at me. This is 8:30 in the morning. I suppose this is what it's like being in a mad-house, living in close proximity, unable to escape from the other inmates. This is not a rare experience in Brighton. It's a regular occurrence.

9 January 1997

Is there a future, an on-going task, an existence, a performance for a body that walks the streets of Brighton and London, that observes, that recollects, that records the happenings that go on before its eyes? Who are the people? Are they just bodies, mirages or phantoms that appear? The others, that authorise our existence? They believe they're real? Their energies, their cells, their material, are they real? Do they really exist?

I feel I will try and go back to London and become anonymous. I am becoming too well-known here. Return and become the real Urban Robinson Crusoe...

25

Ross Reeves finds his home

Born in Twickenham, London, in 1981, Ross Reeves left home at 18 to explore the world. He travelled in Asia, spending several months in South Korea, and then moved to Australia where he stayed a year. Returning to England in 2004, he spent a few months in London and then Ireland before visiting Brighton. As a young gay man, interested in art and music, it didn't take long for Brighton to feel like home. Here is an early entry about the city:

> **August 2004**
> I got off the train & walked straight down to the beach without any side tracking & sat there for a good 5 mins under the heavy clouds taking it all in. My new home. I always knew I'd end up here at some point. It doesn't even seem a question of liking the place. I almost feel like it's my natural habitat. As though we share all of the same characteristics. Being here is a natural progression. Neither a surprise nor particularly fascinating. It's obvious & certain. I get a particular pleasure from feeling so casual about Brighton. It's like having a sibling & taking the friendship with them for granted, because the bond is so strong.

Initially, Reeves worked in bars, and did call centre work, but before long he found an interesting job helping in a gallery. He also took up working in the social services sector as a support worker for people with learning disabilities.

What am I saying?

Since Reeves began travelling, writing a diary has been important, and although he didn't plan to continue when living in one place, he found he couldn't help himself. It was as though he needed to carry on writing, for otherwise, when he started travelling again, there were too many gaps about his life to be filled in. By the time he settled in Brighton, the habit was firmly in place; though rather than writing daily he makes long entries once a week or once a month. Sometimes, however, he has doubts about how often he should be writing, as in this entry:

December 2005
I've been thinking – again. None of this matters. . . does it? What am I saying? Why is there a need to say it? Would I ever have written such trivial matters in life if I were travelling? So much of what I write probably does little in opening up the world. To open up the world properly it would have to be so detailed as to actually live it. But summaries explain even less. Why do I bother? Should I write every day again? Or not at all.

Reeves writes lucidly and in great detail about his life in Brighton, his friends and relationships, his hopes and disappointments, as well as making more general observations about the world around him. The diaries themselves are a kaleidoscopic collection of artistic books of many sizes and colours, and are often accompanied by photos, song lyrics, and scrapbook material such as maps and leaflets.

A gay couple out for lunch

25 August 2004
We had a lovely lunch as the sun shone through the window to the chilled cafe. What was instantly noticeable to me & refreshing was the fact that we were clearly a gay couple out for lunch & no one batted an eyelid. Such a tiny thing but for me it amounts to a great deal. I hope the entire world is this blasé one day.

1 September 2004
Almost forgot, seeing as so much is going round in my head. Spent a lovely hr wandering around Brighton Pavilion. It really is a unique place. To me the outside looks like it's made of plastic & could do with being jazzed up in an array of colours. The actual shape & design of it is so striking, nestled in the middle of such a very British sea-side resort. It's fantastic really.

9 September 2004
From work I made my way to 'Punctured', a friendly piercing shop to get my lip done. I love it! It's tiny & pretty. But as I soon found out, I have no clue how to eat with it! It really is proving a struggle which I wasn't expecting at all. Hopefully it's just coz it's new & I'll get used to it.

A great place for music

15 October 2004
Later in the day I headed home where I had an appointment. A guy called Kevin was coming over to see me with a guitar and a couple of CDs. I'd put an ad in the 'Friday Ad' just a few days ago [. . .] 'Young male singer looking for eclectic group of musicians to start avant garde band with roots in funk and soul.' And actually had quite a good response – Kevin being the first.

It's becoming clear that Brighton is a great place for music. It's funky enough, got the scene, but it's still small enough to have a community about it. It's not so big & impregnable as say London might be.

29 October 2004
Somehow managed to get to the gallery on time for opening, in fact earlier (I'm taking my new responsibilities very seriously) and have pottered about all day doing bits and pieces. [. . .] I've been polishing up replica 'regency' furniture and loving it. The sun's shining, I have Mozart playing, and I'm now flicking between diary writing & people watching. I love this job.

30 October 2004
Had an excellent day at work in fact. Selling well over £800 worth of stuff. A very good day. And the customers were typically friendly as ever. Even had a lovely girl called Kate come in and interview me for half an hour on men's fashion for her dissertation.

Bills, and band news

12-18 October 2005
In fact my first day off in just over 2 weeks was on the Thursday when Mum visited for the day and we spent the day enjoying Brighton. Checking out Bill's. The new cafe in [North Laine], part cafe part green-grocers. Bloody brilliant. And very Brighton. [. . .]

Right. Band news. Where to start. Well at some point the name changed . . . again. Warwick while away in Berlin came across the word – 'Super Soul', which we all fell in love with immediately. And so it has stuck happily. We have learnt that there is a band, or rather a hiphop act, in the US with the same name, but fuck it. The day we're big enough that the name becomes an issue we'll be able to pay someone else to deal with [it]. For now at least it's catchy and suits us perfectly.

Bonfire night at the allotment

2-8 November 2005
Saturday came round and with it Bon Fire night. I'd wanted to go to Lewes, being one of the biggest events in Europe for Bon Fire night. Certainly for Guy Fawkes in the UK. But Stevie and Davey had organised a party up at the allotment for the occasion. Turned out to be a fantastic party. All the group turned out. [. . .] Everyone instructed to bring one big expensive firework each rather than bring scores of little weak things. It worked a treat and we managed to light up the allotment valley in fantastic colours. Had a great night, buzzing and dancing until the early hrs of course.

9-15 November 2005
The demo has now been mastered, copied & given out to us band members, and we've been really happy with the result. REALLY happy in fact. And the more people it gets passed to the greater the response.

From Super Soul to August

16–22 November 2005

I've asked Maz to take the photos for the band. Which she's happily agreed to. And so it's all set, & though it will be a few weeks to have everyone in the same place at the same time, we should hopefully be getting them done at the allotment on Dec 10th. Brilliant. It seems the perfect place. Unique, earthy, in Brighton, but with any luck it's never been done before.

A drummer was trying out for the band, and Maz was in tow, to get a feel for our music (and unexpectedly taking shots throughout rehearsals as well). Ian, the drummer, was bloody good, it has to be said [. . .] and the band went from 5 to 6. And we are now complete. Fantastic. No stopping us now! [. . .] The final issue to solve in the pub was the name. 'Super Soul' had indeed been copyrighted & we need another name – after seemingly going through every word in the English language, we came back to our roots. We're 'August' once more.

Bingo, and 80s Frocks

23-29 November 2005

A night of gay Bingo with Stevie's lot and a rowdy crowd at the fringe on Kensington Gdns. Not a camp affair as you might expect but instead lots of stubbly, hairy men in outrageous drag screaming out numbers faster than you could ever decipher. Cabaret shows inc. lesbian geisha ... the whole thing went from mad to chaotic with penis kissing, naked compering, and vodka jellies being replaced by cotton balls downs in poppers. All too much for Stevie who soon left. The rest of us had a ball however.

December 2005

The band's been going great. I've been working my arse off trying to get gigs everywhere. We've got some – Joogleberry Playhouse [now called Latest MusicBar] in Jan, one or 2 others and then Pressure Point in March – a biggy. Other Brighton venues – good venues – are interested. [. . .] Ian's fitted in like a glove on a hand. I can't believe it's only been a month that he's been with us. [. . .]

Before long it was 7pm, New Year's Eve, in Nina's kitchen, where we were all doing our make-up. We were off to join all Stevie's lot at 'Brighton Rocks' for an '80s Frocks' evening. Stevie was less than impressed to see his fella dressed up to the 9s in a tight-fitting red lycra dress, fish-net tights, false eye-lashes and the rest, but me & the girls were loving it.

26

Brighton and Me

I have a long association with Brighton. As a young couple, in their mid-20s, my parents came here for a weekend in late summer 1951 – and went home with more than they bargained for. Marriage followed. Many years later, I found a photograph of them sitting in deckchairs on the beach – probably a few hours before or after the moment my life began.

The first time I came to Brighton as an adult was only a few months after returning from a three-year round-the-world adventure. I was still in travelling mode which explains my willingness to kip down in a cemetery (Woodvale). And by the following year, I'd become a regular visitor, drawn by the personal warmth and social excitement I found in the home of friends – Rosy and Andrew. For several years in the 1990s, my partner and young son lived in North Laine. Since 2006, I've been living near Preston Circus.

I have written diary entries regularly since 1974. For a short while, when I was travelling, in 1974 and 1975, I tried to write every day. For most of my life, however, I've written more freely, reflecting in retrospect on my actions and behaviour and thoughts, on average, probably about twice a week. From 1973 until 1987, I kept handwritten journals, usually in hard-back books. Since 1987, I've written most of my entries directly onto a computer. I do still hand-write journals when on holiday.

The following entries – covering a period of twenty-five years – have been chosen for their 'Brighton' quality, if I can put it that way, describing, among other things, the festival, the sea, a bomb scare, fireworks, the veteran car rally, and a *Brighton Rock* writing workshop!

Sleeping in Woodvale Cemetery

4 June 1977
No, that's not all I want to say about Brighton. The wind blows cold. And I hate amusements. [. . .] Met a Dutch lady and brother in Brighton – a psychiatric nurse and a potter – Arianne and Ari. A very fresh lady, sad to leave her. Cold

winds and rains. Such a homely cemetery protected my soul for two nights. Waking one morning to see the sun rising above a small hill and Gaelic cross, somewhere from the middle of the film 'Barry Lyndon', and so many dreams undreamt between the waking squalls of rain. And yet not one cry, not one mutter from the dead. The dead stones around with their dead engravings and short cropped grass. When the wind made no noise through the holes in my sleeping bag, I could not know if I was in my bed at home or in a guest's heavenly eiderdown. [. . .]

Poetry, theatre, dance and jazz were all part of the Brighton festival, none of it excellent to me, but all very interesting. The jazz was hyper-modern, full of screeches, there was one guy playing his cello as though he was in a frenzied 'It's a knockout' race to destroy it. The theatre was full of surprises.

In the sea and on the beach

26 December 1978
Boxing Day. How the sea carried me off, into the spacious realms of ecstasy, how the waves tumbled me into their dreams. The brown turgid froth − alive, how alive with stones coming to life, leaping out at me, with me towards the sea.

29 July 1979
Brighton felt good − a day of shimmering violet. The swimming me, tiptoeing among fully dressed men on the sand.

    The People Show [a theatre group] came to the sea. They stood and looked pretty with their slow, slow movements. Taking photos on the sand, and asking strangers to choose with whom they'd like their photo taken. To me it was a take-off, of the young men with tiny monkeys and fast cameras. The People Show give all their photos away free, and their music too, the bluesy jazz. Hoorah for the People Show.

My favourite church of the year

21 April 1980
Quite a splendid day passed in Brighton on Saturday. [. . .] Yes the splendour of St Bartholomews is the balance afforded by the enormous expanse of unadorned brickwork with Catholic ornamentation of silver, gold, colours, statues, candles etc. There is no constructed structure within the church, it is essentially an empty hall; the chairs are laid out in the centre as if in a park. How large an expanse of wall is needed to balance a silver cross? This church does it. My favourite church of the year.

Bomb scare at the theatre

11 September 1990
I must report that last weekend at the theatre in Brighton, I was victim of a bomb scare. This was an amusing incident and probably added to the evening rather than

detracting from it. The long play – 'Soldiers' – in three acts totalling three hours, fictionalises a few related events, with Churchill at the centre, in the Second World War. It is a wordy, almost tedious play, though never crass or trivial. Well it did become trivial about ten minutes into Act Two. Without any warning to the actors – Churchill was theorising through a cigar – when the front of house manager walked on in front of them and told the audience that they were to leave immediately. [. . .] We all forgathered on the pavement and, every few minutes, were pushed back further and further by the policemen until, finally, we were all bunched up behind a ribbon cordoning off the entire street. [. . .] The main entertainment came from watching streams of people – some holding bottles of wine – emerging from restaurants along the same street having been told by the police to leave. One man resisted and was forcibly dragged along the road until pushed behind the ribbon. I was that close I could see the resentment on the man's face and the combination of fear and power on the face of the policeman. While the very last of the diners were making their way towards the ribbon, the green light was given somewhere by someone and we all streamed back to our respective entertainments. Brighton is no stranger to bomb attacks.

Fireworks in Wild Park

4 November 1990

Brighton. Bright, bright Brighton. Clear blue skies yet again; a north wind brings a colder nip in the air than of late, signifying the embrace of autumn and the closeness of winter. Such a lot of activity in this town. Last night we went to a magnificent firework display, more akin to an artist's show than the traditional spark and bang outburst. This morning we are about to leave for the seafront to watch the vintage cars arriving from London in the annual rally. Also in town is a toy collectors fair and a large gift and craft fair. [. . .]

We arrived [at Wild Park] round about 7pm, the time the display was due to start and found ourselves streaming up the park, inland so to speak, with hundreds of other groups of people. As we approached the arena so we could make out the white and coloured lanterns, and the white shapes, and the sparklers and torches and the lights from one or two stalls – B remarked how pagan it all seemed. It was true, I felt as though we could have been characters from a Hardy or Eliot novel. A man and his wife and child going to the fair.

Groups of people parked themselves along the side slopes and many stood in the arena near the stalls and close to the cordons around the bonfire pile and as close to the fireworks as they could get. [There was] a truly mellow and peaceful atmosphere; a large crowd, but no crowding. B had made some watercress soup and brought it in a thermos with bread rolls. A band assembled in the boat, the show boat, and gave us a couple of jazz numbers and one folk melody. We danced; that is B and I danced, while A sat around, lazily, on my shoulders enjoying the ride. Several giant heads wandered into sight while an enormous anemone hovered close by the show boat. After the musical intro, the fireworks began with the loudest crackles and bangs of the evening.

The show ended with a traditional display of golden-exploding, silver-raining, sky-filling giant rockets but in between we were treated to simple and effective lighting of the set pieces – prehistoric creatures, other monsters and giant glow-worms, which turned out to be under the control of puppeteers who moved eerily. The lighting was effected by fireworks which had been chosen in style with the giant puppets, one frizzy angled creature for example had a silver cracker that frizzed at angles through the sky, another one with a circular rim to its head was lit by a vertically-orientated circle of roman candles. The glow worms were just giant paper cylinders slowly lit from inside.

The veteran car rally

Later. This morning we trooped down, again with crowds of people, to Madeira Drive on the seafront to look at the vintage cars arriving. At the finish line, a radio DJ or broadcaster of some description interviews the drivers or owners of the machines on a loudspeaker system that stretches from one end of the Drive to the other. He has briefing notes on the cars and their owners so we usually know where the car has come from, how old it is and how many times it has entered the race. The interviewees talk about their "best run ever", or the "brilliant day" or "our record time" or the fan belt that had to be changed. Sometimes the owners are asked for a pocket history of the car – "well it was bought by my family in 1901; in 1904 a gasket went and it was pushed to the back of the garage until the 1950s when my grandfather restored it."

I don't suppose I had quite realised how big an event this rally is. Rich fanatics ship their prize cars all the way from the Continent, the US and Mexico. Imagine the expense, and people are proud of – not embarrassed by – the trouble they've gone to. I find it an extraordinary display of I'm not quite sure what, pretension I suppose, of money. At the other end of Madeira Drive there are hundreds of cars with trailers, vans with trailers, mini-car-transporters, lorries big enough to carry a small car and so on. Many if not most of the cars neither drive back to London nor even come from there, but are rather shipped one way or another back to their garages where their owners or owner's mechanics clean them, work on them, mend them, shine them ready for the next outing. My son was given a badge and a flag. Both sported the names of the sponsors – Kenco and the RAC – in letters bigger and bolder than the name of the race. He waved the flag merrily around.

Brighton Festival events

4 May 1992
The last weekend passed in a fervour of writing activity but as with everything at the moment any pleasure or enjoyment is undermined by a growing sense of emptiness. Friday saw the opening of the Brighton festival with a splendid procession of children and their school-made dragons. And on Saturday, I had a 'Brighton Rock' writing workshop, though beforehand I'd had little idea what it would be like. I dutifully arrived on the Palace Pier a little before 10 and took a couple of photos – the light was astonishingly bright and clear and the pier furbishings were looking as spanking new and clean as I've seen them; they must have had a coat of paint within the last few weeks, and the glass in the

windows had been spotlessly cleaned. The photos I took were similar to some I'd taken ten years ago.

At 10 exactly, I approached the tiny group of people in the centre of the pavement at the entrance to the pier. The literature event organiser was there holding a wad of tickets; there was a large well-built man of around 50 who was introduced to me as Tony Masters. There were only two other punters like me – Jake and Bob. Tony, who turned out to be quite a well known and prolific writer, never really recovered from the fact that so few people had signed up for his day long workshop.

Sensing the sleaze and squalidness

We removed to a banquet suite in the Albion Hotel where Tony talked a while about his working methods, about 'Brighton Rock' (he had known Graham Greene) and about what we were going to do during the day – i.e. a walk in the morning and a writing session in the afternoon. It turned out that Bob had never read the book 'Brighton Rock' and had never penned a word of fiction in his life; while Jake who found it almost impossible to stop talking, never strayed from his favourite subject of films. Both these characters added much to the day.

The walk was a disappointment – we walked up and down the pier, passed Forte's cafe on the corner directly opposite the pier which had been the setting for Snow's [in the film]. Tony insisted it would have been more sleazy in the time Greene researched the book but I thought otherwise – Rose says she couldn't get another job as good and I suspect it was quite posh then, even more so than now. Tony said the same thing about the pier and the Albion hotel (where Greene stayed when in Brighton) but again I would have thought the pier would have been quite rich in those days given the amount of visitors it used to get. Our resident writer seemed determined to impose the sense of sleaze and squalidness that exudes out of the whole book on all the locations. We then walked up to Nelson Place which is where Pinkie grew up and where Rose's parents lived. Tony seemed to insist he could really feel "a sense of place" (the title of the workshop) in this location but I didn't get anything from it at all.

Brighton Rock writing workshop

For a while we sat in the pub Dr Brighton's (formerly, and in the book, the Star and Garter where Ida was often found). We were given five minutes to write down the bone of an idea based on any inspiration we had had on the walk; and then less than an hour to actually write up the idea.

Apart from general thoughts about the gaudiness of the attractions on the pier and the similarity perhaps with Brighton itself in some respects, three pictures on the pier had struck me: the sight of a lanky youth, standing silent and motionless staring at a video machine; a small boy who refused to walk over the slats of the pier because he could see water below and chose instead to walk along the boards laid down for pushchairs; and the colour of the sea – a translucent turquoise which seemed to have a light source of its own – as spotted between the slats when walking through a covered part of the pier.

Pressed into creating a story line and taking my cue from a simple example put forward by Tony himself, I turned the youth into a rather lonely character yet to leave home, addicted to the video machines, his only pleasure, and on the edge of making an important decision in his life. I have him watching the small boy choose the safe path over the boards and seeing himself.

Jake wrote three sentences in Tom Wolfe style about a film star who has come to Brighton to film a few scenes but falls over on the pier and is going to have an affair with a young street-wise lad. Bob also wrote just a few words about a tailor's shop he'd seen. They were highly descriptive and emotive even and promised well.

We talked for an hour or so about these attempts. Jake found my writing Kafkaesque, Bob liked it and Tony explained that I wrote rather economically without much description, that I didn't waste words. The cost of the workshop also includes the chance to send in a story (max 3,000 words) to the organisers who will then award a £50 price as well as provide some constructive criticism. I shall certainly take advantage of that offer.

Barbie went with Freddie

5 July 1992

On my mother's birthday, B, A. and I took her out for a meal to a Greek restaurant in Primrose Hill. We got to talking about my father, Fred, and how she had met him in the Cosmo. [. . .] The next weekend, the very next weekend, (i.e. within days of meeting) Barbie went with Freddie for a weekend to Brighton. Barbie says she had no idea that Freddie would try and seduce her, after all the men she had known up until then had all been respectable and even perhaps rather naive with respect to sex. Because Barbie had not become pregnant after three years or so with [her first husband], she had begun to wonder whether she was, in fact, sterile; and this explains, perhaps, a rather irresponsible attitude to taking precautions. Freddie duly seduced Barbie in Brighton, and I was the result.

First prize for Helter Skelter!

1 August 1992

"I am delighted," Adrian Slack, organiser of the literature part of the Brighton Festival, writes, "to inform you that you have won first prize in the short story competition. I enclose a cheque for £50." Well, well, well. My first ever literature success. Well, it would be if I wasn't reasonably sure that I was probably the only entrant. Shame I didn't get second and third prize as well. The story – 'Helter Skelter' – was supposed to be read by several judges and a critique provided, that might have been more useful than the £50 prize.

Skinny dipping on Christmas Day

26 December 1993

The very best thing about spending Christmas Day in Brighton is that I can go for a skinny dip before breakfast and wake myself up truly and properly to the day. We drove down to Madeira Drive at about 8:30. Apart from one group of teenagers and a man with a dog on the beach, the town was deserted. I raced onto the beach stripping off my clothes as I went, like they do in the movies in summer, and raced into the icy cold water. Since it took just a few minutes to get from my warm bed to the sea, I was protected by an aura of heat for about 90 seconds, then my toes started to ice up, and the soles of my feet went into deep pain. I had had the forethought to bring my flip-flops, because I always suffer most in the feet, however, the undertow/tow grabbed one of them and it floated so far out to sea, I thought I had better let the other one join it. Because of the pain in my feet I didn't get right in, but I did wet myself all over and scream a little bit as the physical stress hit me. Meanwhile, B went for a run along the promenade, and A ran up and down the stones, jumping down the big drops. As I had neither towel nor spare clothes, he took great pleasure in running off with my only jumper, which I was trying to use for warmth and to dry myself. Although the entire length of the beach was empty, a man with a dog managed to find himself on our bit; but, fortunately, I had already put my clothes back on. An early morning dip on Christmas day – wonderful.

A seaside album

30 August 2003

I strolled down to Brighton on Wednesday. I've been meaning to go all summer, to swim, to look at the shops, to look at the people. But I was prompted to go by reading a review of a photographic exhibition at the Brighton Museum. I set off before six, wanting an easy drive and the chance of getting a free parking place where I always used to park when visiting B in Tidy Street. I had the road to myself almost through to Pulborough, and made Brighton in one hour. I parked and then strolled through North Laine to the beach and then looked for a paper and a place to breakfast. I thought I would settle down in Food for Friends, but it didn't open for breakfast (it used to be the best breakfast place in Brighton) and nor were there any signs saying when it would open. So I took a coffee and pan de chocolate at an Italian coffee place near Churchill Square.

The (free) exhibition was no disappointment. It was called 'A Seaside Album' and was put together by a man called Philippe Garner, who grew up in Brighton and has worked in the art market (he's published books on Cecil Beaton, Sixties Design) and curated photographic exhibitions in London, Paris and Tokyo. This one contains photographs from 1846 to 2000, many of them not published before. It's a sort of combined tour of Brighton's history and the history of photography (with daguerreotypes, calotypes, salt prints, albumen prints) managing just enough of both to do a good job. The earliest photographs are by William Constable, Calvert Richard Jones, Edward Fox, William Mason Junior and William Cornish Junior.

There is a glorious study of Brighton fishermen by William Mason Junior and some beautiful seascapes, beachscapes and treescapes by Edward Fox. (In fact, Edward Fox seems to have the same kind of photographic eye as I do, but some 150 years earlier!). William Henry Fox Talbot makes an appearance too with several portraits of the Royal Pavilion taken in 1846. The exhibition does skip quickly through 150 years of history but it's an enjoyable romp.

Philippe Garner adds a personal postscript to the exhibition (but it's more of a prologue in the catalogue) with some of his own contemporary pictures of Brighton and with two photographs of him and his girlfriend on a Brighton promenade in 1976, and his parents on a Brighton promenade in 1947. (This idea is similar in concept to the display in my bedroom, where I have a photograph of my parents in Brighton, probably taken on the day I was conceived, and another photo of a poster advertising dirty weekends in Brighton!).

I sat in the Pavilion Gardens for a while, drinking tea and reading a book, and watching the people, then I walked back through North Laine, picking up a sandwich at Forfars, before returning to my car and driving home.

References

General sources/resources

Internet Archive – http://www.archive.org/details/texts
Oxford Dictionary of National Biography – http://www.oxforddnb.com/
Ponsonby, Arthur – *English Diaries*, Methuen, London 1923
Ponsonby, Arthur – *More English Diaries*, Methuen, London 1927
The Diary Junction – http://www.thediaryjunction.co.uk/
The Diary Review – http://thediaryjunction.blogspot.com/
Wikipedia – http://www.wikipedia.org/

Introduction

Erredge, John Ackerson, *History of Brighthelmston or Brighton as I View it and Others Knew it with a Chronological Table of Local Events*, printed by E. Lewis, Observer office, Brighton, 1862
Farrant, John H. 'Visitors to Eighteenth–Century Sussex', in *Sussex Genealogist and Local Historian*, 1983
Horsfield, Thomas Walker, *The History, Antiquities, and Topography of the County of Sussex*, Sussex Press, Lewes, 1835

1 – Samuel Pepys

Blount, Thomas, *Boscobel or The History of the Most Miraculous Preservation of King Charles II after the Battle of Worcester, September the Third, 1651* Tylston and Edwards, London, 1894
Dale, Anthony, *Brighton Churches*, Routledge, London, 1989
Hutton, Ronal, *Charles II*, Oxford University Press, Oxford, 1989
Sawyer, F.E., 'Captain Nicholas Tettersell and the Escape of Charles II', *Sussex Archaeological Collections* vol. xxxii, Sussex Archaeological Society, Lewes, 1882
Pepys, Samuel, *The Diary of Samuel Pepys* – http://www.pepysdiary.com/

2 – Peregrine Phillips

Phillips, Peregrine, *A Diary Kept in an Excursion to Little Hampton, near Arundel, and Brighthelmston, in Sussex, in 1778; and also to the latter place in 1779*, printed for the author, London 1780
Women of Brighton – http://womenofbrighton.co.uk/contents.htm

3 – Fanny Burney

Barrett, Charlotte Frances (ed.), *Diary and Letters of Madame d'Arblay, 1778-1840*, Henry Colburn, London, 1842-1846 (7 vols)
Burney Biographies – http://burneycentre.mcgill.ca/bio_frances.html

4 – Joseph Farington

Greig, James (ed.), *The Farington Diary*, Hutchinson & Co, London, 1922-1924 (4 vols)

5 – John Erredge

Erredge, John Ackerson, *History of Brighthelmston or Brighton as I View it and Others Knew it With a Chronological Table of Local Events*, printed by E. Lewis, *Observer* office, Brighton, 1862
Erredge, John Ackerson, *History of Brighthelmston with a new introduction by John Farrant*, Brambletye Books, Forest Row, 2005

6 – Sylvester Douglas

Bickley, Francis (ed.), *The Diaries of Sylvester Douglas*, Constable, London, 1928 (2 vols)
Sichel, Walter (ed.), *The Glenbervie Journals*, Constable, London, 1910

7 – Thomas Creevey

Maxwell, Herbert (ed.), *The Creevey Papers*, John Murray, London, 1903 (2 vols)

8 – John Wilson Croker

Jennings, Louis (ed.), *The Croker Papers*, John Murray, London, 1884-1885 (3 vols)

9 – Gideon Mantell

Curwen, E. Cecil (ed.), *The Journal of Gideon Mantell, Surgeon and Geologist*, Oxford University Press, Oxford, 1940

10 – Charles Greville

Gash, Norman, *Wellington: Studies in the Military and Political Career of the First Duke of Wellington*, Manchester University Press, Manchester, 1990
Hibbert, Christopher, *Queen Victoria: A Personal History*, HarperCollins, London, 2000

Monypenny, William Flavelle, *The Life of Benjamin Disraeli: Earl of Beaconsfield*, John Murray, London, 1920

Reeve, Henry (ed.), *The Greville Memoirs: A Journal of the Reigns of King George I. and King William IV, Longmans, Green*, London 1874 (3 vols)

Reeve, Henry (ed.), *The Greville Memoirs: A Journal of the Reign of Queen Victoria 1837-1852*, Longmans, Green, London 1885 (2 vols)

Reeve, Henry (ed.), *The Greville Memoirs: A Journal of the Reign of Queen Victoria 1852-1860*, Longmans, Green, London 1887 (3 vols)

11 – Henry Edward Fox

Earl of Ilchester (ed.), *The Journal of the Hon. Henry Edward Fox, Afterwards Fourth and Last Baron Holland*, Thornton Butterworth, London, 1923

12 – Walter Scott

Lockhart, John Gibson, *Memoirs of the Life of Sir Walter Scott*, Robert Cadell, Edinburgh, 1837-1838 (4 vols)

Scott, Walter, *The Journal of Sir Walter Scott, from the Original Manuscript at Abbotsford*, David Douglas, Edinburgh, 1890 (2 vols)

13 – Thomas Raikes

Raikes, Thomas, *A Portion of the Journal kept by Thomas Raikes, Esq. from 1831 to 1847*, Longman, Brown, Green, Longmans, & Roberts, London, 1856-1857 (2 vols)

14 – William Tayler

Wise, Dorothy (ed.), *Diary of William Tayler, Footman, 1837*, Marylebone Society, London, 1962

15 – Henry Crabb Robinson

Beardsley, Christina, *Unutterable Love: The Passionate Life and Preaching of F.W. Robertson*, Lutterworth Press, Cambridge, 2009

Sadler, Thomas (ed.), *Diary, Reminiscences and Correspondence of Henry Crabb Robinson*, Macmillan, London, 1869 (3 vols)

16 – Xue Fucheng

Howland, Douglas (ed.) and Helen Hsieh Chien (trans.), *The European diary of Hsieh Fucheng: Envoy Extraodinary of Imperial China*, St Martin's Press, New York, 1993

17 – Henry Peerless

Fenton, Edward (ed.), *A Brief Jolly Change*, Day Books, Oxford, 2003

18 – Arnold Bennett

Bennett, Arnold, *Hilda Lessways*, Methuen, London, 1911
Flower, Newman (ed.), *The Journals of Arnold Bennett 1896-1928*, Cassell, London 1932-1933 (3 vols)

19 – Cynthia Asquith

Asquith, Cynthia, *Lady Cynthia Asquith Diaries 1915-1918*, Hutchinson, London, 1968
Beauman, Nicola, *Cynthia Asquith*, Hamish Hamilton, London, 1987

20 – Virginia Woolf and Harold Nicolson

Bell, Anne Oliver (ed.), *The Diary of Virginia Woolf*, Hogarth Press, London, 1977-1984 (5 vols)
Woolf, Leonard (ed.), *A Writer's Diary*, Hogarth Press, London, 1953
Nicolson, Harold (ed.), *Diaries and Letters*, Collins 1966-1968 (3 vols)

21 – Olive Stammer

Mass Observation Archive – http://www.massobs.org.uk/index.htm

22 – Tony Simmonds

Brighton Behind the Front, QueenSpark, Brighton, 1990
My Brighton & Hove – http://www.mybrightonandhove.org.uk/
Letter in the Attic – http://catalogue.communitysites.co.uk/lita_about.html

23 – Letter in the Attic

Letter in the Attic – http://catalogue.communitysites.co.uk/lita_about.html

24 – Des Marshall

Marshall, Des, *Journal of an Urban Robinson Crusoe*, Saxon Books, Burgess Hill, 2002

25 – Ross Reeves

Diaries privately held by Ross Reeves

26 – Paul K Lyons

Pikle – http://www.pikle.co.uk/journal.html

Life in Brighton

CLIFFORD MUSGRAVE

Clifford Musgrave, OBE was the director of the Royal Pavilion for over thirty years. The author of many books and articles on Georgian and Regency furniture and architectural design, this is his definitive history of the city of Brighton. Divided into five sections – Fishermen and Farmers, Princes and Palaces, Late Georgian, Victorian Marvels and Mysteries, Battle Scene and Transformation – it shows how Brighton grew from a small fishing village.

978 0 7524 6047 5

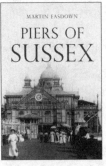

Piers of Sussex

MARTIN EASDOWN

Sussex has a good claim to be the birthplace of the seaside pleasure pier: the famous Chain Pier at Brighton was the first to be used as a fashionable promenade. Brighton even boasted a 'moving pier', the extraordinary Electric Railway, affectionately known as the 'Daddy-long-legs'. The county of Sussex should be proud to have retained six of its piers, including three of Britain's finest.

978 0 7524 4884 8

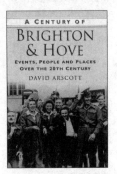

A Century of Brighton & Hove

DAVID ARSCOTT

This fascinating selection of photographs illustrates the extraordinary transformation that has taken place in Brighton & Hove during the twentieth century. Many aspects of Brighton & Hove's recent history are covered, famous occasions and individuals are remembered and the impact of national and international events is witnessed. Illustrated with a wealth of black-and-white photographs, this book celebrates the character and energy of the town.

978 0 7509 4907 1

Haunted Brighton

ALAN MURDIE

With heart-stopping accounts of apparitions of all kinds, this collection of stories contains both well-known and hitherto unpublished cases of hauntings from in and around Brighton. From the ghost of Cary Grant at the Rottingdean Club to the Screaming Skull in the Lanes and the ghost who spelt out 'prove me innocent!' at Preston Manor, this scary selection of ghostly goings-on is bound to captivate.

978 0 7524 3829 0

Visit our website and discover thousands of other History Press books.

www.thehistorypress.co.uk